# FOCKE-WULF Fw190

**1939 onwards (all marks)**

**COVER CUTAWAY:** Focke-Wulf Fw190 A-8.
*(John Weal/Amber Books)*

© Graeme Douglas 2016

All rights reserved. No part of this publication may be reproduced or stored in a retrieval system or transmitted, in any form or by any means, electronic, mechanical, photocopying, recording or otherwise, without prior permission in writing from Haynes Publishing.

First published in April 2016

A catalogue record for this book is available from the British Library.

ISBN 978 085733 789 4

Library of Congress control no. 2015944297

Published by Haynes Publishing,
Sparkford, Yeovil,
Somerset BA22 7JJ, UK.
Tel: 01963 440635
Int. tel: +44 1963 440635
Website: www.haynes.co.uk

Haynes North America Inc.,
861 Lawrence Drive, Newbury Park,
California 91320, USA.

Printed in the USA by
Odcombe Press LP,
1299 Bridgestone Parkway,
La Vergne, TN 37086.

## Acknowledgements

In writing a Haynes Manual, I am once again indebted to a number of people for their help in many fields concerning the story of this fascinating aircraft. Without their knowledge, expertise and information this manual could not have been written.

Flug Werk GmbH – Frank Hohmann, for supplying information and photographs about the Flug Werk replicas.

GossHawk Unlimited – Dave, Connie and Lindsey Goss who, in addition to allowing me to use many photos, were all endlessly helpful and patient both during my visit and also during my many months of queries by email.

Haynes Publishing – again I extend my thanks to Jonathan Falconer for assistance with contacts, supplying photographs and reassurance when needed.

Imperial War Museum, Duxford – thanks again to Sean Rehling for access to the photo archives and to Andy Robinson for his photographs.

Klaus Plasa – who in addition to kindly writing an account of his first flight in a Flug Werk aircraft, answered my many queries and sent many very useful photographs.

Photographs were supplied by Airbus photo archive, Aviation images.com, Brian M. Silcox of Flight of 2 Photography, Bundesarchiv, Gavin Conroy of Classic Aircraft Photography, JaPo and WW2 images.

Other photographs were supplied by Rusty Gautreaux, Bob Harrington, Don Hansen, Andy Thomas, Pavel Turk, Max Weigelin and Andreas Zeitler.

Lastly, another big thank you to my patient wife, Marion, whose constant encouragement, proofreading and checking of all German words and terms has proved invaluable.

# FOCKE-WULF Fw190

1939 onwards (all marks)

## Owners' Workshop Manual

An insight into owning, flying and maintaining
the most outstanding German fighter of the Second World War

Graeme Douglas

# Contents

| 8 | Introduction |
|---|---|

| 14 | Development and production of the Fw190 |
|---|---|

Fw190 V1 (Versuch) 16
Fw190 V2 20
Fw190 V5 and V6 20
Pre-production models (A-0) 20
Production models (A series) 22
Experimental models (B and C series) 25
Pre-production models (D series) 27
Production models 27
Ground attack and fighter-bomber variants (F and G series) 30
Trainer models (S series) 31

| 36 | The Fw190 at war |
|---|---|

Western Front – Europe 38
Hit-and-run tactics 39
Wilde Sau 40
Sturmgruppen 41
D-Day daring 44
Fw190 on the Eastern Front 44
Kursk 47
The North African and Mediterranean campaigns 49
Captured butcher birds 51

| 56 | Anatomy of the Fw190 A-8 |
|---|---|

Fuselage 59
Cockpit 63
Empennage 66
Wing 68
Main undercarriage 69
Systems 74
Armament systems 77
Emergency power systems 81
Engine installation 83
Radio and autopilot installation 83
Oxygen system 83
Camera systems 84
Emergency equipment 84

| 86 | Power for the Fw190 and Ta152 |
|---|---|

BMW801 radial engine 88
Junkers Jumo 213 96

| 104 | The Flug Werk replicas |
|---|---|

The cost of ownership 117

| 118 | Flying the Fw190 |
|---|---|

Maiden flight 120
Fw190 A-series pilots' operating instructions 126

| 128 | The engineer's view |
|---|---|

Periodic maintenance schedule – Fw190 A-series aircraft 147

| 148 | Sources |
|---|---|

| 149 | Appendices |
|---|---|

1 Rüstsatz field conversion kits fitted to the A-8 series 149
2 Surviving, substantially complete FW190 airframes and airworthy Flug Werk replicas 150
3 German terms and abbreviations 153
4 Conversion factors 154
5 Useful addresses 154

| 155 | Index |
|---|---|

**OPPOSITE** Two Fw190 pilots on the Russian Front exchange greetings. Aircraft in this campaign were painted with a yellow fuselage band. *(Bundesarchiv Bild 101I-727-0285-20)*

'Just as the Spitfire IX was probably the most outstanding British fighter to give service in World War Two, its Teutonic counterpart is undoubtedly deserving of the same recognition for Germany. Both were supreme in their time and class; both were durable and technically superb, and if each had not been there to counter the other, then the balance of power could have been dramatically altered at a crucial period in the fortunes of both combatants.' From *Wings of the Luftwaffe* by Eric Brown. This Flug Werk replica carries an underbelly stores rack with 300l drop tank and cannon barrels to add to the authentic look. *(Gavin Conroy)*

# Introduction

The Focke-Wulf Fw190 was one of the great fighter aircraft of the Second World War. It was sometimes known to the Allies as the 'Butcher Bird' after its little-used German manufacturer's name of Würger, meaning Shrike. Although it may lack the grace of the Spitfire or the clean lines of the Mustang, the Fw190 is not an unattractive aircraft, exuding an air of purposeful aggression brought about perhaps by the philosophy of its creator, Kurt Tank: to design a rugged, easily maintained fighter capable of operating in the harshest of combat theatres. Praised by its pilots and respected by its opponents, the Fw190 was constantly evolving to remain at the forefront of fighter technology of the 1940s. It was such an adaptable design that it underwent

**BELOW** One of a number of Fw190 replicas built by Flug Werk, this aircraft is based in New Zealand and is shown here against a spectacular mountainous backdrop. New-build replicas have openings on the top of the cowlings for the engine air intake and oil cooler. 'Stahlgewitter' was damaged in a landing accident in 2015 but is under repair to fly once more. *(Gavin Conroy)*

a myriad of different configurations, some of which fell by the wayside while others, although they showed great promise, ran out of time or resources, or both, in the chaotic last months of the war in Germany. This ongoing experimentation did bear fruit, however. The Fw190's airframe experienced three major, distinct design changes, incorporating a radical change of power plant: the original radial-engined aircraft which spawned the successful A, F and G series was reconfigured to accept an in-line powerplant, which gave rise to the D series with improved altitude performance and finally the stretched fuselage and extended wing Ta152 H series, with a performance to match any other piston-engined fighter of the period. The 20,000-odd examples produced bear testament to the fact that both the radial-engined and the in-line versions proved to be highly successful in their designated roles, proving the soundness and versatility of Kurt Tank's original concept.

In January 1933 Adolf Hitler was appointed Chancellor of Germany and under the Nazi party's aggressive foreign policy he announced barely a month later that the country must rearm despite this being forbidden under the terms of the Versailles Treaty following the First World War. Initially, this was done in a clandestine fashion to prevent the Allied

**ABOVE** The man behind the Fw190 and Ta152, Professor Kurt Tank in pilot's overalls. Tank not only designed the aircraft but also carried out a good deal of the test flying. After the war he continued his work in aeronautical design, first in Argentina and later in India. Returning to Germany in the 1970s, he died in 1983. *(via Aviation-images.com)*

**BELOW** Allied victory in the Second World War ensured the mass destruction of most Axis airframes. But thanks to the Flug Werk company there are now a number of these replicas flying around the world. Here a German-registered example takes off during a test flight from Manching airbase. *(Andreas Zeitler)*

**RIGHT** Only a single example of an original aircraft is currently airworthy. At the time of writing, this is the only original example flying and it is powered by the only running BMW radial engine. The Flying Heritage Collection's A-5 model is pictured landing at Payne Field, Washington, USA. *(Bob Harrington)*

powers from becoming suspicious, but as Nazi foreign aggression continued throughout the 1930s and went largely unchallenged by Britain and France, the ramping up of military production became obvious to the world. The aircraft industry in Germany underwent huge expansion. In 1932 it employed just over 3,000 workers and produced around 100 aircraft, mostly civilian types. By 1941 it had swollen to 250,000 workers building 10,000 military aircraft per year. The Nazis poured huge amounts of money into their rearmament programme: just two years after Hitler came to power, expenditure on military equipment accounted for 73 per cent of the government's purchases of goods and services. In this environment, German aircraft designers and engineers were able to produce some of the most advanced types of their day and German pilots were able to hone their skills in them in the Spanish Civil War of 1936 to 1939, when Hitler's air force units fought for the Fascist dictator General Franco.

By September 1939, Hitler's aggression had reached the point where his forces invaded Poland and where Britain and France declared war on Germany. Just three months earlier, in Bremen, northern Germany, the first flight of a new single-seat fighter aircraft had taken place; that aircraft was the Focke-Wulf 190, and it was destined to play an enormously important

**BELOW AND OPPOSITE BOTTOM** An airworthy example of a Flug Werk replica shown here flying in Louisiana, in the USA. It is flown by test pilot Klaus Plasa, who has carried out most of the testing of the Flug Werk replicas around the world. This aircraft has since been sold to an Australian organisation. *(Rusty Gautreaux via Klaus Plasa)*

role in the conflict about to follow. That it was born from the military aggression of the Nazis is naturally a source of regret, but it does not diminish our interest in the history of this aircraft and the technical achievements of those who designed and flew it.

In September 1941 RAF pilots flying over occupied France and Belgium reported contacts with a new radial-engined fighter. Some pilots mistakenly identified these aircraft as captured French Curtiss Hawks, but others who had duelled with the new type were more than a little surprised by its performance and were categorical that 'this was no Curtiss Hawk!'. For when the Fw190 first took on the RAF it was more than a match for their front-line fighter of the time, the Spitfire Mk V, capable of outperforming its British counterpart in all performance categories except in its turn radius. For almost a year, it reigned supreme against Allied fighters until the hastily designed stopgap Spitfire Mk IX restored parity. The design team at Focke-Wulf Flugzeugbau GmbH continually adapted the design with a host of variants and sub-variants designated for roles such as photo-reconnaissance, ground attack, high-altitude interception and long-range fighter-bomber, among others, so that the Fw190 was always at the forefront of the Luftwaffe's arsenal of combat aircraft.

The ultimate development of the series, the Ta152 H, with a new wing, lengthened fuselage housing an in-line engine and a host of other improvements, proved to be one of the fastest aircraft of the war. Its true potential can only be guessed at, however, as too few were built, and too late, to have a significant impact on the course of the war.

**BELOW** A Flug Werk replica based in Arizona, USA, comes in to land with full flap lowered. *(Doug Fisher)*

**LEFT** A leader and his wingman in a two-ship Rotte over Ukraine in March/April 1943. Their underbelly stores racks are empty, suggesting these two Fw190 A-5s are returning from a mission. *(via Aviation-images.com)*

**BELOW** A G-3, captured by the Allies displays its Stammkennzeichen (radio code letters) beneath its wings. Evidence of under-wing stores racks can be seen. *(via Aviation-images.com)*

*Chapter One*

# Development and production of the Fw190

The Focke-Wulf Fw190 was a product of the 1930s, a time of expanding rearmament in Germany. Built for a war that many in the industry anticipated, it incorporated the latest technology, which was constantly developed and advanced to counter Allied aircraft design.

**OPPOSITE** A trio of pre-production A-0 aircraft run up their engines at the Focke-Wulf factory at Bremen. The symmetrical teardrop-shaped bulge of the supercharger air duct identifies this particular model. Subsequent models had the bulge flattened at the top. *(Jonathan Falconer collection)*

Before the First World War two German aviation pioneers formed a partnership which would lead in 1924 to the establishment of the Focke-Wulf Flugzeugbau AG at Bremen airport in northern Germany. Heinrich Focke and Georg Wulf were both from the city of Bremen and secured funding for their new company from local businessmen. Despite modest beginnings, they were able to expand their aircraft manufacturing operation in the difficult financial climate of the 1920s. Their personal involvement didn't extend into the Second World War, however. Wulf was killed in a flying accident in 1927 and Focke was ousted from the company in 1936, possibly because the Nazi regime believed him to be unreliable. He went on to pursue a career in helicopter design.

By 1931 the company was on a sufficiently sound financial footing to allow it to acquire the Albatros aircraft company of Berlin–Johannisthal, which provided a great deal more capacity for Focke-Wulf. In the same year, the company appointed a new chief of the design and flight test departments, Kurt Tank, who has become synonymous with the design of the Fw190 and the Ta152, an aircraft which because of his influence bears the first two letters of his surname in its designation.

During 1936 and 1937 the company continuously expanded and became a limited liability company, the Focke-Wulf Flugzeugbau GmbH, and was taken over by the German electrical firm AEG, building a number of aircraft from other manufacturers such as Heinkel, Gotha and Messerschmitt under licence as well as constructing its own designs.

As a result of the expansion of Germany's aircraft industry after Hitler had come to power in 1933, Focke-Wulf grew and benefited greatly from increased orders for several military aircraft types. The company produced a number of successful designs such as the Fw58 Weihe (Harrier), a twin-engined monoplane, the Fw189 Uhu (Eagle owl), a twin-boom, twin-engined reconnaissance aircraft, and the long-range, four-engined Fw200 Kondor. As a result it found itself very much in favour with both the government and the Luftwaffe.

In early 1938 Focke-Wulf was invited by the Reichsluftfahrtministerium (RLM) – the German Ministry of Aviation, which had been charged with developing the Third Reich's aircraft industry – to propose a possible design that could complement or eventually succeed the very successful Messerschmitt Bf109, which had entered service with the Luftwaffe the year before. The specification issued by the RLM came about because of a concern in both the Luftwaffe and the RLM that, good though it undoubtedly was, too much might be asked of the Bf109 as the main German fighter type, when other nations, in the escalating crisis of the late 1930s, were developing more than one front-line fighter type.

# Fw190 V1 (Versuch)

The resourceful and talented engineer and test pilot Kurt Tank was director of the project, and gathered around him a team of designers and engineers comprising Rudolf Blaser, Willy Käther and Ludwig Mittelhuber, who in the summer of 1938 set about designing and building an aircraft to meet the RLM specification. Shortly afterwards, orders came through from the RLM technical bureau that the work should be speeded up. Blaser, who was in charge of the detailed design work, moved his bed into an office at the factory in order to meet the new deadlines. He was later to suffer a collapse from mental and physical exhaustion. From the outset the team chose a totally different approach to Messerschmitt and his Bf109. Tank wanted the fighter to be a tough Dienstpferd (cavalry horse) rather than a racehorse. The design was to be capable of operating in rugged environments and able to carry a variety of weapons. Maintenance was to be easily accomplished and the aircraft was designed to be able to absorb battle damage and still return to base. The approach the team took was innovative and went against established thinking in aeronautical design in Germany at the time. Instead of a liquid-cooled in-line engine, an air-cooled radial engine was chosen to power the new fighter. Conventional wisdom dictated that an in-line engine presented the smallest frontal area and therefore was more efficient than blunt-nosed radial-engined designs. Tank and his team, however, wanted to use a radial because it was more rugged. An air-cooled engine did not have a vulnerable cooling system that was prone to battle damage – it was not unknown for an aircraft with an air-cooled engine to have a cylinder knocked out in combat and still return home.

It has often been stated that the designers faced opposition from the RLM in their desire to use a radial engine. However, Tank himself always denied that this was the case, and in fact Ernst Udet, the Luftwaffe's Director General of equipment at the time, actively encouraged the proposal and promoted the Focke-Wulf design to the Luftwaffe leadership. Contrary to common belief, during this period there was a strong interest among a number of German aircraft designers in developing air-cooled radial fighters. In 1938, a captured Russian Polikarpov I-16 used in the Spanish Civil War was brought to Germany. This small, crudely constructed, single-seat radial-engined machine was tested against the best that the Luftwaffe had at the time, the Bf109, and surprisingly, the results showed that the I-16 (nicknamed Rata or the rat), although unable to match the speed of the Messerschmitt, could out-turn the German machine to the extent that it could never in this manoeuvre bring its guns to bear on the Russian aircraft. The Russian design, thanks to its small size and short wings, was able to out-manoeuvre its larger foe. Designers could see the possibilities of a small fighter designed to German technical standards and built around a powerful radial engine.

Another benefit of choosing a different engine for the new design was that the Bf109 was powered by the in-line DB601. The two fighters would not be competing for the same powerplant and thus it would potentially alleviate future supply problems. The engine they chose was a 14-cylinder 2-row radial design, the BMW139, early examples of which had bench-tested in 1937 at 1,570ps. As part of the prototype's engine installation, the three-bladed VDM propeller was surrounded by a large ducted spinner through which cooling air was designed to pass. Behind the spinner a ten-bladed engine-driven fan forced the air over the engine. The engine was surrounded by a NACA cowling, an aerodynamically shaped ring designed to accelerate air over the engine cylinders to assist cooling. The cowling itself was a particularly close fit around the cylinders in order to make the installation as aerodynamic as possible. Additionally, the individual ejector exhaust stubs from the engine were directed rearwards through gaps in the cowling in a way that was designed to draw more air through the front spinner. The new design, given the RLM designation number 190, became the Fw190 V1 (experimental or research). It incorporated an all-round vision canopy and a lowered rear fuselage spine, giving the pilot excellent vision to the rear. A high, wide-track undercarriage was also featured: hydraulically operated in the V1, electrical operation was used in production versions. In line with the rugged approach the designers adopted for their new fighter, the undercarriage, along with other structural components, was over-engineered in order to meet future increases in the weight of the aircraft, inevitable when it entered service. Capable of absorbing a sink rate of 4.5m/sec, almost twice that needed for the prototype's weight, the undercarriage remained virtually unchanged throughout the life of the aircraft. In order to make the Fw190 handle responsively, a lot of care was taken by the designers to balance the control surfaces and minimise the stick forces required by the pilot and to reduce the need to retrim the aircraft when changing power settings. The only movable trim surface was the variable-incidence tailplane, which the pilot operated via an electric motor. An unusual feature was the use of rods to operate the ailerons rather than the normal cable and pulley system. Unaffected by stretch, the system

**ABOVE** Construction of the very first Fw190 nears completion at Bremen probably in the spring of 1939. The V1 was fitted with a ten-bladed fan (seen here before the ducted spinner was installed), carried no armament and had the short-span (9.5m) wing. The aircraft is suspended from its undercarriage fixing points and from a tail trestle. In the background are cockpit canopies for Fw189 aircraft. *(Airbus photo archive Bremen)*

**ABOVE** The V1 shown with the short-lived ducted spinner. The undercarriage doors differ from production aircraft and the inner wheel doors are also missing at this stage. The aircraft carries a civilian registration. *(via Aviation-images.com)*

provided a very direct and crisp response to the pilot's inputs.

Otherwise, Tank's design was a conventional low-wing monoplane of all-metal, semi-monocoque construction. The pilot sat directly behind the engine and the oil tank; behind his seat was a large fuel tank. Armament at this stage was planned to be two MG17 machine guns and two MG131 machine guns in the wing roots, synchronised to fire through the propeller arc.

Construction of the V1 began in the autumn of 1938 and was completed by early summer of the following year. On 1 June 1939, Hans Sander conducted the first test flight from Bremen airport. The company test pilot found that the aircraft handled very well – an endorsement of the careful design of the control surfaces. There were a number of problems, however. The undercarriage up-lock was not strong enough to hold the legs up during all manoeuvres, and the hydraulically actuated legs tended to sag down. This was fairly easily fixed by designing a more substantial lock catch. Another issue concerned the aerodynamic 'locking' of the canopy above about 430kph, which made it impossible for the pilot to abandon the aircraft above this speed because of the air pressure exerted on it. After some trials, Focke-Wulf engineers came up with a mechanism that used an explosive charge firing against a piston to force the canopy to the rear and break the lock. Another serious problem was not so easily remedied: the BMW engine was prone to overheating, mainly in the area of its rear cylinders. This in turn led to very high cockpit temperatures, reported by Sander to be 55°C: he said that he felt as though he was sitting with his feet in a fire. Additionally, poor sealing allowed carbon monoxide gas into the cockpit, and Sander had to wear an oxygen mask throughout the flight. Despite the engine-related problems, the V1 was sent to the Luftwaffe testing airfield at Rechlin. It was found that the large ducted spinner designed to force air in to cool the engine was not really working as had been hoped, and it was subsequently abandoned in favour of a conventional spinner.

**RIGHT** The same aircraft after the removal of the ducted spinner and the fitting of a conventional aerodynamic spinner. *(via Aviation-images.com)*

# THE REICHSLUFTFAHRTMINISTERIUM (RLM)

Nazi Germany's Ministry of Aviation, the Reichsluftfahrtministerium (RLM), was the government department responsible for all aviation matters of both military and civil design during the era of the Third Reich, 1933–45. The Ministry was formed in April 1933 with Reichsmarschall Hermann Göring at its head. An early action was to requisition all patents and companies within the Junkers group, which included all rights to the important Ju52 transport aircraft. In May of the same year, the German army's military aviation department was transferred to the RLM, giving rise to the Luftwaffe proper.

Over the next six years, the Ministry expanded greatly to coincide with the policy of rearmament pursued by the Nazis. The military department was run by Erhard Milch, the Secretary of Aviation, who operated personal vendettas against some of Germany's most important aircraft designers: he tried to prevent Willy Messerschmitt from gaining government contracts for new designs, and Hugo Junkers was forced out of his own company because of his socialist and pacifist views. Personal infighting at the top and the settling of scores plagued the Ministry during the 1930s and throughout the war years, affecting aircraft and engine output and delaying new designs. Aircraft manufacturers were constantly forced to change the specifications of their designs, which in turn prevented them from concentrating on just a few successful types. The prototype system for each new model variant of a proven design was also a protracted process, requiring 20 to 30 test aircraft and extensive test flying programmes. During peacetime this might have been an acceptable practice, but in the increasingly desperate times that Germany found herself in, it was something the Luftwaffe could ill afford. Milch was succeeded in 1943 by Albert Speer and production output improved, but it was all to no avail: the Nazi war machine progressively succumbed to a lack of fuel, raw materials and a shortage of experienced pilots.

Today, the RLM building still stands in Berlin, one of the few remaining structures of the Third Reich era to have survived Allied bombing, an impressive building in a style that is sometimes termed 'intimidation architecture'. Running along Wilhelmstrasse and Leipziger Strasse, it was at the time of its construction in 1935–36 the largest office building in Europe. After the war, as it was in the Soviet zone of Berlin, the building was used by the Soviet military administration, and after the founding of the German Democratic Republic, it housed the Council of Ministries. Since German reunification, it has had a number of uses, and since 1999 it has housed the German government's Finance Ministry.

**LEFT** The entrance to the former RLM building as it is today in Berlin. It was here that all key Luftwaffe decision-making took place. *(Max Weigelin)*

19

DEVELOPMENT AND PRODUCTION OF THE FW190

## Fw190 V2

The second experimental aircraft, also with the BMW139 installed, flew in late 1939 and was used to test the wing-mounted armament. The aircraft was fitted with a conventional propeller spinner from the outset and retained the ten-bladed cooling fan. Despite this new arrangement, the engine overheating problems persisted and could have threatened the entire project had it not been for the fact that BMW had been developing a newer engine of virtually the same size and capacity since October 1938. The BMW801 was also a 14-cylinder 2-row radial which developed slightly more power, around 1,620ps, with the promise of more to come. More importantly, it was expected to be less prone to overheating and to be more reliable. The decision to re-engine the Fw190 with the BMW801 was taken. As a result, the next two planned experimental models, the V3 and V4, never flew.

## Fw190 V5 and V6

The V5 had to be redesigned to accommodate the new BMW engine, which required stronger mounts and a strengthened fuselage as the unit weighed some 160kg more than the 139. In order to retain the centre of gravity, the cockpit was moved further back, with the fuel tanks relocated to a position under the pilot's seat. This moved the pilot further from the engine, thus relieving him from the worst of the high temperature problems experienced on the earlier aircraft. In addition, as the oil tank was moved from ahead of the instrument panel to within the cowling, a space was created ahead of the cockpit for a forward armament compartment. With the new engine came the fitting of a 12-bladed cooling fan, a feature retained by almost all radial-engined production models.

When the V5 flew for the first time in April 1940 the aircraft's handling and manoeuvrability was found to have deteriorated because of the higher wing loading. This required a major redesign of the wing. The original centre section with bolt-on outer sections was changed to a through spar 'carry-through' design on subsequent models, with a 1m-longer span taking it to 10.5m, and this together with a reduced taper increased the wing area and brought the wing loading back to an acceptable figure. Handling was restored but at the expense of a slightly reduced maximum speed. The new wing was designated the 'g' wing, with its predecessor redesignated the 'k' wing. Later in the programme, the tailplane and fin areas were increased in order to match the larger wing.

The Fw190 V6 is sometimes included among the pre-production aircraft (see below), but it was a prototype and used in a number of development programmes; these included testing the new larger wing design as with the V5.

## Pre-production models (A-0)

### Fw190 A-0

From the successful testing of the first two experimental aircraft, the Focke-Wulf Company received an order from the RLM in 1940 for a batch of pre-production machines, initially numbered 40, but later revised to 28 aircraft. In anticipation, the company had already started construction, and consequently the first nine aircraft were fitted with the early, small 'k' wing. These aircraft, built during the second half of 1940, were fitted with a pre-production version of the new engine, the BMW801 C-0 or C-1. These proved to have their fair share of problems, as discovered by the RLM pilots of the Erprobungsstelle (E-Stelle) at Rechlin. Under service evaluation trials the engines were still found to be overheating, and problems with the new engine control unit (Kommandogerät) compounded the issues with the new fighter. Only by the combined efforts of Focke-Wulf, BMW and the Rechlin staff was the programme saved and the Fw190 passed for service introduction.

Many of these pre-production A-0 aircraft were later converted into prototypes for other later series aircraft and were, from spring 1941 onwards, engaged in a variety of service trials and test programmes, trialling equipment fits, various weapons testing and ground handling procedures. A key feature of the programme was the proving of a variety of factory-installed modification kits for specific tactical roles. These 'U' or Umrüst-Bausatz sets became a feature of the Fw190 programme, spawning a myriad of sub-versions for almost every conceivable role.

**ABOVE** The BMW 'power egg' is hoisted into position for connection to the engine mounts of either an A-0 or A-1 model. *(Airbus photo archive, Bremen)*

**ABOVE** A line-up of early BMW801 C-1 engines for fitting to production Fw190 A-1 fuselages to the left. The second engine has its oil tank and cooler already installed. These early engines were still prone to overheat, and were unreliable. *(Airbus photo archive, Bremen)*

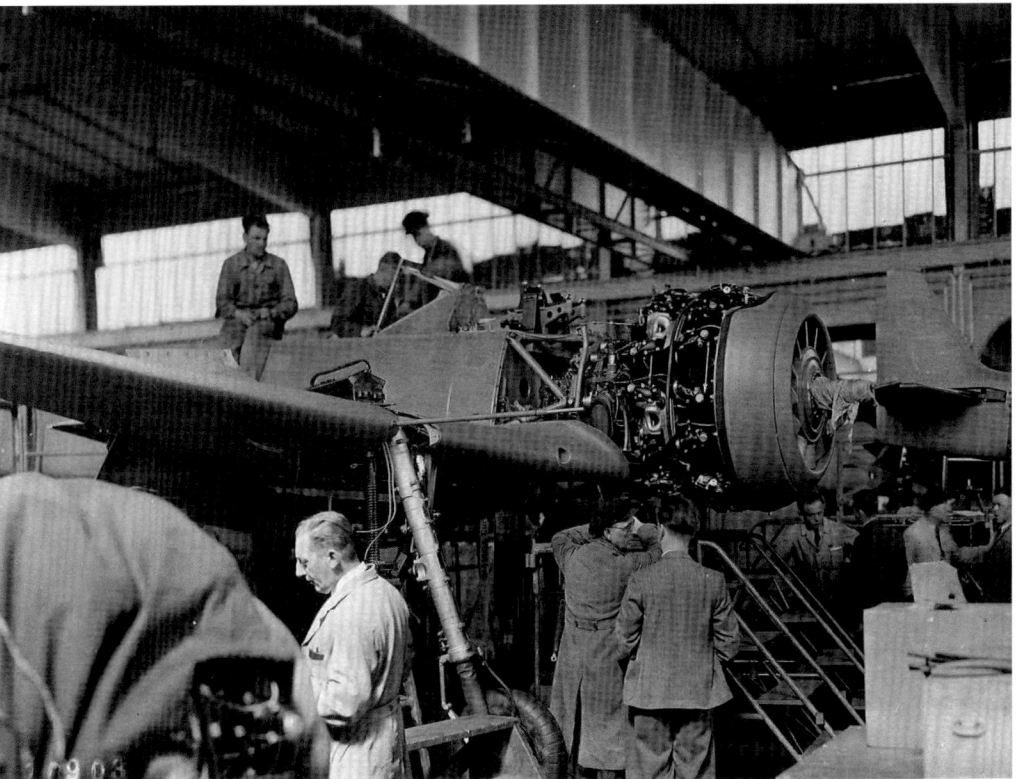

**LEFT** An engine installed on an A-0 model. The gun mounts for the two MG17 guns can be seen behind the engine. *(Airbus photo archive, Bremen)*

**LEFT** Final fitting out on the production line at Bremen. The aircraft are supported on jacks: this was still a small-scale-production operation, therefore there was no need for moving production lines. *(Airbus photo archive, Bremen)*

## Production models (A series)

The nine production versions of the A series are described below; they gave rise to numerous sub-variants with U or R suffixes that fall outside the scope of this account, which only deals with the main models. A list of R versions for the A-8 model can be found in Appendix 1.

### Fw190 A-1

Produced between May and September 1941, both at the Bremen factory and at a new dispersed plant at Marienburg, then in Prussia but now situated in Poland, the initial production version was powered by the BMW801 C-1 engine and armament consisted of four MG17 machine guns of 7.92mm calibre. Two were mounted in the upper fuselage bay and two in the wing roots. These weapons were synchronised to fire through the propeller disc. In the outboard wing, two 20mm MGFF cannon packed a heavier punch. The A-1 model began to equip Jagdgeschwader (JG) 26 from July 1941 and it was from this unit, operating from the Low Countries, that the first examples saw action against the RAF. Around 100 A-1 models were completed.

### Fw190 A-2

The A-2 was produced between August 1941 and September 1942, by the parent company and a number of outside contractors at dispersed locations. As well as Focke-Wulf at Bremen and Marienburg, Arado and AGO

**CENTRE AND LEFT** Two photos showing the hoisting and attaching of the VDM wooden-bladed propeller; the aircraft is resting on its undercarriage in the final assembly area. This is an A-0 pre-production aircraft. *(Airbus photo archive, Bremen)*

**RIGHT** In this Bremen factory shot, an early A-1 (W Nr 110005) has the propeller already attached. Of interest is the dimpled finish stiffening to the fuselage armament panel, something of a Focke-Wulf trademark. The ducting tube passing through the leading edge over the undercarriage leg feeds hot air from the engine to the outboard wing cannon ammunition boxes. *(Airbus photo archive, Bremen)*

at Oschersleben helped to contribute to the 420-odd examples built. The main differences between it and the earlier model was the fitting of the improved BMW801 C-2 engine and the installation in the wing roots of MG151/20 20mm cannon in place of the two MG17 guns. The cannon barrels protruded from the wing root, which served to distinguish this model from the A-1. It was not uncommon for some aircraft to have the outboard MGFF cannon omitted.

### Fw190 A-3

As well as the companies that built the A-2 model, Fieseler at Kassel also contributed to A-3 production. The major change over the previous model was the fitting of the much improved D-2 version of the BMW801. In addition to producing slightly more power, 1,725ps, the overheating problems and the issues encountered with the functioning of the Kommandogerät seemed to have been resolved. The engine installation included vertical cooling slots on the fuselage sides behind the exhaust ports, which aided recognition of this particular model. Produced between August 1941 and approximately August 1942, around 580 examples were built, some of which were involved in the development of the aircraft into different roles such as ground attack and fighter-bomber models which carried a variety of underwing and underbody stores. These variants paved the way for specialised models in the Fw190 F and G ranges.

### Fw190 A-4

Built between June 1942 and August 1943, production ran to some 900 aircraft; this version was the first to feature a distinctive fin post for attaching the aerial for the FuG16 radio

equipment. Armament fit remained the same as for the A-2 and A-3, again some aircraft having the outboard wing cannon omitted. This version usually carried an under-fuselage ETC501 stores rack for carrying a drop tank or bomb, as well as the factory-produced conversion kits, the Umrüst-Bausatz, which gave rise to the A-4/U suffix to denote various equipment fits for specialist roles such as armed photo-reconnaissance and long-range fighter-bomber (the Jabo-Rei). Other kits for fitting in the field, known as Rüstsätze (literally, armament options), gave rise to the A-4/R suffix, which denoted a specialised weapon fit.

### Fw190 A-5

The Fw190 was now proving to be such a versatile aircraft, capable of carrying a variety

**ABOVE** Final fitting out and inspection before flight testing. These A-1 models appear to have been retrospectively converted with the addition of engine cooling slots in the fuselage sides and are framed between balanced propeller assemblies in the foreground. *(Airbus photo archive, Bremen)*

**BELOW** The A-5 was the first model to have the engine moved forward. This can be seen at the wing root where an extra fairing has been added to cover the gap in this area. Also visible are the cockpit adjustable cooling shutters. This example is operated by the Flying Heritage Collection in Seattle, and is the only original example flying with a BMW radial engine.
*(Bob Harrington)*

of equipment and armament, that it became necessary with the A-5 model to move the engine 150mm forward to compensate for the change in centre of gravity brought about by the increasing amount of stores. The overall length of the aircraft was increased to 8.95m, the added length being obvious at the wing root where an extra fairing cover was installed to cover the gap when the engine cowling was moved forward. A distinguishing feature of the A-5 was the replacement of the vertical cooling slots with adjustable shutters, which became standard on the rest of the A-series aircraft. Again, numerous sub-variants with /U and /R designations covered everything from a radar-equipped night fighter to heavily armed bomber attack fighters equipped with underwing gun pods, bringing total armament to two machine guns and six cannon. Between November 1942 and June 1943 around 1,720 A-5s are believed to have been built.

### Fw190 A-6
Originally developed as a heavy fighter operating on the Eastern Front, armament was increased by fitting two MG151/20 cannon in the outer wing positions in place of the less effective MG FF weapons. The wing required a redesign and strengthening to accommodate the new cannon and their larger ammunition boxes. Manufactured by Fieseler, Arado, AGO and Norddeutsche Dornier, Wismar, between May 1943 and March 1944, production amounted to around 570 examples, possibly more.

### Fw190 A-7
This model introduced two 13mm-calibre MG131 machine guns in the upper fuselage in place of the smaller MG17 weapons. The access panels for these guns included distinct bulges in front of the windscreen. Built between November 1943 and March 1944, only around eighty of this particular model appear to have

been constructed by AGO, Fieseler and the Focke-Wulf plant at Cottbus.

### Fw190 A-8

The major production version of the series, the A-8, was built in greater numbers than any other, more than 1,300 examples being completed. It retained the weapons fit of the A-7 but the under-belly ETC501 stores rack was moved forward 200mm and in later versions was replaced by the improved ETC504 rack. Mountings for fitting underwing unguided mortar rockets (W.Gr21) were fitted as standard. The inner undercarriage doors were omitted from this model onwards. Later examples were designed to be fitted with one of two systems to boost engine power; either a GM-1 nitrous oxide set or a MW50 methanol-water system allowed the engine to maintain power at high altitude, although neither system was widely used and instead a 115l fuselage fuel tank was fitted in their place in the rear fuselage. The pitot tube was moved from a mid-wing position to the starboard wingtip. Focke-Wulf factories at Cottbus and Aslau built the A-8, as did Fieseler, Arado, AGO and Norddeutsche Dornier, who were joined by Weserflug at Tempelhof in a production run that lasted between February 1944 and January 1945. Some versions of this model were fitted with the more powerful and heavier armoured version of the BMW801 D-2 engine, the 801TU, which featured thicker armour around the annular cowling to protect the oil cooler. Other versions were equipped with outer-wing MK108 30mm cannon. This weapon required a bulge on the top surface of the wing, which was a feature that was retained in all subsequent models whether or not fitted with the MK108.

### Fw190 A-9

This version, the last of the A series, was equipped with the BMW TS engine which boosted power to around 2,230ps. A different propeller with wider blades was fitted and a 14-blade cooling fan installed. Some examples were fitted with an enlarged, round-topped cockpit canopy such as those fitted to ground attack versions. Armament remained similar to the A-8. Production was shared between Focke-Wulf at Cottbus and Aslau, Arado at Warnemünde,

Mimetall and Erfurt, and Norddeutsche Dornier at Wismar. Production took place between August 1944 and February 1945.

A further model, the A-10, was planned, which would have had four 30mm outer-wing cannon. It is possible that some earlier airframes were modified to this specification, as was frequently the practice with Focke-Wulf, which in turn makes it almost impossible to say for certain how many of each model were actually constructed and how many were rebuilt versions of earlier airframes.

## Experimental models (B and C series)

Kurt Tank studied ways to improve the 190's altitude performance, looking at a number of alternative powerplant options and turbo-supercharger installations. This led to the B, C and D series of the Fw190. The first two were ultimately failures and no production aircraft were produced. The work involved cost Focke-Wulf a great deal of time and resources, which in hindsight could have been better spent. The RLM development demands for new and pre-production models were torturous to say the least, with a requirement for many different development aircraft to test not only the various power plants but also new wing layouts, armament options, pressurised cockpits and so on. This protracted process was maintained throughout 1944 when the situation for the Third Reich was continuing to deteriorate, and

**ABOVE** Most numerous of the A series, the Fw190 A-8; this is 'White 11' of 5./JG4 but captured and in American hands. The aircraft was flown during Operation Bodenplatte on 1 January 1945 and was hit by flak during the attack over St Trond airfield. The pilot had to make an emergency landing. The weapons have been removed. The photo was taken by the resident USAAF 404th Fighter Group. *(USAF)*

it almost seemed as if the RLM hierarchy was living in a bubble when those in the industry were hoping to supply the Luftwaffe with what it most desperately needed – an effective Höhenjäger (high-altitude fighter) able to take on the Allied bombers and escorts that were increasingly successful in their attacks on German cities and infrastructure. Instead, much time and effort was wasted on quite needless projects such as a torpedo-armed version of the Fw190.

A telling contrast was the Allies' approach to developing a high-speed, high-altitude fighter. In 1942 the RAF took the decision to re-engine the Allison-engined Mustang with a Rolls-Royce power plant. The first test flight of the British engine in the Mustang airframe was in October 1942 and the first production examples were completed in the USA in April 1943, with only five development aircraft being built along the way. In contrast, the Luftwaffe test centre at Rechlin demanded between 20 and 30 development aircraft for each distinct mark, a requirement that became increasingly impossible to meet as the war wore on and Allied forces pressed on into Germany.

## Fw190 B-0

The first attempt at improving high-altitude performance was to fit four experimental aircraft with a pressurised cockpit and to study ways of boosting the power of the BMW801 engine. One example was unarmed and had a new wing with a span of 10.24m, while another was fitted with GM-1 nitrous oxide boost.

## Fw190 B-1

Similar to the GM-1-equipped B-0 but with armament changes, only a single example appears to have been constructed. All of these B series were extensively tested during 1943, but problems were encountered with cockpit heating and cockpit glazing that tended to shatter at altitude. These led to the abandonment of the project.

## Fw190 C-0 and C-1

A total of 13 prototypes of the C series aircraft were constructed; they were converted from earlier A-0 and A-1 aircraft and most were powered by versions of the Daimler-Benz DB 603 engine, which had better high-altitude performance than the BMW. Different aircraft tested a variety of features such as pressurised cockpits, armament options, shorter-span wings, a four-bladed propeller and, most interesting of all, a turbo-supercharger in an under-belly fairing. The turbo-supercharger installation failed because, unlike the Americans, the Germans did not have unlimited access to raw materials such as tungsten, which would have allowed them to design a sufficiently heat-resistant exhaust system for the turbos.

Generally, with the DB 603 engine fitted to the Focke-Wulf airframe, high-altitude

**RIGHT** The first prototype of the unsuccessful Fw190 C series. In an attempt to improve high-altitude performance, this early A-0 airframe was fitted with a DB603 engine and given the designation number V13. Although the DB engine did indeed improve performance as planned, there were problems with the installation and the project was abandoned. *(JaPo)*

performance was enhanced considerably over the standard 801-engined aircraft. However, this development did not perform as well as expected, and problems with the pressurisation system and the cockpit canopies led to this programme being abandoned in 1944.

## Pre-production models (D series)

The D series pioneered the use of the Junkers Jumo 213 in-line liquid-cooled engine. Developed from the Jumo 211, that was used primarily as a powerplant for bomber aircraft, the 213 engine was a speeded-up version with an improved cooling system. By 1944, when most factories had switched to fighter production, sufficient numbers were being produced to power the Fw190 series.

The Jumo 213 A-1 developed 1,795ps, which could be increased to 2,130ps by the use of MW50 boost; importantly, the engine's supercharger maintained power at 1,620ps up to 6,000m. The 213 offered what the 801 had lacked: more power at altitude. It also offered the possibility of mounting a gun that fired through the centre of the spinner.

### Fw190 D-0

Completed in the spring and summer of 1944, the first three experimental D-series aircraft with the Jumo 213 A-1 installation were based on conversions of earlier airframes, as was often the case with Focke-Wulf. The cowling was annular, housing the coolant radiator, giving the appearance of a radial installation. However, the nose was considerably longer (hence the nickname Langnasen-Dora (Long-nose Dora). The exhaust ports of the inverted V-12 Jumo exited six on either side of the cowling, and ahead of these the adjustable cowl flaps controlled the airflow through the radiator. There was some experimentation on the pre-production models with a pressurised cockpit, a feature desirable in a high-altitude fighter but one that caused Focke-Wulf some difficulties in design. Early D-1 and D-2 series were abandoned, and the designations D-3 to D-8 were never allocated because Focke-Wulf wanted to base the production D series on the A-9 airframe; hence the series continued with the D-9.

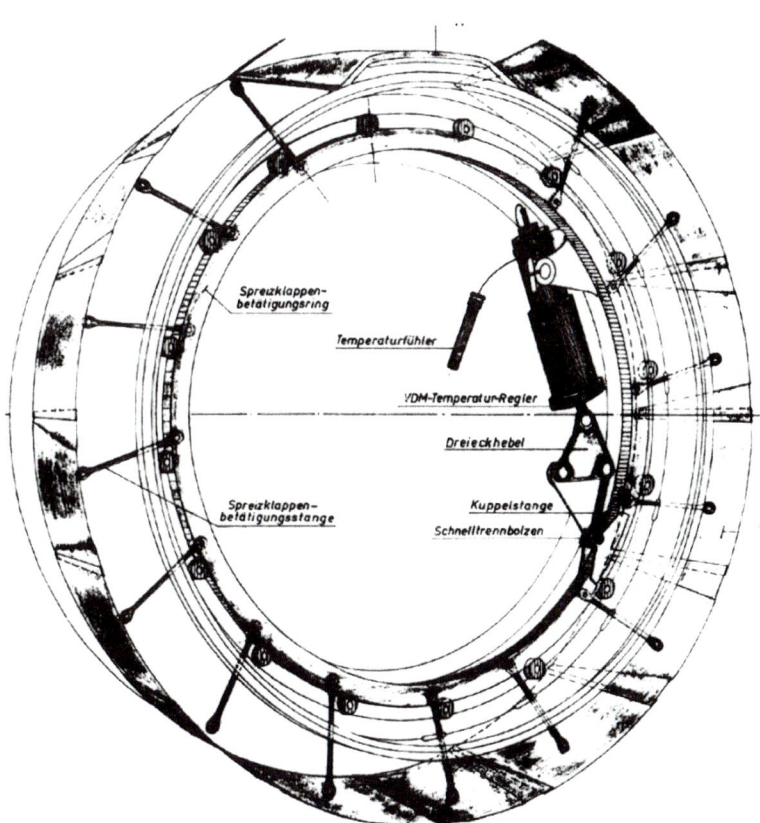

ABOVE The adjustable cowl flap arrangement for the D and Ta152 series. Jumo-powered aircraft automatically adjusted the position of the flaps dependent on the coolant temperature. *(Airbus photo archive, Bremen)*

## Production models

### Fw190 D-9

The longer Jumo engine required an extension to the aircraft's fuselage in order to control the changed centre of gravity. A fuselage extension section of 500mm was added just ahead of the tailplane, and the vertical fin was slightly enlarged and given a squarer top; these changes and the longer engine increased the overall length from 8.95m to 10.24m. Internally there were adjustments to the position of the oxygen bottles, which were now housed in the fuselage extension just ahead of the tail. In order to strengthen the airframe to cope with the extra weight of the Jumo engine, external horizontal stiffeners were added to the fuselage below the cockpit along with strengthening to the firewall and fuselage gun area. The wing had additional longitudinal stiffening added. Apart from these changes, the wing and fuselage centre section were basically unaltered from the late A-series aircraft. Production began in the summer of 1944 at the Focke-Wulf factory at Cottbus; the aircraft was also built by Fieseler and Mimetall.

RIGHT New, early production D-9 built by Focke-Wulf, Cottbus, demonstrating the lengthened nose of the Jumo installation and the additional lengthened rear fuselage. *(via Aviation-images.com)*

Many earlier A-8 airframes were modified to D-9 standard, thus the total number of aircraft produced is unclear, although around 700 are thought to have been completed. Armament was unchanged from standard A-7/A-8 models. The D-9 had a better rate of climb and dive, a higher top speed and an overall superior performance at altitudes above 6,000m than the radial-engined models. The fighter gave the Luftwaffe pilots something they had previously lacked, an aircraft that was on a par at altitude with Allied fighters such as the P-51 Mustang.

### Fw190 D-11

The D-10 version did not proceed beyond the design stage, but the D-11 was built in small numbers and was supplied with a different version of the Jumo engine, the 213 F-1, which replaced the single-stage, two-speed unit fitted to the 213 A-1 with a two-stage, three-speed device. Fuselage guns were removed and instead two MG151/20 cannon in the wing roots were supplemented by two outer-wing MK108 30mm cannon.

### Fw190 D-12

The major difference between this and the D-11 was the addition of a MK108 cannon firing through the propeller spinner and the deletion of the outer-wing MK108s. This version was also powered by the 213F or the 213E engine, which differed only by the addition of an intercooler. Again, only a small number of this version was produced.

### Fw190 D-13

The final production D model was equipped with the 20mm MG151/20 Motorkanone firing through the nose of the Jumo 213 F-1 engine, but was otherwise similar to the preceding model. Production commenced in March 1945, with around 30 aircraft being built.

RIGHT The ultimate model of the D series, the D-13 differed mainly from the D-9 in the installation of a nose-mounted 20mm cannon firing through the spinner. *(GossHawk Unlimited Inc.)*

## AMERICAN PILOTS' REPORT ON THE FW190 D-9

In a report issued by the US Air Materiel Command in 1946, a group of test pilots gave their opinions of a captured D-9. In this rare assessment, the aircraft is seen through the critical eyes of its one-time opponents. The results are favourable in some areas, while critical in others.

The report describes the limited shoulder and arm room in the cockpit and the seat position. The layout of the instrument panels also comes in for criticism in the way that the upper panel blanks out some of the instruments on the lower one. Otherwise, the layout of the cockpit is generally praised for its neatness. The single power lever operation comes in for particular approval.

Of handling and control the report states: 'The controls are highly effective at most speeds. Forces are moderate and control feel is good up to approximately 605kmh. When the aircraft turns at this speed, elevator forces become quite heavy and lateral forces are excessive. ...

'The outstanding characteristic of this aircraft that affects its manoeuvrability is its rate of roll. In this respect it compares well with the P-51D Mustang or the P-47 Thunderbolt but it cannot match the rate of roll of the P-80 Shooting Star or P-38J Lightning. The radius of turn, however, is poor and elevator forces in tight turns are excessive. Constant stabiliser adjustments are required in turns, which, if pulled too abruptly, result in a fast stall with little warning.'

It goes on to criticise the high noise level in the cockpit and the discomfort that would be experienced by a pilot flying for two hours or more. Forward vision on the ground is described as poor and taxiing is problematic because of the poor brakes. Landing and approach are described as 'not difficult', while landing roll is short and directional control is easy to maintain.

The report praises the Jumo 213 engine, saying that its functioning is excellent and that it 'seems to provide ample reliable power to make the Fw190 a high-performance aircraft comparable with Allied types of fighters of the same date'. However, more criticism is levelled at the electric switches that operate the flaps and undercarriage, which often fail to retract the wheels or to extend the flaps. The hydraulic system for actuating the coolant flaps is also said to be very difficult to operate and to function poorly.

In conclusion, the report states: 'The Fw190 D-9, although well armoured and equipped to carry heavy armament, appears to be much less desirable from a handling standpoint than the other models of the Fw190 using the BMW 14-cylinder radial engine.

'Any advantage that this aircraft may have in performance over other models of the Fw190 is more than offset by its poor handling characteristics.'

Perhaps the report's conclusions are not so surprising considering that Kurt Tank always thought of the D series as a 'stopgap' range before the fully developed and proven Ta152 family was supposed to take over multiple roles from ground attack to high-altitude interceptor. The D-9 was basically an A-series airframe with the Jumo engine in front, whereas the Ta152 was designed from the outset for an in-line engine and with different wing designs for various roles.

In contrast to these conclusions, Captain Eric Brown (a pilot who knows more than virtually anyone when comparing Second World War types) in his book *Wings on my Sleeve* included the Focke-Wulf Fw190 D-9 in his list of top twenty aircraft he has flown, stating that it was 'German fighter technology at its best'.

# Ground attack and fighter-bomber variants (F and G series)

The flexibility of the radial-engined A series led to the development of these two specialist series. The F series were designed to offer short-range ground attack and battlefield support operations. Often known by the term Jabo, short for Jagdbomber (fighter-bomber), different variants were equipped with a selection of stores and weaponry to support this role.

The G-series Jabo-Rei, for Jagdbomber mit vergrösserter Reichweite (long-range fighter-bomber), was designed specifically for longer-range fighter-bomber missions and often carried drop tanks to increase their range.

## Fw190 F1 and F2

Both families of variants derived from trials of A-series airframes. In the case of the ground attack machines there had been experimentation with an A-0 pre-production machine designated A-0/U4. Production A-4 and A-5 series with various U conversion kits formed the basis for the first two models in the F series; these configurations were retrospectively designated the Fw190 F-1 and Fw190 F-2 respectively. Additionally, approximately 271 new-build F-2s were constructed between late 1942 and mid-1943, some with 'tropical' air filters. All the F series featured additional armour protecting the underside of the engine, cockpit and fuel tanks along with armour on the cockpit sides. They only carried the MG151/20 inboard wing cannon but retained the fuselage weapons as well as a ventral stores rack or wing racks, or both.

## Fw190 F-3

Using the strengthened wing of the A-6 along with features from the A-5 model, the F-3 could carry a 300l drop tank under the fuselage. It was produced by Arado at Warnemünde between May 1943 and April 1944, and during this period between 450 and 500 aircraft were produced.

## Fw190 F-8

The F-4 to F-7 designations were used for projects that never went into production. The F-8 was similar to the A-8, but had a modified round-topped canopy to improve visibility along with a modified fuel injection system to boost short-term power at low altitude where the aircraft mostly operated. Produced mainly by Arado at Warnemünde and Norddeutsche Dornier at Wismar, numbers of this version are not known, because of the practice of rebuilding earlier airframes to later specifications. Records are far from complete but production seems to have begun in March 1944. The date for completion is not known.

## Fw190 F-9

The final model of the series, based on the A-9, was produced by the same factories that made the F-8. Production began in October 1944 and continued until the end of the war; production figures are unknown. All examples were equipped with a bulged canopy and some aircraft were built with a wide-span tail unit, as fitted to the Ta152. There were variations in the under-belly and underwing racks, some allowing the aircraft to carry two 250kg bombs.

## Fw190 G-1 and G-2

The first two models were redesignations of the early A-series fighter-bomber versions. The A-4/U8 became the G-1 and the A-5/U8 was then listed as the G-2. An indeterminate number of new-builds were constructed of each of these models, some converted from older airframes, with construction ending sometime during the summer of 1943. A characteristic of the G-series Jabo-Rei models was the fitting of three stores racks which allowed the carrying (typically) of two 300l underwing fuel tanks and either a 250 or 500kg bomb on the fuselage centre line. This cannot be used as a reliable recognition feature, however, as the underwing racks were often removed in the field if combat conditions necessitated it. All G-series aircraft were built without the fuselage guns and the gun troughs panelled over, distinguishing them from the F series.

## Fw190 G-3

Based on the layout of the A-6, and produced directly after the two preceding models, the G-3 model incorporated an autopilot. Some versions were built as night fighters with flame-damped exhausts. Like most models in the F and G series, only the inboard wing cannon were retained as a weight-saving measure, but one version of this model also carried two double-mounted cannon pods beneath each wing.

## Fw190 G-8

The designations G-4 to G7 never went into production and so the final model of the series was the G-8, based on the A-8. Production of an unknown number (but at least a few hundred) models took place between September 1943 and March 1944. The G series was finally abandoned in favour of the F-8, which was in more demand thanks to the deteriorating military situation facing the Nazi regime by this time.

# Trainer models (S series)

Conversions of A-5 and A-8 airframes into two-seat trainer aircraft were accomplished by removal of the auxiliary tank fitted behind the pilot's seat to make room for the second cockpit. A different three-piece canopy hinged to the side was fitted. The models were retrospectively designated as S-5 and S8.

## Ta152 series

Although the series is mainly remembered today for the only version to go into production, the 152 H, the Ta152 family was originally intended to include a range of other variants for specific roles, most of which did not progress beyond a few experimental examples. All of the Ta152 series had a fuselage lengthened further from that of the D series by extending the nose an extra 0.58m, in order to accommodate the longer MK103 cannon as a possible alternative to the MK108 engine-mounted weapon.

The Ta152 A (Jumo 213E engine) was to be a low- to medium-level fighter and the Ta152 B was designed as a heavy fighter for ground attack roles, powered by the Jumo 213 or Daimler Benz DB603 engine. Neither progressed beyond a handful of prototypes.

The most important member of the series that never quite made it was the low- to medium-level Ta152 C with the DB603L engine. It was to have a completely new wing housing fuel cells to increase range. The wing was also

**ABOVE** A prototype for an important series that never quite made it into production – the Ta152 C series was to be powered by the DB603L engine. It was fitted with a new 11m-span two-piece wing and featured a hydraulically operated undercarriage. It would probably have been a formidable aircraft. *(ww2 images)*

**BELOW** A drawing showing the fuselage and wing fuel tank arrangement for the Ta152 C and H-1 models, which shared a two-piece wing design. The extension of the wing is for the H model only. *(Airbus photo archive, Bremen)*

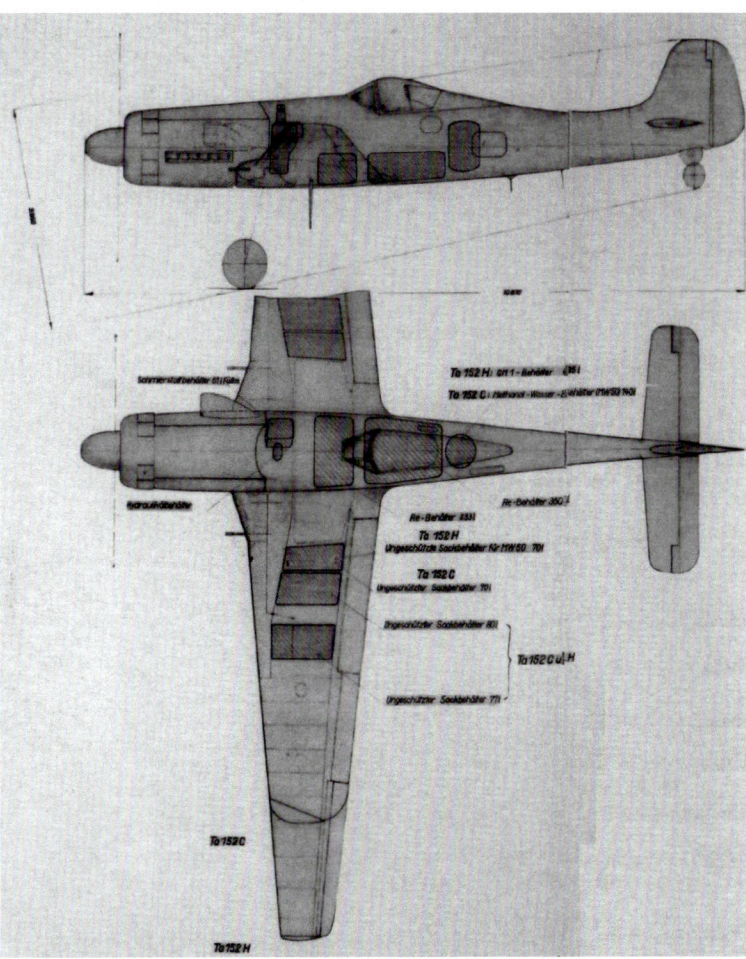

DEVELOPMENT AND PRODUCTION OF THE FW190

## Focke-Wulf Ta152 H-1.
*(Mike Badrocke)*

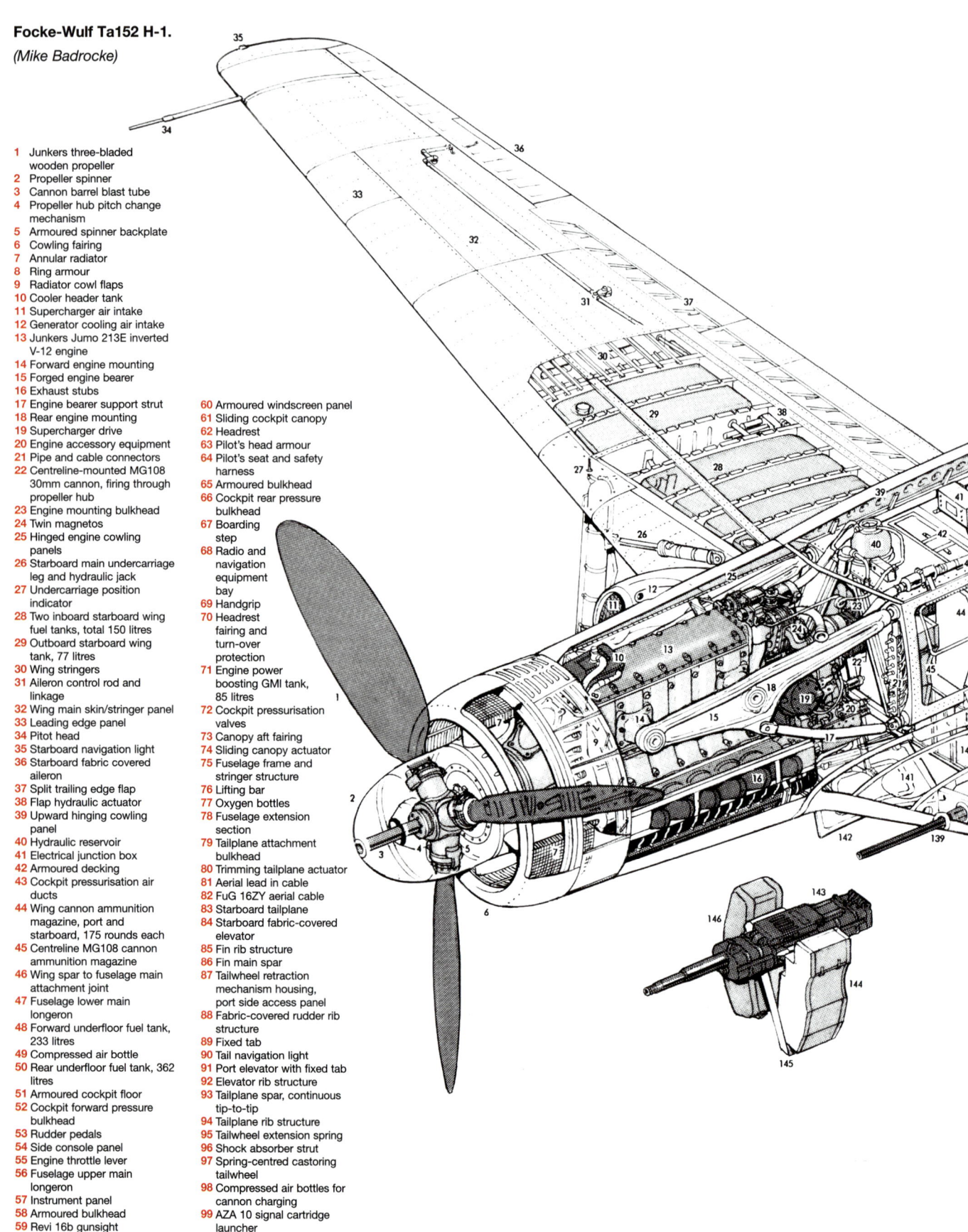

1 Junkers three-bladed wooden propeller
2 Propeller spinner
3 Cannon barrel blast tube
4 Propeller hub pitch change mechanism
5 Armoured spinner backplate
6 Cowling fairing
7 Annular radiator
8 Ring armour
9 Radiator cowl flaps
10 Cooler header tank
11 Supercharger air intake
12 Generator cooling air intake
13 Junkers Jumo 213E inverted V-12 engine
14 Forward engine mounting
15 Forged engine bearer
16 Exhaust stubs
17 Engine bearer support strut
18 Rear engine mounting
19 Supercharger drive
20 Engine accessory equipment
21 Pipe and cable connectors
22 Centreline-mounted MG108 30mm cannon, firing through propeller hub
23 Engine mounting bulkhead
24 Twin magnetos
25 Hinged engine cowling panels
26 Starboard main undercarriage leg and hydraulic jack
27 Undercarriage position indicator
28 Two inboard starboard wing fuel tanks, total 150 litres
29 Outboard starboard wing tank, 77 litres
30 Wing stringers
31 Aileron control rod and linkage
32 Wing main skin/stringer panel
33 Leading edge panel
34 Pitot head
35 Starboard navigation light
36 Starboard fabric covered aileron
37 Split trailing edge flap
38 Flap hydraulic actuator
39 Upward hinging cowling panel
40 Hydraulic reservoir
41 Electrical junction box
42 Armoured decking
43 Cockpit pressurisation air ducts
44 Wing cannon ammunition magazine, port and starboard, 175 rounds each
45 Centreline MG108 cannon ammunition magazine
46 Wing spar to fuselage main attachment joint
47 Fuselage lower main longeron
48 Forward underfloor fuel tank, 233 litres
49 Compressed air bottle
50 Rear underfloor fuel tank, 362 litres
51 Armoured cockpit floor
52 Cockpit forward pressure bulkhead
53 Rudder pedals
54 Side console panel
55 Engine throttle lever
56 Fuselage upper main longeron
57 Instrument panel
58 Armoured bulkhead
59 Revi 16b gunsight
60 Armoured windscreen panel
61 Sliding cockpit canopy
62 Headrest
63 Pilot's head armour
64 Pilot's seat and safety harness
65 Armoured bulkhead
66 Cockpit rear pressure bulkhead
67 Boarding step
68 Radio and navigation equipment bay
69 Handgrip
70 Headrest fairing and turn-over protection
71 Engine power boosting GMI tank, 85 litres
72 Cockpit pressurisation valves
73 Canopy aft fairing
74 Sliding canopy actuator
75 Fuselage frame and stringer structure
76 Lifting bar
77 Oxygen bottles
78 Fuselage extension section
79 Tailplane attachment bulkhead
80 Trimming tailplane actuator
81 Aerial lead in cable
82 FuG 16ZY aerial cable
83 Starboard tailplane
84 Starboard fabric-covered elevator
85 Fin rib structure
86 Fin main spar
87 Tailwheel retraction mechanism housing, port side access panel
88 Fabric-covered rudder rib structure
89 Fixed tab
90 Tail navigation light
91 Port elevator with fixed tab
92 Elevator rib structure
93 Tailplane spar, continuous tip-to-tip
94 Tailplane rib structure
95 Tailwheel extension spring
96 Shock absorber strut
97 Spring-centred castoring tailwheel
98 Compressed air bottles for cannon charging
99 AZA 10 signal cartridge launcher

| 100 | FuG25A IFF aerial |
| 101 | Master compass housing |
| 102 | Autopilot controller |
| 103 | Aft fuselage access hatch |
| 104 | D/F loop aerial |
| 105 | Retractable boarding step |
| 106 | Wing root trailing edge fairing with boarding step |
| 107 | Wing rear spar attachment joint |
| 108 | Port wing root MG151/20 20mm cannon |
| 109 | Hinged cannon bay access panel |
| 110 | Ammunition feed chute |
| 111 | Wing auxiliary spar |
| 112 | Port inboard wing fuel tanks, 80 litres, and MW50 tank, 70 litres |
| 113 | Port trailing edge flap shroud ribs |
| 114 | Hydraulic flap actuator |
| 115 | Port outboard fuel tank, 77 litres |
| 116 | Aileron control rod linkage |
| 117 | Wing rear spar |
| 118 | Port aileron geared tab |
| 119 | Aileron rib structure |
| 120 | Wing tip fairing |
| 121 | Port navigation light |
| 122 | Leading edge ribs |
| 123 | Wing lower skin/stringer panel with structural access hatches |
| 124 | Extended auxiliary centre-spar |
| 125 | Outboard leading edge spar |
| 126 | Wing rib structure |
| 127 | Tank bay end rib |
| 128 | Main undercarriage leg pivot mounting |
| 129 | Mainwheel leg doors |
| 130 | Torque scissor links |
| 131 | Wheel hub and brake |
| 132 | Port mainwheel |
| 133 | Mainwheel leg strut |
| 134 | FuG 16ZY antenna |
| 135 | Leading edge leg mounting access panel |
| 136 | Hydraulic retraction jack |
| 137 | Gun camera |
| 138 | Mainwheel leg up-lock |
| 139 | Cannon barrel |
| 140 | Wing main spar |
| 141 | Mainwheel bay |
| 142 | Wheel bay door |
| 143 | Centrally-mounted MK108 30mm cannon firing through propeller hub |
| 144 | Ammunition magazine, 90 rounds |
| 145 | Cartridge case ejector chute |
| 146 | Starboard side engine oil tank, 61 litres |

33

DEVELOPMENT AND PRODUCTION OF THE FW190

to be built in two pieces. All of these changes constituted a totally new design, at a time when the German aircraft industry was struggling to keep up with production outputs for existing types. Nevertheless, it was built, not only in experimental examples but also in a number of prototype versions, and it is just possible that one example was on operational strength at the end of the war.

There are believed to have been only two examples of the Ta152 E-series fighter-reconnaissance version, but fuselages of uncompleted models discovered after the war by Allied forces appeared to have been earmarked for conversion to Ta152 C specification.

Focke-Wulf spent a lot of time and effort trying to develop the Ta152 series but only had one type, the Ta152 H, on squadron strength right at the end of the war to show for it. Much of the delay was due to the RLM's poor decision-making and failure to take the need for improved types sufficiently seriously until far too late. If things had been different, the Ta152 C and H might have appeared in numbers in 1944, and the air war in Europe might well have taken a different course.

### Ta152 H

Kurt Tank and his team had long been aware of the altitude limitations of the radial-engined versions of the Fw190. Tank always regarded the 190 D as something of a stopgap machine until a more advanced high-altitude fighter could be designed. There was, until fairly late in the war, indifference towards high-altitude fighter development among senior Third Reich officials. Only when the level of American bombing raids (almost always from above 6,000m) began to significantly impact German industry did official attitudes start to change. Many in the aircraft industry believed this decision was made too late; the fact that the Ta152 H only entered service in January 1945, and then not in the high-altitude role for which it had been designed and in such small numbers that it had no significant impact, tends to bear out the designer's concerns. The Ta152 was one of the Second World War's most advanced piston-engined designs, and had it been available earlier in significant numbers it might not have changed the outcome but could have extended the duration of the war.

In order to increase high-altitude performance significantly, Tank and his team choose to radically redesign the Fw190 D as well as make use of its proven layout, along with results of technical experiments from various development projects, to incorporate improvements in the new fighter. The first prototype of what was to become the H series first flew in July 1943, and in August Focke-Wulf were officially allocated RLM number 8-152, using the first two letters of Tank's name as a prefix for the new design, in recognition that he now headed his own design bureau at Focke-Wulf. Work progressed slowly, largely because of official hesitation about the project. Eventual production did not get under way until November 1944. By this date, time was running out for the Luftwaffe – and ironically, considering the slow pace of previous development, the H was rushed into production without proper development having taken place.

Despite this, the performance of the Ta152 H has become renowned, perhaps helped by an account related by Kurt Tank himself. He tells of an occasion when he had just taken off in an unarmed Ta152 and received a radio message from the airfield tower that two Mustangs had just flown over the airfield in pursuit. Tank says that he pushed the throttle fully forward and switched on the MW50 injection. The aircraft surged forward and the Mustangs disappeared as specks in his rear-

**BELOW** Layout drawing of the instrument panel for the Ta152 H. *(Airbus photo archive, Bremen)*

view mirror. This was an aircraft with a quite exceptional performance and very much at the peak of piston-engined fighter design.

In his book *Wings of the Luftwaffe*, Eric Brown, Britain's most experienced test pilot, says of the Ta152:

*In my view, the Ta152 H was every bit as good as any of its Allied piston-engined counterparts and, from some aspects, better than most. It was unfortunate for the Jagdflieger, but undoubtedly fortunate for the Allies, that it arrived on the scene too late to play any serious role in the war.*

## Ta152 H-0

This pre-production series saw limited operational use, at the very end of the war in Europe. The H model was designed from the outset as a high-performance, high-altitude fighter. Although drawing on the overall layout of the D series, and fitted with a similar Jumo engine, it was in fact a very different aircraft. The forward fuselage extension necessitated moving the wing assembly forward to retain a workable centre of gravity envelope. This repositioning led to a redesign of the fuselage bulkhead at the front of the forward fuel tank, which in turn led to the fitting of a larger (362l) rear tank. The cockpit was pressurised, the canopy being sealed by rubber foam-filled tubes inflated by compressed air; the system maintained a pressure of 0.36 atmospheres at 8,000m.

Although the fuselage was clearly developed from the generic Fw190 design, the wing fitted to the H series was of an entirely new design. It was a high-aspect-ratio all-metal construction with a span of 14.44m. The thickness of the wing skinning was increased to take the increased loads imposed by the extra span, and extra half ribs were placed between each main rib at the leading edge. The new wing on the H-0 was different internally to that of the H-1 in that it did not hold fuel cells. Additionally, no GM-1 or MW50 boost systems were fitted to the H-0 series. The slightly wider tracked and strengthened undercarriage, instead of being electrically operated, was hydraulically actuated, as were the wing flaps. The oxygen bottles were retained in the fuselage extension as they had been in the D series, and a 5l compressed air bottle for operating the engine cannon was added to this area. Because the cabin was now pressurised, the flare gun in the cockpit was removed and replaced by electrically operated flare launchers in the rear fuselage. Production was at the Focke-Wulf Cottbus factory and began in November 1944, with 20 examples of this pre-production version known to have been completed. Standard armament consisted of one MK108 30mm engine-mounted cannon and two MG151/20 20mm cannon in the wing roots.

## Ta152 H-1

Externally very similar to the H-0 series, the 23 examples produced differed mainly by having a wing which was now built in two pieces and attached at the centre line by large flanges fixed to the top and bottom of the front wing spar. The internal structure was different to the H-0, in order to house bag-type fuel cells. The port inboard cell of the six fuel cells was allocated as a tank for the MW50 system, and a separate tank in the fuselage was used for the GM-1 boost. The engine was a Jumo E with a rated power of 2,080ps with boost. Performance was impressive, with a speed of 718kph at an almost unprecedented 10,700m altitude. Armament was the same as the H-0. Production was based at Cottbus late in the war, but only 23 examples appear to have been delivered before the surrender of Germany in May 1945.

**BELOW** This is probably Ta152 H-1 W Nr 150168, captured from JG301 and flown to Britain. It was scrapped in 1946. *(via Aviation-images.com)*

Chapter Two

# The Fw190 at war

When the new German fighter burst on to the scene of the air war over north-west Europe, it came as a surprise to British pilots who encountered it. Although RAF intelligence were aware of the existence of a new fighter type, very little was known of this deadly foe. Until an example could be obtained intact to study, Allied pilots found they were at a disadvantage.

**OPPOSITE** This pilot of an Fw190 A-2 is strapped into his aircraft at an airfield in France during the spring of 1942. The unusual unit markings relate to the pilot's initials – Bruno Hegenauer, of Stab. JG26. Wk Nr 20202 was only the second A-2 model built by Focke-Wulf at Bremen. *(Bundesarchiv Bild 101I-604-1528-17)*

## Western Front – Europe

The first aircraft to enter operational service were the A-1 models belonging to II Gruppe of JG26, based in northern France and the Low Countries from July 1941. Although these early models still suffered from engine problems, and were prohibited initially from flying over the Channel, they still proved more than a match for the Allied fighters. By the spring of 1942, with the engine problems resolved and given free rein over the sea, the increasing numbers of Fw190s were coming into ever more frequent contact with British fighters, the RAF's Spitfire Mk Vs, whose pilots struggled to combat the manoeuvrable and well-armed German machines.

Fighter pilot and top-scoring British ace of the war in Europe, Air Vice-Marshal James 'Johnnie' Johnson, records his initial encounters with the Fw190 in his book *Wing Leader*:

*We were puzzled by the unfamiliar silhouettes of some of the enemy fighters, which seemed to have squarer wing-tips and more tapering fuselages than the Messerschmitts we usually encountered. One pilot swore that one of the enemy aircraft which fastened on to him had a radial engine, and another pilot had distinctly seen a mixed armament of cannon and machine guns, all firing from wing positions.*

*Whatever these strange fighters were, they gave us a hard time of it. They seemed to be faster in a zoom climb than the 109, far more stable in a vertical dive, and they turned better than the Messerschmitt, for we all had our work cut out to shake them off. …*

*Back at our fighter base and encouraged by our intelligence officer, we drew up our chairs and sketched plan and side views of this strange aircraft…We were all agreed that it was superior to the Messerschmitt 109F and completely outclassed our Spitfire Vs. Our sketches disappeared into mysterious intelligence channels and we heard no more of the matter, but fighter pilots reported increasing numbers of these outstanding fighters over northern France.*

*Later we were given the novel explanation that the new enemy fighters were probably some of a batch of Curtiss Hawk aeroplanes which the French had bought from the United States shortly before the war. It was suggested to us that the Luftwaffe had taken over the Curtiss Hawks and were using them operationally. This was an absurd theory, for no pre-war aircraft had a performance to compare with these brutes, and it was not for some months that our intelligence admitted the introduction of a completely new fighter, the redoubtable Focke-Wulf 190, designed by Kurt Tank.*

**RIGHT** A rare sketch of RAF pilots' impressions of the Fw190 after their first encounters with the new fighter over France in the summer of 1941. These early combats were the cause of considerable alarm to the British pilots, who found their Spitfire Vs were completely outclassed by the latest German fighters. *(ww2 images)*

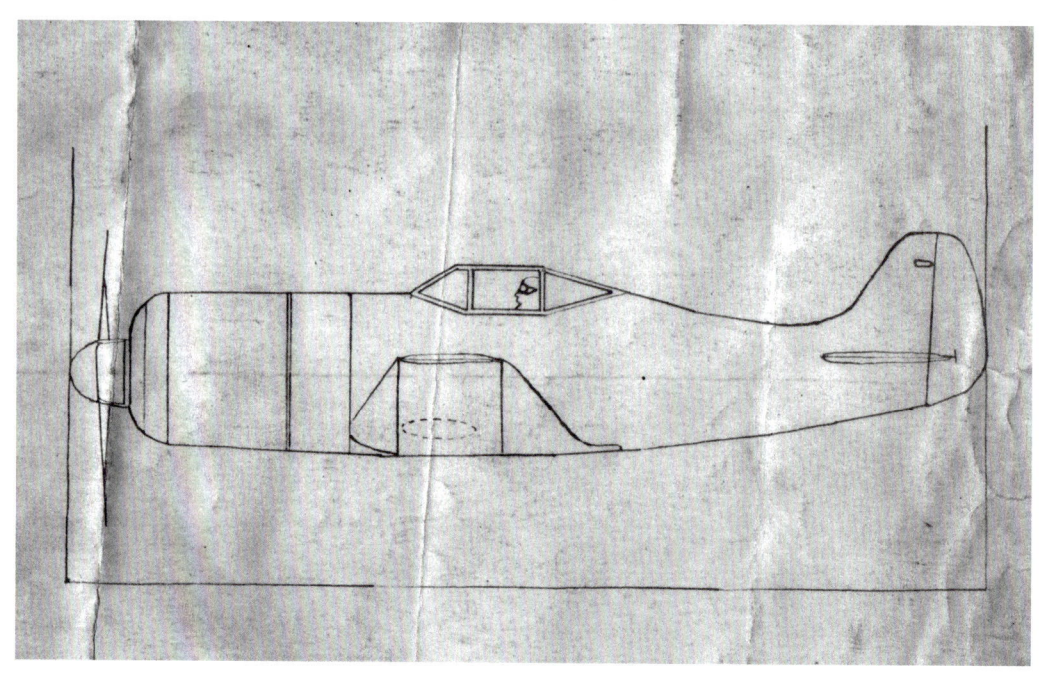

Incursions into European skies by British aircraft were often met by large groups of Fw190s that inflicted heavy casualties. On 1 June 1942, seven squadrons of Spitfire Vs providing cover for Hurricanes over Belgium were attacked by 40 Fw190s and 8 Spitfires were lost and 5 more damaged with no Focke-Wulf being seriously damaged. On the following day, a large RAF fighter sweep over St Omer in northern France was set upon by Fw190s. This time the outcome was seven Spitfires lost and two seriously damaged for no German losses.

One of the first major actions in which the Fw190 was involved was Operation Zerberus, also known as the Channel Dash. Between 11 and 13 February 1942, the German Kriegsmarine battleships *Scharnhorst* and *Gneisenau*, accompanied by the heavy cruiser *Prinz Eugen*, ran a British naval blockade of the Channel to reach their home ports on the north German coast. Air support was given by 250 fighters, including Fw190s, which provided daylight fighter cover to fend off heavy RAF attacks on the German ships. The operation was entirely successful for the Germans, with all ships arriving almost unscathed in port.

In August 1942, the Focke-Wulfs took part in their first significant mass air battle during Operation Jubilee, the ill-fated Allied raid on the French port of Dieppe. Two Fw190 JGs comprising over 100 aircraft defended the port from a British/Canadian seaborne assault with support from the RAF. The Allied airborne support comprised a mixed force of Spitfire Mk V and Spitfire Mk IX and Hawker Hurricane fighters along with Douglas Boston bombers and North American Mustang fighters. Fighting close to their home bases, the Axis fighters had the advantage of being able to stay in the air and fight for longer, whereas the Allied fighters had only enough fuel to stay over the combat area for a few minutes. Casualties are disputed, but it seems the Luftwaffe lost around 23 fighters and about 25 Dornier Do217 bombers against around 100 of all types lost by the RAF.

## Hit-and-run tactics

During 1942 and 1943 Jabo versions of Fw190s based in northern France were engaged in sporadic hit-and-run raids on British towns and coastal shipping. Towns attacked included those on the south coast of England, such as Bournemouth, Hastings and Torquay, which were within easy reach of the French airfields. These targets were generally of little if any military significance, but were difficult to defend as the attackers flew fast and low across the Channel to avoid radar detection. Often, only small numbers of aircraft took part (four to ten), and with each one typically equipped with a 250kg bomb

**LEFT** This Fw190 A-4 W Nr 147155 landed in error in April 1943 at West Malling airfield in the UK. It was a night fighter from II./SKG10 sent to attack targets in London. The pilot became lost and landed at the RAF base. The aircraft has been painted in a sooty black finish, which clearly did not weather well; the fairings under the wings were for the extra fuel tanks which were dropped before the aircraft landed. Note the message on the cowling – officials were keen that no one should interfere with their prize before it could be properly examined. *(Jonathan Falconer collection)*

**RIGHT** Based near Berlin, this A-9, 'White 11' operated by 1./NJG10, has a fairing over the exhausts to cut down glare at night and the numerous aerials are for a FuG217 airborne radar set to assist interceptions with enemy bombers. On the cowling is the badge showing the boar's head emblem of the Wilde Sau units. *(Alfred Price via Andy Thomas)*

the damage inflicted tended to be slight and was designed more to depress the morale of the civilian population than to strike at any specific target. However, in retaliation for Bomber Command raids on German cities, JG2 and JG26 Fw190s were ordered to hit at the historic city of Canterbury in south-east England. On the evening of 31 October 1942, just as dusk was falling, around 70 aircraft crossed the Channel at very low altitude and attacked the city. With the aid of surprise, the raiders dropped about 30 bombs on to built-up areas. Barrage balloons were deployed quickly, so some of the aircraft dropped their bombs short of the target. There were 32 people killed on the ground and 116 injured, while one Fw190 was shot down over land and another over the sea. This raid was the most significant attack on Britain by the Luftwaffe since the Battle of Britain more than two years earlier.

A specialised unit was formed in December 1942 to concentrate the Jabo assets of JG2 and JG26 into the new Schnellkampfgeschwader 10 (SKG10) which, equipped with Jabo versions of the Fw190, continued daylight operations over southern England as well as launching some night-flying operations, which were not particularly successful. On one occasion, four aircraft from this unit became lost at night and three of them landed at RAF West Malling, Kent. Two aircraft were destroyed and another was captured, while the fourth crashed elsewhere in Kent.

## Wilde Sau

In the constant battle against the night raids of Bomber Command, the Luftwaffe looked for ways to improve interceptions of bombers by its night fighters. A new method to allow the fighters to locate and shoot down bombers was proposed by Oberst Hans-Joachim Hermann. Previously, fighters had been guided by radar ground controllers to the area of the bomber stream where they would then use their airborne interception (AI) radar to locate individual aircraft to engage. The new method code named Wilde Sau allowed the fighters free rein to operate at a higher altitude than the bombers in the general area of the target. By using illumination from below, from searchlights, flares or fires, ideally on to an undercast of clouds, the enemy aircraft could be easily identified and attacked from above out of the darkness. The newly formed JG300 Wilde Sau unit comprising a mixed force of Fw190 and Bf109 night fighters saw action for the first time in early July 1943 when RAF bombers targeted Cologne. The fighters claimed 12 aircraft downed. Wilde Sau gained more credibility after the British captured a Junkers Ju88 night fighter and were able to work out the wavelength of its Lichtenstein radar. They were then able to drop small strips of aluminium foil (chaff) from their aircraft in order to produce 'clutter' on the German night fighters' radar screens. This they did over Hamburg in late July 1943, when the radar defence system was swamped by false echos, preventing the night fighters from locating the bomber stream, and most of the city was destroyed by a horrifying fire storm. As a result, Hermann's experimental force was expanded further, with JG301 and 302 forming a Jagddivision (JD). The new system had its limitations, though, as it was very much dependent on the right weather conditions: the cloud undercast had to be at the correct height. The Fw190s used were initially borrowed from day-fighter units and were not really suitable in the night-fighter role. Without effective flame-damped exhausts and with a lack of radar homing aids, many aircraft were lost in landing accidents or the pilots were forced to bail out after failing to locate an airfield at which they could land. The units eventually received specially adapted night fighters, but by the beginning of 1944, with losses of pilots and aircraft increasing as a result of the winter weather conditions and the development of a VHF version of the Lichtenstein radar, which was immune to jamming, the need for the Wilde Sau units diminished.

## Sturmgruppen

By the spring and early summer of 1944 daylight raids by American heavy bombers were having increasingly devastating effects on German industry. The bombers were now being escorted by long-range fighters for most if not their entire journey deep into the Reich territory. The Luftwaffe, in order to have the best chance to shoot down as many of the bombers as possible, needed to employ fighters with heavy armament and protective armour – the Fw190 A-8/R8 armed with two 13mm machine guns, two 20mm cannon and two 30mm cannon was the natural choice as a bomber destroyer. Additionally, this version carried extra armour protection in the form of 30mm-thick glass side panels on the canopy, 5mm-thick steel plates attached to the cockpit side panels and various thickness steel plates in the wings protecting the ammunition magazines of the 30mm cannon. This was in addition to the standard protection fitted to the aircraft surrounding the pilot's seat and the armour shielding the nose-mounted oil cooler. With the extra weight of armour and armament (around 200kg), the Focke-Wulf became heavy and less responsive, and was certainly no match for the American P-51 Mustang or P-47 Thunderbolt fighters. So to protect the Sturmgruppen (storm groups), more lightly armed and agile Begleitgruppen (escort groups), usually comprising Bf109 Gs, would seek to engage the American fighters while the Fw190s attacked the B-17 Fortress and B-24 Liberator bombers.

**LEFT** An aircraft from JG26 being loaded with a W.Gr 21cm mortar at Lille-Vendeville, France, in May 1944. These weapons were mainly intended to be used against American heavy bombers, but were also sometimes deployed against ground targets. *(Bundesarchiv Bild 101I-674-7772-13A/ photo Grosse)*

OPPOSITE **The often typical fate of many Luftwaffe aircraft as Allied forces overran airfields in Europe in their advance eastwards. This almost new A-8 from II./JG26 looks to have had its weapons removed, either by the retreating Luftwaffe or the Allies, and rendered unflyable by damage to the flying surfaces and removal of the cockpit canopy.** *(JaPo)*

In order to maximise the effectiveness of the A-8/R8s' formidable fire-power, the Sturmgruppen employed some unconventional tactics. A Staffel comprising around 12 aircraft would form in a broad arrowhead formation with the leader at the head of the arrow and each aircraft staggered back by 2 or 3m. The leader then selected which part of the enemy formation to attack, for example the high, middle or low squadron. As the fighters closed in on their targets from the rear, they would only begin firing at extreme close range, around 100m. This was to maximise the effectiveness of the MK108 cannon, the 30mm shells from this range having a devastating effect. On average it took only three hits to bring down a bomber. Of course the German pilots were under attack themselves from the massed guns of the Fortress and Liberator formations, but generally they suffered surprisingly few fatalities even at such close range, because of the very heavy armour protection they carried. Another unusual feature of the Sturmgruppen was that each pilot who volunteered to join was asked to sign a declaration to the effect that if necessary he would be willing to ram his aircraft into an enemy bomber in order to bring it down. It was not compulsory for a pilot to sign this document, but any who did, and failed to press home their attack by ramming, if for example they had run out of ammunition, could be liable to face a court martial. As it transpired, few pilots found it necessary to commit to ramming, and of those who did it is believed that about

## FOCKE-WULF DOWN

In the deadly combat encounters with American daylight heavy bombers, timing of attacks was crucial and could be the difference between the German fighter pilot claiming an Abschuss (a confirmed kill) or himself falling victim to the massed guns of the bombers.

Lt Eberhard Burath was an Fw190 pilot flying with I./JG1 based at Schipol in Holland during the summer of 1943. He recounts an incident in which he participated in an attack on B-17 bombers from the 95th Bomb Group based in England:

*On 28 July, the commander wanted to observe from a distance how an attack from ahead should really be carried out and I was to take his place as the leader. We overtook a formation entering the north of Holland, and then Hauptmann Schnoor sheared off to get a good view from above. Now it was my turn. Far enough ahead, about 3km, then right wing down to give the signal and a 180° turn to face the centre of the formation. Good, so far, and I am approaching from dead ahead. A glance to the side and I am struck dumb – way ahead of the others I am hurtling all alone at the viermots. Now good night! Instead of spreading the defensive fire evenly to all, the Yanks concentrate on the lone cheeky one and the tracer comes flying at my breast. I make myself very small, get the B-17 I was aiming for briefly into my sights, and press the trigger. Then it rattled into the kite like at a fireworks. Curtains and exit!*

LEFT **A Western Front Experten, Oberleutnant Josef Wurmheller, Staffelkapitän of 9./JG2 at Beaumont-le-Roger, France, summer 1943, with British and American victory symbols on the rudder of his Fw190 A-6 'Yellow 2'. He was killed on 22 June 1944 over Normandy, with a tally of 102 victories.** *(Bundesarchiv Bild 101I-483-2896-35A/photo Engelmann)*

*Smoke! Shear off. The prop stops, but fortunately no fire. Handy that the Dutch have such nice fields. I select a convenient one and approach, somewhat too fast, the kite refuses to sit down, I pass the end of the field, a pity that the Dutch have so many canals, I pass over them with the nose into the opposite bank, tail up and I ready for a somersault. But then my guardian angel gives my port wing a tiny nudge, my kite turns 180° and slaps neatly down, potatoes rain down on the fuselage and then a wonderful calm after the storm. I thank my guardian angel and crawl out of the cockpit into the potatoes. The machine looks quite sound, only 20cm shorter at the nose.*

(Source: Theo Boiten and Martin Bowman, Battles with the Luftwaffe)

Eberhard Burath was shot down twice more, but ended the war as a Staffelkapitän with seven victories, six against American heavy bombers and one Russian twin-engined bomber on the Eastern Front.

**LEFT** This ground attack F-8 W Nr 586875 was one of several from 6./SG10 flown in to Neubiberg airfield near Munich to surrender to American forces after they captured the base in April 1945. It wears the late war outlined style of Balkenkreutz and Hakenkreuz. *(JaPo)*

THE FW190 AT WAR

**ABOVE** One of several of Major 'Pips' Priller's mounts, all marked as 'Black 13', which he flew during the Normandy campaign. This A-8 with a drop tank may or may not have been the one he flew over the beaches on D-Day while commanding JG26 in France. *(Bundesarchiv Bild 101I-493-3370-36A/photo Engelmann)*

half survived. Indeed by late 1944, the shortage of pilots had become so severe that it was no longer considered necessary to use the Fw190 as a Sturmbock (battering ram).

The Sturmgruppen could and did register spectacular gains, such as on 7 July 1944, when around 23 B-24s including 12 from one group alone, the 492nd BG, were shot down when located by JG3 over Bernburg, Germany, without fighter cover. But as the Allied forces gradually gained dominance in the air battles over Germany, the Luftwaffe found itself losing more and more of its top pilots, whose experience could not be replaced, while the American war machine produced seemingly endless supplies of heavy bombers and fighters along with a continuous stream of men to fly them.

## D-Day daring

In a rare demonstration of the Luftwaffe's presence on D-Day, 6 June 1944, Fw190 pilots Josef 'Pips' Priller and his wingman Heinz Wodarczyk from JG26 carried out a single strafing attack on Sword Beach during the Normandy landings. Although this didn't constitute the only action launched by the Luftwaffe on this day when the Allied forces overwhelmed the skies over the landing beaches; there were in fact 170 sorties flown by the Luftwaffe. But in comparison to the Allies' 14,000 sorties, the German air activity went almost unnoticed. Priller's daring dash over the beach is recreated in the famous film *The Longest Day*. Priller was an adviser on the film. He finished the war with 101 victories, including 68 over the Spitfire, making him the highest-scoring Spitfire-Experte.

## Fw190 on the Eastern Front

As a result of the German forces' ultimately disastrous invasion of the Soviet Union in May 1941, code named Operation Barbarossa, and its failure to take Moscow, the German armies in the east had retreated but had stabilised their front line. In July 1942, they began their summer offensive to take important oilfields in the Russian Caucasus. Hitler, however, intervened to expand the original objectives to include the capture of Stalingrad. The resultant battle for the city dragged on for many months, through into the bitter Russian winter. Eventually, the German forces, decimated by cold and hunger, were

ABOVE Rare colour image of 6 Staffel of II./SchlG1, January 1943, displaying 13 new Fw190 A-5/U3s based on the Eastern Front at Deblin-Irema, Poland. This version of the A-5 carried additional protective armour and was capable of carrying 4 × 50kg bombs under the wing. Later, it was redesignated as the F-2 ground attack model. *(John Weal via Andy Thomas)*

LEFT Major Walter Nowotny in the cockpit of his Focke-Wulf on the Eastern Front. Norwotny scored most of his 255 confirmed kills in the Fw190; for long periods he averaged two kills per day. He died in November 1944 at the controls of an Me262 jet aircraft. *(Bundesarchiv Bild 101I-654-5830-18A/ photo Erlz)*

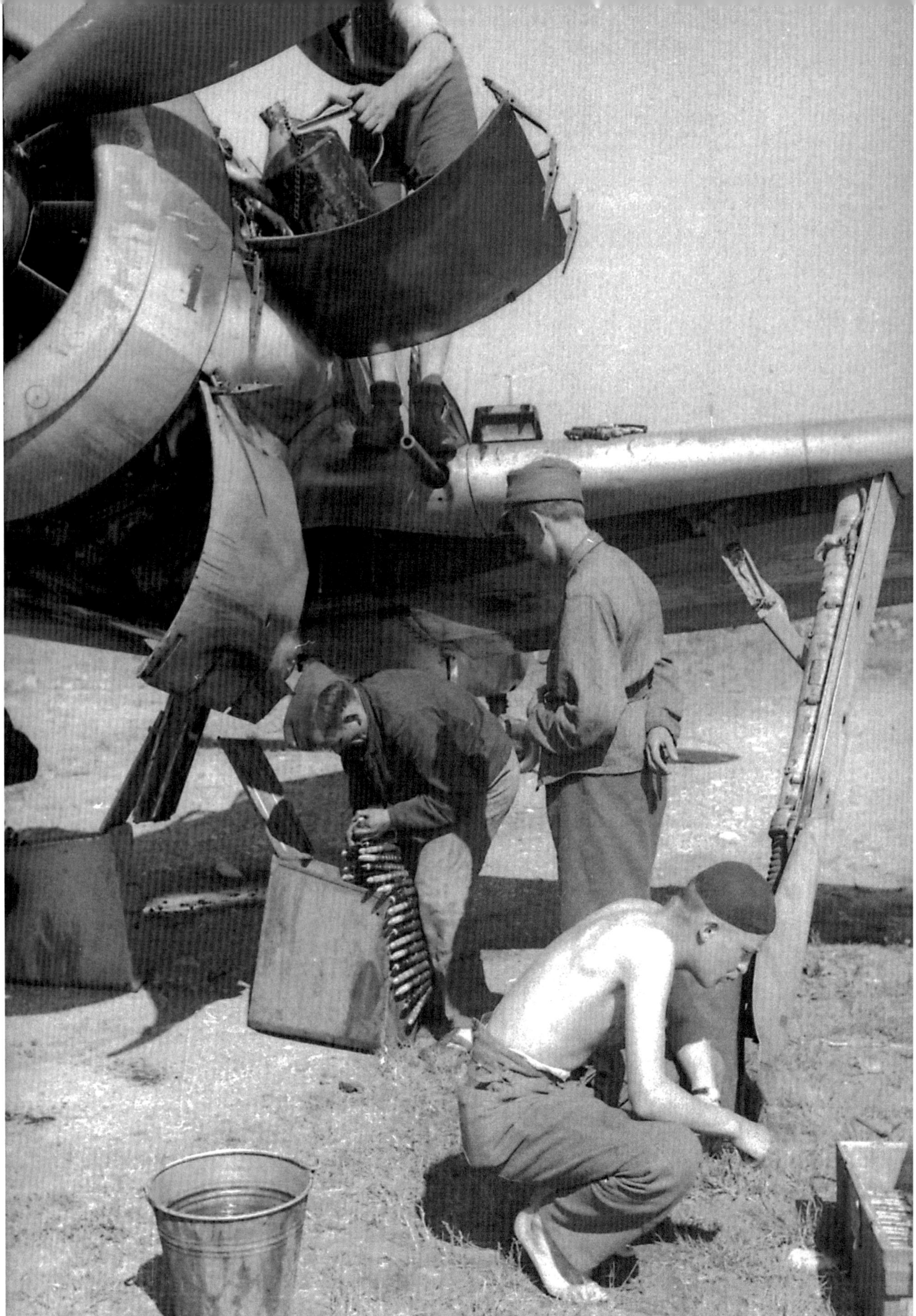

forced to surrender in February 1943. It was during this campaign that the Fw190 made its first appearance on the Eastern Front in September 1942, during the strategically important battle of Stalingrad. The first unit to use the fighters in combat was JG51; the Fw190s were engaged initially in supporting transport aircraft and bombers (often Junkers Ju87 Stuka dive-bombers), dropping supplies to pockets of isolated German troops that had become surrounded by Russian forces. By December, they were joined by JG54, which was converting to the Fw190. There were plenty of opportunities to engage defending Russian fighters, such as Petlyakov Pe-2s and Ilyushin Il-2s, which were easy prey for the better armed and faster German machines. Between them, these two units produced some of the top-scoring aces of the war. Many of these pilots, Experten such as Otto Kittel, Walter Nowotny and Joachim Brendel, scored all or almost all of their kills on the Eastern Front while flying the Fw190, having previously flown other types of aircraft.

The air campaign on Germany's Eastern Front was often characterised by aircraft having to make use of rough landing strips in very hostile winter conditions. Sometimes they were forced to use the frozen surfaces of lakes. In these circumstances, the Fw190 was an ideal choice, with its wide-track undercarriage, robust construction and relatively straightforward field maintenance. It proved to be superior in these environments to the narrow-track Messerschmitt Bf109 with its liquid-cooled engine.

# Kursk

During the summer of 1943, the German forces launched Operation Zitadelle (Citadel) on the Eastern Front using armour with air support to punch through the salient in the Kursk area, 450km south-west of Moscow. Fw190s equipped eight Jagdgruppen in both ground attack and fighter variants. The Luftwaffe, notably JG51 and JG54, scored highly over the inferior Russian aircraft, whose pilots were under orders to remain as escorts for the Soviet bombers and not to engage freely with German fighters. The air battle was a one-sided affair with losses on a single day for the Soviet 16th Air Army running to 30 against only 3 Fw190s lost. On the ground, though, it was a different story as the Nazi offensive came to a halt, overwhelmed by sheer numbers of men and tanks. The Russians then launched their own counter-attacks, threatening to cut off the German Ninth Army and the Second Panzer Army. The Fw190-equipped Geschwader with bomb-carrying Jabo variants were initially successful in slowing the Soviet advance, but it was a temporary reprieve for the exhausted ground forces below and the Panzerdivisions were eventually overwhelmed. The Fw190 had shown itself to be a formidable weapon both in its pure fighter form and as a bomb-carrying Jabo battlefield attack aircraft, its heavy armament being particularly valuable. But for the Nazi leadership the loss of the battle was to be a turning point, marking the last strategic offensive they would launch in the East.

## Flying the Fw190 in Russia

Lt Fritz Seyffardt of II./SchlG1 ended the war with 30 victories and was one of the first pilots to fly the Fw190 operationally on the Eastern Front. Here he gives his assessment of the aircraft in comparison to the Bf109.

*In 1942, I saw and flew my first Fw190; I was thrilled with this machine. During the war I flew the Fw190 A, F and G models, and also the Messerschmitt Bf109. The difference between the Fw190 and the Bf109 was that there was more room in the Focke-Wulf's cockpit and the controls were simpler – for example, landing flaps and trim were electric. Another pronounced difference was the stability of the Fw190. Thanks to its through-wing spars and wide landing gear the machine was substantially more stable in flight, and especially in landing on rough fields. At great height, engine performance was inadequate. Normal range of the later F models was approximately 600–680km. The average mission on the Russian Front lasted 45–60 minutes. Firepower was very good. As a rule we had two 20mm cannon and two machine guns. There was also provision for two additional 20mm cannon in the outer wing panels. As a flying tactic, we had the*

**OPPOSITE** A German detachment was sent to aid Finland against the Soviet Union during 1944. Operating from Immola airfield in southern Finland, sorties were flown by German pilots supported by Finnish ground crew. Here, a Fw190 A-6, belonging to 4./JG54, is being rearmed at Immola in June 1944. *(Bundesarchiv Bild 101I-727-0297-32A/ photo Doege)*

**ABOVE** Operating from Hungary from late 1944 through to early 1945, II./SG2 flew ground attack missions in appalling weather to support the German army's attempt to break through Soviet defences surrounding Budapest. This F-8 carries a yellow underwing chevron identification symbol painted on all Luftflotte 4 aircraft. *(ww2 images)*

*greatest success when we flew in open formation, in other words with approximately 80 to 100m separation between aircraft. In the target area we split into two-plane Rotte elements for the attack, only re-assembling into larger formations on the return flight. In altogether about 500 frontline missions, I had to make several belly landings on differing terrains, something that could be done without undue difficulty.*
(Source: John Weal, *Focke-Wulf Fw190 Aces of the Russian Front*)

### 'Beethoven' and 'Mistel'

A novel use of German technology on the Russian Front was the creation of the unusual 'Beethoven' combination of aircraft. It comprised a fighter, usually a Fw190 or sometimes a Bf109, mounted on struts above a twin-engined Junkers Ju88 bomber. The bomber's stripped-out fuselage contained 3,500kg of high explosive. The combination was controlled by the fighter above via electrical signals to the bomber's autopilot. When approaching the objective, the Focke-Wulf pilot aligned the combination with the target, locked the bomber's autopilot and detonated the explosive bolts to separate his aircraft from the warhead-laden lower component. The theory was that the bomber flew on directly to the target where the explosives detonated. The Beethoven–Gerät, as it was officially known, was also referred to as Mistel (Mistletoe) and was developed during 1944 in order to strike at the Russian armament industry. Key targets had been identified in the Moscow and Gorky regions, namely power stations supplying armament factories. These installations were difficult to hit with conventional bombs and were well protected by concrete. The Beethoven combinations gave the Luftwaffe the opportunity to deliver a much larger than normal warhead with high precision.

Two bomber units were chosen to fly these missions, code named Eisenhammer (Iron hammer) Kampfgeschwader 30 and 200. KG30 was based at an airfield near to Prague and began training former bomber pilots to fly the ungainly looking combination. Special training versions were built with the Ju88 retaining its cockpit, which allowed a second pilot in the bomber to land at the end of a training session for the Fw190 pilot. A fully armed Beethoven combination was never designed to land once it had taken off. Most pilots found little difficulty mastering the strange-looking aircraft combination, despite its appearance. The pilot sat some 5.5m from the ground and a long ladder was required to reach the cockpit, yet the combination was reported to handle similarly in the air to a normal Ju88.

48
FOCKE-WULF FW190 MANUAL

Control was effected by the pilot's stick and rudder pedal movements, which were relayed by electrical signals to the servo system of the Ju88's autopilot; thus the flying controls of the two aircraft were synchronised in flight. During manoeuvring, the autopilot was set to Reiseflug (cruise flight) allowing the pilot to control the combination in this manner. When switched to Automatik, the autopilot took over, allowing the combination to maintain heading and altitude and also to keep the Ju88 on course during its final run-in to the target. A panel containing engine instruments for the powerplants of the Ju88 was added to the Fw190 cockpit along with controls for the engines of the bomber.

The plan for Operation Eisenhammer was to fly from airfields as far to the east as possible and at night, to try to avoid detection. Some of the targets were almost 1,600km distant, so the attacks were to be timed to take place at first light. Extra fuel was contained in a 1,200l tank beneath the Fw190, but during the flight the Fw190 consumed fuel from the tanks of the Ju88 so for the return flight it had almost full tanks. Stripped of armament, the fighter was to rely on its speed to escape to the west and land at German-held airfields in Latvia. In the event, before sufficient crews could be trained and readied for missions, the speed of the Russian advance overwhelmed the airfields that Operation Eisenhammer would have used, and the targets were put beyond reach of the combinations.

Instead, those Beethoven combinations which survived were withdrawn to the west and were used in the last months of the war against the Red Army encroaching on Berlin. In an effort to hold off the Soviet forces, attacks were launched on vital bridgeheads across the Oder river. Several assaults by KG200 damaged the Steinau railway bridge in March 1945 and several others were attacked and damaged during April, but none was destroyed.

It is interesting to compare the German approach to delivering a remotely guided bomb to that of the American USAAF, which attempted a similar objective but using radio control from another aircraft flying close to the explosive-packed drone. In the event, neither system was developed sufficiently to be very successful.

## The North African and Mediterranean campaigns

The 190 made its debut in North Africa in November 1942, just after the Allies had defeated Germany's Afrika Korps at El Alamein in Egypt and their forces had landed in North Africa under Operation Torch. In an

**ABOVE** One of the more unusual uses of the Fw190 was in the Mistel concept, in this case comprising a Fw190 mounted above a Junkers Ju88 bomber. This is a captured pair in British markings after the war. It is a training combination as the Ju88 has retained its cockpit and not had its nose replaced by a warhead. *(via Aviation-images.com)*

**LEFT** During the North African campaign, a Focke-Wulf flies over a British tank. The road is the Via Balbia, now known as the Libyan Coastal Highway. A doctored version of this photograph shows the tank engulfed in smoke and flames, in an obvious Nazi propaganda attempt. *(Bundesarchiv Bild 101I-146-1994-065-11/photo unknown)*

**BELOW** Ground attack Fw190 G-3, Wk Nr 160043, was left behind by the retreating Luftwaffe as the Allies pushed northwards towards Rome. This aircraft, complete with a 250kg bomb and several spares, was left at Montecorvino airfield, September 1943. *(Jonathan Falconer collection)*

effort to establish a bridgehead and resupply it, the Axis rapidly moved ground and air forces into Tunisia while the Allies fought to gain air superiority and to prevent a build-up of German troops. Tropicalised versions of the A-4 and A-5 operated along with specialised F and G models equipped for desert conditions by the fitting of a large tropical air filter into the bulge of the cowling air duct. Flying from airfields in Tunisia and Algeria, these aircraft were primarily employed attacking ground targets such as vehicles, tanks, anti-aircraft guns, shipping and airfields as well as engaging American, British and French aircraft such as the Spitfire, P-40 Warhawk and P-38 Lightning. The Fw190 was particularly effective against the American twin-engined P-38 fighter, whose slow rate of roll made it particularly vulnerable to the agile and fast-turning German fighter. The campaign, though, was brief, for after six months the Axis forces surrendered following defeats at the battles of Bizerte and Tunis in May 1943.

Only a few weeks later, Fw190 fighter-bomber units flying from bases in Sicily resumed full-scale operations, mainly against Allied shipping sailing between Sicily and North Africa, along with attacks on Allied airfields. However, in July, Allied forces from Britain, United States and Canada successfully landed in Sicily and the Focke-Wulf units faced difficult times as they attempted to stem the Allies' advance inland towards the north-east corner of the island. Despite increasingly superior Allied air cover, the Luftwaffe pilots flew often successful missions against shipping, harbours and troop concentrations. This only served to delay inevitable defeat, however, and German and Italian forces withdrew to mainland Italy in August 1943, opening the Mediterranean sea lanes.

The Allied invasion then continued in early September 1943 on the southern Italian mainland, where the main Fw190-equipped unit, SchlG4, flew ground-support missions for the German army, which was attempting to hold back the Allied force's advance toward Rome. The unit's pilots flew many sorties against armoured vehicles, bridges, airfields and troops through deteriorating weather conditions during the autumn and into the winter of 1943–44; the battle for southern Italy finally ended in January 1944.

### Dogfight over the desert

In February 1943, Oberleutnant Erich Rudorffer was a Fw190 pilot with II./JG2 based at Kairouan airfield in Tunisia. He flew one of six aircraft ordered to scramble to intercept enemy aircraft flying a reconnaissance mission in the area:

*When we started for the bombers the Curtiss fighters came down on us and that's when the dogfight began. After a time the P-40s, which were not as fast as us, went into a 'Lufbery circle' and I began to slip in from low and high and shoot them down. I managed to shoot down six in about seven minutes. As I recall the combat report, I got one at 13:59 and the last at 14:06. By that time the fight had broken up and everyone had scattered. Then I saw some P-38s strafing below us, and though I only had about four Fw190s with me at this time, I went down at them and surprised them. I got one coming from above and then went up again and came down on another and shot him down. That gave me eight for the day – I remember it because it was one of the best days I ever had.*

(Source: Andrew Arthy and Morten Jessen, *Fw190 in North Africa*)

## Captured butcher birds

The RAF made full use of the Fw190s which fell into its hands during the course of the war. Others followed the first example, the Fw190 A-3 that mistakenly landed in Wales. Aircraft landed in error following disorientated night sorties, and later, when the Allies invaded Europe, many were captured on former Luftwaffe bases. Each was extensively tested to find weaknesses that might be exploited by Allied pilots.

Among the pilots whose job it was to test and evaluate captured enemy aircraft was Captain Eric Brown, whose experience in flying a world record 487 different types of aircraft places him in a unique position to assess the strengths and weaknesses of the Focke-Wulf design.

**BELOW A prize for the RAF was the fortunate acquisition of an intact Fw190 A-3 when in June 1942 Oberleutnant Faber mistook the Bristol Channel for the English Channel and, believing himself over France, landed instead at RAF Pembrey in Wales. The timing could not have been better for the British.**
*(Andy Thomas)*

## COMPARISONS WITH ALLIED FIGHTERS

**BELOW RAE Farnborough's captured Fw190 A-4 in RAF markings (PE882) is flying alongside a Fleet Air Arm Spitfire Mk Ia (Y1-M, R7193) from the Naval Fighter School at Yeovilton, 8 March 1944.** *(via Aviation-images.com)*

Since the first Fw190s appeared in combat in August 1941, the RAF were very keen to obtain an example of the fighter and learn more about the new combat type that was proving more than a match for its best front-line fighter at the time – the Spitfire V. So eager was Fighter Command to learn more of the Fw190's secrets, that a commando raid on a French airfield was proposed in order to steal a Fw190 and fly it intact back to England. This daring plan was never put into action, however, as events superseded it. On 23 June 1942, a disorientated German pilot, Oberleutnant Arnim Faber, having mistaken the Bristol Channel for the English Channel after engaging Spitfires over the south of England, inadvertently landed his Fw190 A-3, Wk Nr 135313, at Pembrey, South Wales. This unexpected windfall for the RAF was exactly what they wanted, and they wasted no time in examining their new 'war booty' in every detail. In doing so they were very anxious to find any weakness in the design that RAF pilots might exploit in combat situations. For this reason comparison combat flights were made by the A-3 and a number of Allied combat types.

In their detailed report of the aircraft, the RAF's Air Fighting Development Unit (AFDU) lavished praise on many features of the design and performance; they were particularly complimentary regarding the layout and comfort level of the cockpit, the general flying characteristics which they described as being 'extremely light and positive' and the fact that retrimming of the flight controls was rarely necessary. The all-round vision from the cockpit was also praised, and described as 'the best that has yet been seen by this unit', although it was not considered helpful that the hood could not be opened in flight. On the debit side, the report notes that the view ahead on the ground was poor, making taxiing difficult, take-offs and landings also presenting the pilot with a restricted view ahead. Furthermore, the report noted that the glare from the exhaust ejector stubs at night would compromise the night vision of the pilot.

## FLIGHT-TESTS – FW190 AGAINST THE SPITFIRE MK VB

The German fighter was found to be faster by between 30 and 55kph at a range of heights between 600 and 6,400m. It also demonstrated a better climb performance at all heights and, being faster in the dive, could easily leave the Spitfire behind. When it came to manoeuvrability, the Fw190 was found to have a superior rate of roll, but the Spitfire could easily out-turn it. In order to reduce the chances of being 'bounced' by the 190, the report recommended that Spitfire pilots should cruise at high speed in the combat zone, and if intercepted while returning home, they should enter a shallow dive. The Fw190 would eventually catch up, but not before the aircraft had been drawn a long way from its base.

## AGAINST THE SPITFIRE MK IX

In combat trials against the improved Spitfire IX, with the Merlin 60-series engine, both aircraft were found to be closely matched in terms of speed over a range of heights, the difference being no more than 13kph in favour of the Focke-Wulf at 600m. Parity in the climb was restored, and above 6,500m the performance of the Fw190 fell off rapidly in comparison. However, in the dive the Focke-Wulf could still outstrip its British counterpart, and its acceleration was better.

## AGAINST THE RAF MUSTANG MK IA (P-51A)

When pitted against the Allison-engined Mustang, it was found that the Fw190 had a similar top speed at various heights except between 3,000 and 4,500m, when the P-51 was about 25kph faster. The German fighter could out-climb its American counterpart easily, although in a dive the two were quite evenly matched. When it came to turning, the Fw190 was inferior to the Mustang. However, the German fighter possessed a superior rate of roll. Acceleration of the Fw190 was found to be slightly better. Overall, the two combatants were considered to be fairly evenly matched. The report found that the 190 performed best against the Mustang below 900m and above 6,100m, whereas between 1,500 and 4,500m the Mustang had the edge.

## AGAINST THE P-38 LIGHTNING

When compared to the P-38F, the Fw190 was found to be faster at heights up to 6,700m, at which point the two aircraft were approximately equal. Above this the P-38 was slightly faster. In the climb, the Focke-Wulf was superior up to 4,500m, above which the American fighter improved its rate of climb rapidly until at 6,000m it was the better performer. In the dive, the German fighter was found to be better and its acceleration was faster than that of the P-38. In terms of manoeuvrability, the Fw190 was better in all respects except for turns at or below 225kph, when the P-38 could out-turn its German foe. Allied pilots flying the Lightning were advised that if 'bounced' by the 190, they should pull up into a spiral climbing turn, flying at the lowest possible airspeed.

## AGAINST THE TYPHOON

Limited trials flown against the Typhoon found that the British fighter was slightly faster at all heights and that it was able to out-climb and out-dive the Fw190. The tests revealed that both aircraft possessed similar turning circles but the 190 had a faster rate of roll.

## AGAINST THE SPITFIRE MK XII

When pitted against the prototype Griffon-engined Spitfire, limited tests showed that the British aircraft had a significant speed advantage and better acceleration as well as the ability to out-turn the Focke-Wulf. Although not compared at the time, it is very likely that the 190 still possessed a better rate of roll.

ABOVE British engineers and pilots lost no time examining every detail of this captured machine. The results of their findings proved invaluable in developing tactics to combat the threat of the Focke-Wulf fighter. *(via Aviation-images.com)*

Eric Brown summarises his thoughts on flying the Fw190:

*I was to fly the Fw190 many times and in several varieties – among the last of the radial engined members of Kurt Tank's fighter family that I flew was an Fw190 F-8 on 28 July 1945 – and each time I was to experience that sense of exhilaration that came from flying an aircraft that one intrinsically knew to be a top-notcher, yet, at the same time, demanded handling skill if its high qualities were to be exploited. Just as the Spitfire IX was probably the most outstanding British fighter to give service in World War Two, its Teutonic counterpart is undoubtedly deserving of the same recognition for Germany. Both were supreme in their time and class; both were durable and technically superb, and if each had not been there to counter the other, then the balance of power could have been dramatically altered at a crucial period in the fortunes of both combatants.*

(Source: Eric 'Winkle' Brown, *Wings of the Luftwaffe*)

## Blitzkrieg in the Ardennes – Operation Bodenplatte

The winter of 1944–45 was particularly harsh in Europe, and following the invasion of Normandy in June 1944, the Allies had advanced as far as the forested Ardennes region situated between France, Belgium and Luxembourg.

In order to support the Axis forces in their counter-offensive against the Allied land forces that were pushing eastwards towards the German border in north-west Europe, a large-scale counter-attack was planned that would split the British and American armies. For his part, Reichsmarschall Hermann Göring ordered a massive air assault to be scheduled to coincide with the land offensive on 16 December 1944. Bad weather prevented the planned air attack on this date, but the Nazi land offensive initially gained success in what

RIGHT A casualty of Operation Boddenplatte, this is Fw190 A-8/R2, 'White 11' from JG4 being examined by American pilots. The aircraft made a wheels-up landing near St Trond airfield in Belgium. It was repaired and flown by the 404FG. *(John Weal via Andy Thomas)*

became known as the 'Battle of the Bulge'. The air assault had to be put off until the weather conditions improved and it finally happened on New Year's Day 1945, when the order was given for Operation Bodenplatte (base plate) to commence at dawn. The attack on 16 RAF and USAAF airfields in Belgium, Holland and France was to be led by night-fighter wings flying Ju88 bombers to act as navigational pathfinders for some 34 Gruppen of fighters, consisting of Fw190 A and D series and Bf109s. In total over 1,000 aircraft took part.

Although the Luftwaffe achieved an element of surprise as they attacked the Allied bases flying at very low level, the mission was poorly conceived and executed. Several groups were jumped by Spitfires, Mustangs and Typhoons flying reconnaissance patrols, which inflicted heavy losses. German flak gun crews had not been fully informed of the operation and as a result a number of aircraft were victims of friendly fire. Many of the German pilots lacked experience and training, and amid the secrecy surrounding the mission, they received a very cursory briefing just before they were due to fly. Additionally, all aircrews had been ordered to maintain radio silence during the mission even when attacking enemy bases, by which time the secret had already been revealed to the Allies. This added to confusion during the attacks.

Most of the Allied losses were of unmanned aircraft on the ground, and these were rapidly replaced; such was the commitment to armaments production at this time. Figures are disputed but Allied personnel losses are believed to be in the low teens, with around 320 aircraft destroyed and 200 damaged. German casualties invariably meant the loss of both man and machine, and totalled 143 pilots killed or missing with 70 captured and 21 wounded, and 271 fighters destroyed and 65 damaged. At this critical time skilled and experienced pilots were already in short supply, and the German aircraft industry was struggling to produce aircraft in its war-ravaged factories.

The Fw190, as potent a ground attack aircraft as it was, when hampered by poor planning and inexperienced hands, was as vulnerable as any other type.

Despite achieving some tactical surprise, the operation did not fulfil its aim of gaining air superiority in the Ardennes; it was to be the Luftwaffe's last large-scale strategic offensive of the war. In the remaining weeks, the fighter force was unable to mount an effective defence of German air space after such a severe depletion both of aircraft and experienced pilots.

## FOCKE-WULF EXPORTS

Nazi Germany supplied several of its allies with the Fw190 during the course of the Second World War. Deliveries to the Royal Hungarian National Air Force (MKHL) began in November 1944, and eventually totalled 72 ground attack Fw190 F and G versions. Originally intended to fly against the Soviet forces on the Eastern Front with their German counterparts, the Hungarian Air Force only ever deployed them against the USAAF and the Soviet Air Force (VVS) in defence of their own country. Operations continued until late April 1945, when a shortage of fuel finally grounded the aircraft.

Turkey, a neutral country during the Second World War, received between 60 and 70 Aa-3 models between 1943 and 1944, the extra 'a' in the designation referring to a foreign (ausland) model. The Turkish Air Force operated the Fw190 alongside British and American types during the war, including the British Spitfire.

Another of Germany's initial allies, Romania, captured 22 Fw190 F models. These were originally obtained from the Luftwaffe. After the country changed sides in August 1944, the Romanian Air Force took ownership of the fighters but did not use them operationally. They were quickly confiscated by the Red Army.

During the war, a production facility to build the Fw190 was planned in France, fairly close to Paris. However, the plant did not reach production fruition by the time it was liberated by the Allies in 1944. Nevertheless, after the war in French hands, the SNCAC aircraft company completed 64 aircraft under the designation of NC900. These A-5/A-6 model equivalents flew briefly after the war with various units of the Armée de l'Air.

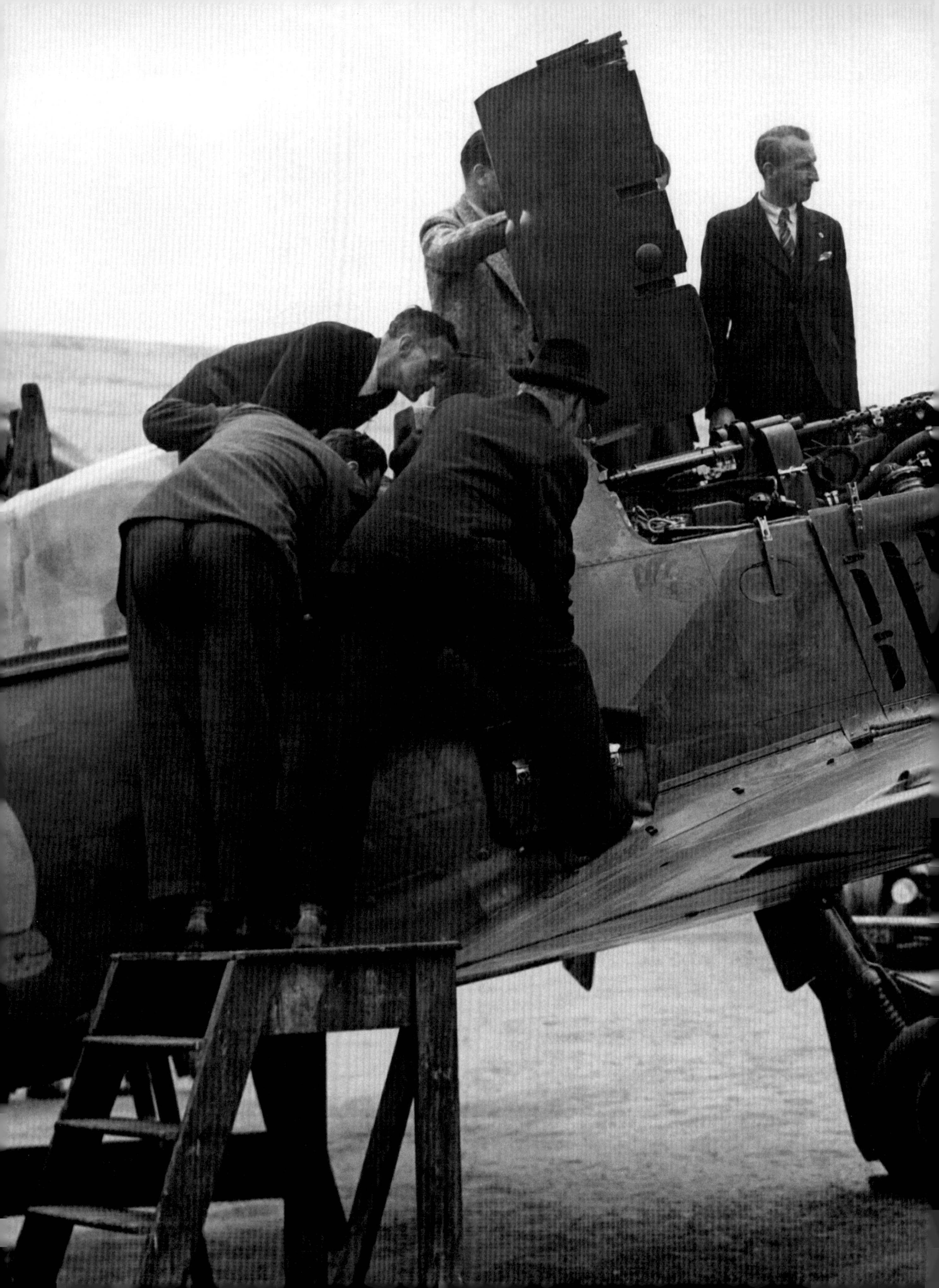

*Chapter Three*

# Anatomy of the Fw190 A-8

With a design brief that from the outset dictated that it should be both easy to maintain in the field and robust in combat, the team that created the Fw190 used conventional technology in the construction and assembly of their fighter.

**OPPOSITE** Suited experts pore over what is very likely the captured Fw190 of Oberleutnant Faber. The aircraft, here repainted in British markings, would yield much valuable information to the RAF. The scientists and engineers were generous in their praise of the quality of engineering of this deadly foe. *(via Aviation-images.com)*

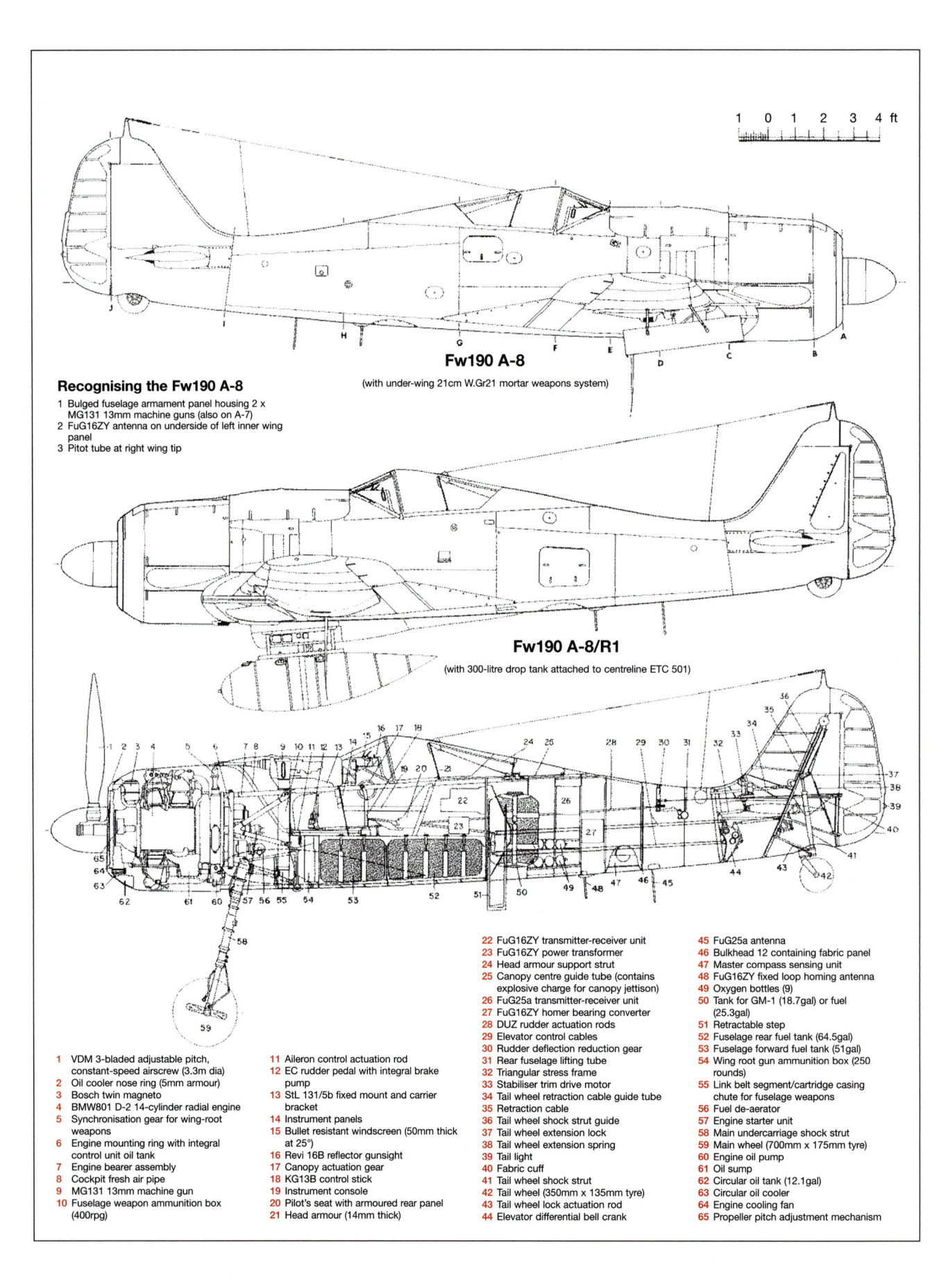

## Fw190 A-8
(with under-wing 21cm W.Gr21 mortar weapons system)

**Recognising the Fw190 A-8**
1. Bulged fuselage armament panel housing 2 x MG131 13mm machine guns (also on A-7)
2. FuG16ZY antenna on underside of left inner wing panel
3. Pitot tube at right wing tip

## Fw190 A-8/R1
(with 300-litre drop tank attached to centreline ETC 501)

1. VDM 3-bladed adjustable pitch, constant-speed airscrew (3.3m dia)
2. Oil cooler nose ring (5mm armour)
3. Bosch twin magneto
4. BMW801 D-2 14-cylinder radial engine
5. Synchronisation gear for wing-root weapons
6. Engine mounting ring with integral control unit oil tank
7. Engine bearer assembly
8. Cockpit fresh air pipe
9. MG131 13mm machine gun
10. Fuselage weapon ammunition box (400rpg)
11. Aileron control actuation rod
12. EC rudder pedal with integral brake pump
13. StL 131/5b fixed mount and carrier bracket
14. Instrument panels
15. Bullet resistant windscreen (50mm thick at 25°)
16. Revi 16B reflector gunsight
17. Canopy actuation gear
18. KG13B control stick
19. Instrument console
20. Pilot's seat with armoured rear panel
21. Head armour (14mm thick)
22. FuG16ZY transmitter-receiver unit
23. FuG16ZY power transformer
24. Head armour support strut
25. Canopy centre guide tube (contains explosive charge for canopy jettison)
26. FuG25a transmitter-receiver unit
27. FuG16ZY homer bearing converter
28. DUZ rudder actuation rods
29. Elevator control cables
30. Rudder deflection reduction gear
31. Rear fuselage lifting tube
32. Triangular stress frame
33. Stabiliser trim drive motor
34. Tail wheel retraction cable guide tube
35. Retraction cable
36. Tail wheel shock strut guide
37. Tail wheel extension lock
38. Tail wheel extension spring
39. Tail light
40. Fabric cuff
41. Tail wheel shock strut
42. Tail wheel (350mm x 135mm tyre)
43. Tail wheel lock actuation rod
44. Elevator differential bell crank
45. FuG25a antenna
46. Bulkhead 12 containing fabric panel
47. Master compass sensing unit
48. FuG16ZY fixed loop homing antenna
49. Oxygen bottles (9)
50. Tank for GM-1 (18.7gal) or fuel (25.3gal)
51. Retractable step
52. Fuselage rear fuel tank (64.5gal)
53. Fuselage forward fuel tank (51gal)
54. Wing root gun ammunition box (250 rounds)
55. Link belt segment/cartridge casing chute for fuselage weapons
56. Fuel de-aerator
57. Engine starter unit
58. Main undercarriage shock strut
59. Main wheel (700mm x 175mm tyre)
60. Engine oil pump
61. Oil sump
62. Circular oil tank (12.1gal)
63. Circular oil cooler
64. Engine cooling fan
65. Propeller pitch adjustment mechanism

FOCKE-WULF FW190 MANUAL

Built in sections, the Fw190 pre-empted the need for subcontractors and dispersed factories, which became more necessary as the war went on. A design philosophy which gave priority to ease of maintenance is often in evidence: it was found more desirable to change components quickly in the field than to repair them *in situ*.

## Fuselage

This consists of two sections, the forward one containing the cockpit: it begins at the firewall or bulkhead 1 and ends at bulkhead 8 just behind the pilot's seat. The rear section begins at bulkhead 8 and ends at the empennage. Although called bulkheads by Focke-Wulf, most are frames in the conventional sense, but are referred to here according to their original description.

The front section comprises an upper and lower bay, forming the cockpit above and the fuel tanks below. Bulkhead 1 is built up from light sheet steel backed by aluminium alloy sheet riveted to built-up steel flanges that extend from the top two engine mount fittings to the lower fittings, which also serve as front spar mounts. Four longerons extend

**OPPOSITE** Profiles and sectioned view of the Fw190 A-8 from an English translation of the aircraft handbook. The profile view shows at the top an aircraft fitted with the 21cm W.Gr mortar and below with a 300l drop tank. *(D. (Luft) T.2190 A-8)*

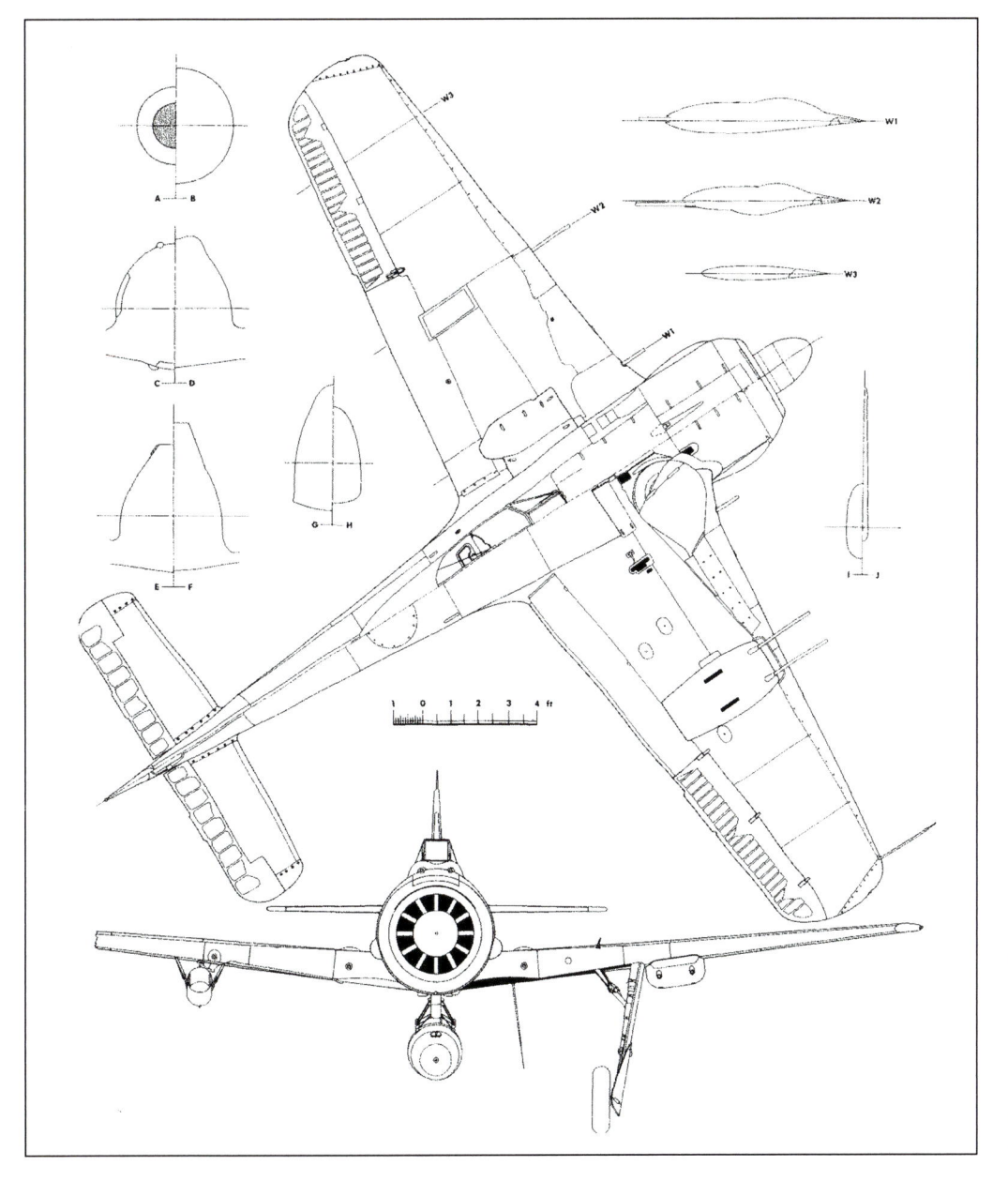

**LEFT** Plan and head-on view illustrating armament options of the 21cm mortar and the dual cannon underwing gondola. *(D. (Luft) T.2190 A-8)*

59
ANATOMY OF THE FW190 A-8

**Focke-Wulf Fw190 A-8.**

*(Amber Books/John Weal)*

1. Pitot head
2. Starboard navigation light
3. Detachable wingtip
4. Pitot tube heater line
5. Wing lower shell floating rib
6. Aileron hinge points
7. Wing lower shell stringers
8. Leading edge ribs
9. Front spar
10. Outermost solid rib
11. Wing upper shell stringers
12. Aileron trim tab
13. Aileron structure
14. Aileron activation/control linkage
15. Ammunition box (125rpg)
16. Starboard 20mm MG151/20E wing cannon (sideways mounted)
17. Ammunition box rear suspension arm
18. Flap structure
19. Wing flap under skinning
20. Flap setting indicator peephole
21. Rear spar
22. Inboard wing construction
23. Undercarriage indicator
24. Wing rib strengthening
25. Ammunition feed chute
26. Static and dynamic air pressure lines
27. Cannon barrel
28. Launch tube bracing struts
29. Launch tube carrier strut
30. Mortar launch tube (auxiliary under-wing armament)
31. Launch tube internal guide rails
32. 21cm (WfrGr 21) spin-stabilised Type 42 mortar shell
33. VDM three-bladed adjustable-pitch constant-speed propeller
34. Propeller boss
35. Propeller hub
36. Starboard undercarriage fairing
37. Starboard mainwheel
38. Oil warming chamber
39. Thermostat
40. Cooler armoured ring (6.5mm)
41. Oil tank drain valve
42. Annular oil tank (55 litres)
43. Oil cooler
44. 12-bladed engine cooling fan
45. Hydraulic-electric pitch control unit
46. Primer fuel line
47. Bosch magneto
48. Oil tank armour (5.5mm)
49. Coolant air pipe
50. BMW 801D-2 14-cylinder radial engine
51. Cowling support ring
52. Cowling quick-release fasteners
53. Duct for ram-air to supercharger
54. Fuel pump (engine rear face)
55. Oil filter (starboard)
56. Wing root cannon synchronisation gear
57. Gun troughs/cowling upper panel attachment
58. Engine mounting ring
59. Cockpit ventilation pipe
60. Exhaust pipes (cylinders 11–14)
61. MG131 link and casing discard chute
62. Engine bearer assembly
63. MG131 ammunition boxes (400 rpg)
64. Fuel filter recess housing
65. MG131 ammunition cooling pipes
66. MG131 recoil mount
67. Ammunition feed chute
68. Twin fuselage 13mm MG131 machine guns
69. Windscreen mounting frame
70. Emergency power fuse and distributor box
71. Rear hinged gun access panel
72. Engine bearer/bulkhead attachment
73. Control column
74. Transformer
75. Aileron control torsion bar
76. Rudder pedals (EC pedal unit with hydraulic wheel-brake operation)
77. Fuselage/wing spar attachment
78. Adjustable rudder push rod
79. Fuel filler head
80. Cockpit floor support frame
81. Throttle lever
82. Pilot's seat back plate armour (8mm)
83. Seat guide rails
84. Side-section back armour (5mm)
85. Shoulder armour (5mm)
86. Oxygen supply valve
87. Steel frame turnover pylon
88. Windscreen spray pipes
89. Instrument panel shroud
90. 30mm armoured glass quarter-lights
91. 50mm armoured glass windscreen
92. Revi 16B reflector gunsight
93. Canopy
94. Aerial attachment
95. Headrest
96. Head armour (12 mm)
97. Head armour support strut
98. Explosive charge canopy emergency jettison unit
99. Canopy channel side
100. Auxiliary tank: fuel (115 litres) or GM-1 (85 litres)
101. FuG 16ZY transmitter-receiver unit
102. Handhold cover
103. Primer fuel filler cap
104. Autopilot steering unit (PKS 12)
105. FuG 16ZY power transformer
106. Entry step cover plate
107. Two tri-spherical oxygen bottles (starboard fuselage wall)
108. Auxiliary fuel tank filler point
109. FuG 25a transponder unit
110. Autopilot position integration unit
111. FuG 16ZY homer bearing converter
112. Elevator control cables
113. Rudder control DUZ flexible rods
114. Fabric panel (bulkhead 12)
115. Rudder differential unit
116. Aerial lead-in
117. Rear fuselage lift tube
118. Triangular stress frame
119. Tailplane trim unit
120. Tailplane attachment fitting
121. Tailwheel retraction guide tube
122. Retraction cable lower pulley
123. Starboard tailplane
124. Aerial
125. Starboard elevator
126. Elevator trim tab
127. Tailwheel shock strut guide
128. Fin construction
129. Retraction cable upper pulley
130. Aerial attachment strut
131. Rudder upper hinge
132. Rudder structure
133. Rudder trim tab

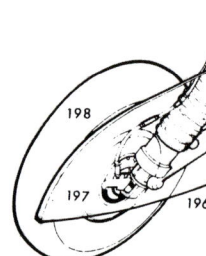

60

FOCKE-WULF FW190 MANUAL

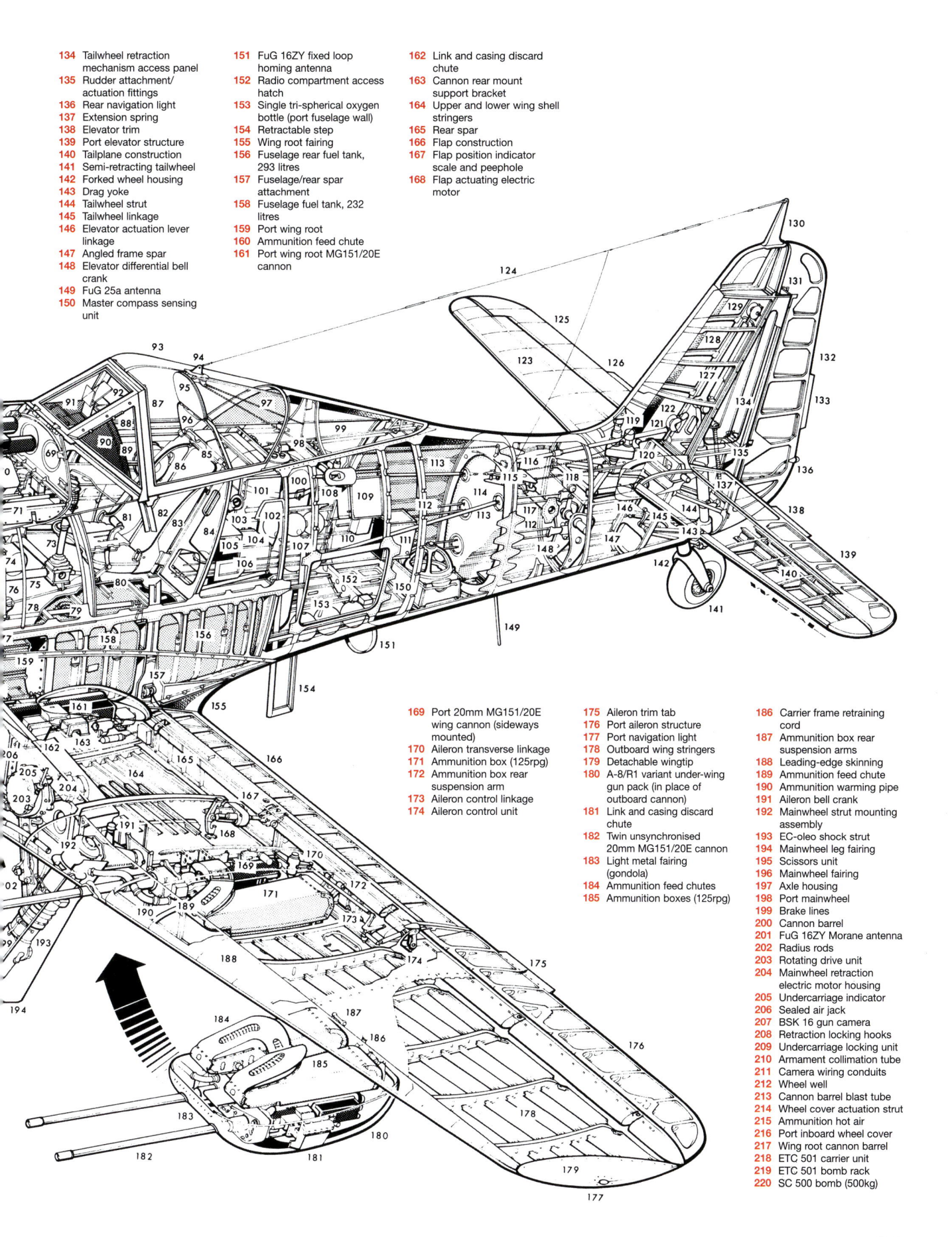

|  |  |
|---|---|
| 134 | Tailwheel retraction mechanism access panel |
| 135 | Rudder attachment/actuation fittings |
| 136 | Rear navigation light |
| 137 | Extension spring |
| 138 | Elevator trim |
| 139 | Port elevator structure |
| 140 | Tailplane construction |
| 141 | Semi-retracting tailwheel |
| 142 | Forked wheel housing |
| 143 | Drag yoke |
| 144 | Tailwheel strut |
| 145 | Tailwheel linkage |
| 146 | Elevator actuation lever linkage |
| 147 | Angled frame spar |
| 148 | Elevator differential bell crank |
| 149 | FuG 25a antenna |
| 150 | Master compass sensing unit |
| 151 | FuG 16ZY fixed loop homing antenna |
| 152 | Radio compartment access hatch |
| 153 | Single tri-spherical oxygen bottle (port fuselage wall) |
| 154 | Retractable step |
| 155 | Wing root fairing |
| 156 | Fuselage rear fuel tank, 293 litres |
| 157 | Fuselage/rear spar attachment |
| 158 | Fuselage fuel tank, 232 litres |
| 159 | Port wing root |
| 160 | Ammunition feed chute |
| 161 | Port wing root MG151/20E cannon |
| 162 | Link and casing discard chute |
| 163 | Cannon rear mount support bracket |
| 164 | Upper and lower wing shell stringers |
| 165 | Rear spar |
| 166 | Flap construction |
| 167 | Flap position indicator scale and peephole |
| 168 | Flap actuating electric motor |
| 169 | Port 20mm MG151/20E wing cannon (sideways mounted) |
| 170 | Aileron transverse linkage |
| 171 | Ammunition box (125rpg) |
| 172 | Ammunition box rear suspension arm |
| 173 | Aileron control linkage |
| 174 | Aileron control unit |
| 175 | Aileron trim tab |
| 176 | Port aileron structure |
| 177 | Port navigation light |
| 178 | Outboard wing stringers |
| 179 | Detachable wingtip |
| 180 | A-8/R1 variant under-wing gun pack (in place of outboard cannon) |
| 181 | Link and casing discard chute |
| 182 | Twin unsynchronised 20mm MG151/20E cannon |
| 183 | Light metal fairing (gondola) |
| 184 | Ammunition feed chutes |
| 185 | Ammunition boxes (125rpg) |
| 186 | Carrier frame retraining cord |
| 187 | Ammunition box rear suspension arms |
| 188 | Leading-edge skinning |
| 189 | Ammunition feed chute |
| 190 | Ammunition warming pipe |
| 191 | Aileron bell crank |
| 192 | Mainwheel strut mounting assembly |
| 193 | EC-oleo shock strut |
| 194 | Mainwheel leg fairing |
| 195 | Scissors unit |
| 196 | Mainwheel fairing |
| 197 | Axle housing |
| 198 | Port mainwheel |
| 199 | Brake lines |
| 200 | Cannon barrel |
| 201 | FuG 16ZY Morane antenna |
| 202 | Radius rods |
| 203 | Rotating drive unit |
| 204 | Mainwheel retraction electric motor housing |
| 205 | Undercarriage indicator |
| 206 | Sealed air jack |
| 207 | BSK 16 gun camera |
| 208 | Retraction locking hooks |
| 209 | Undercarriage locking unit |
| 210 | Armament collimation tube |
| 211 | Camera wiring conduits |
| 212 | Wheel well |
| 213 | Cannon barrel blast tube |
| 214 | Wheel cover actuation strut |
| 215 | Ammunition hot air |
| 216 | Port inboard wheel cover |
| 217 | Wing root cannon barrel |
| 218 | ETC 501 carrier unit |
| 219 | ETC 501 bomb rack |
| 220 | SC 500 bomb (500kg) |

ANATOMY OF THE FW190 A-8

**RIGHT** Drawing of the forward fuselage structure and cockpit showing panels and hatches. Panel 3 is for the inboard wing cannon and panel 5 covers the fuselage weapons bay. *(D. (Luft) T.2190 A-8)*

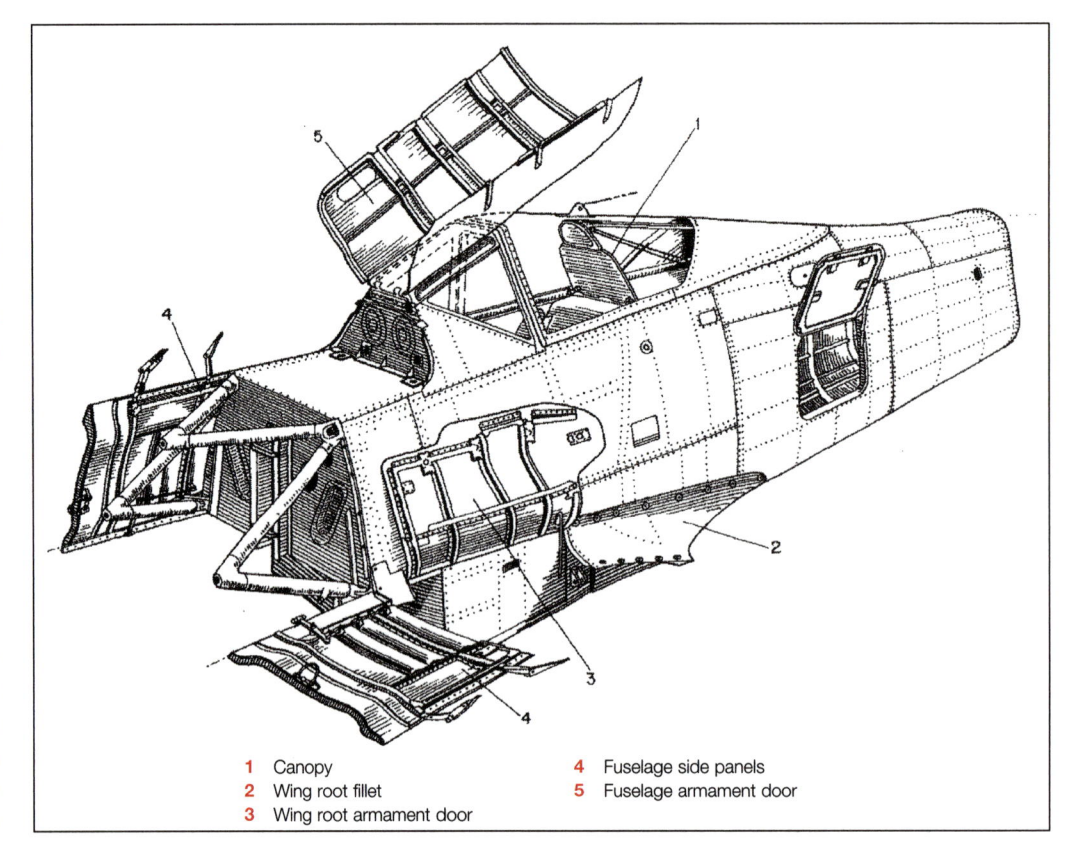

**BELOW** This ghost view of the cockpit illustrates some of the interior fittings in the fuselage. *(D. (Luft) T.2190 A-8)*

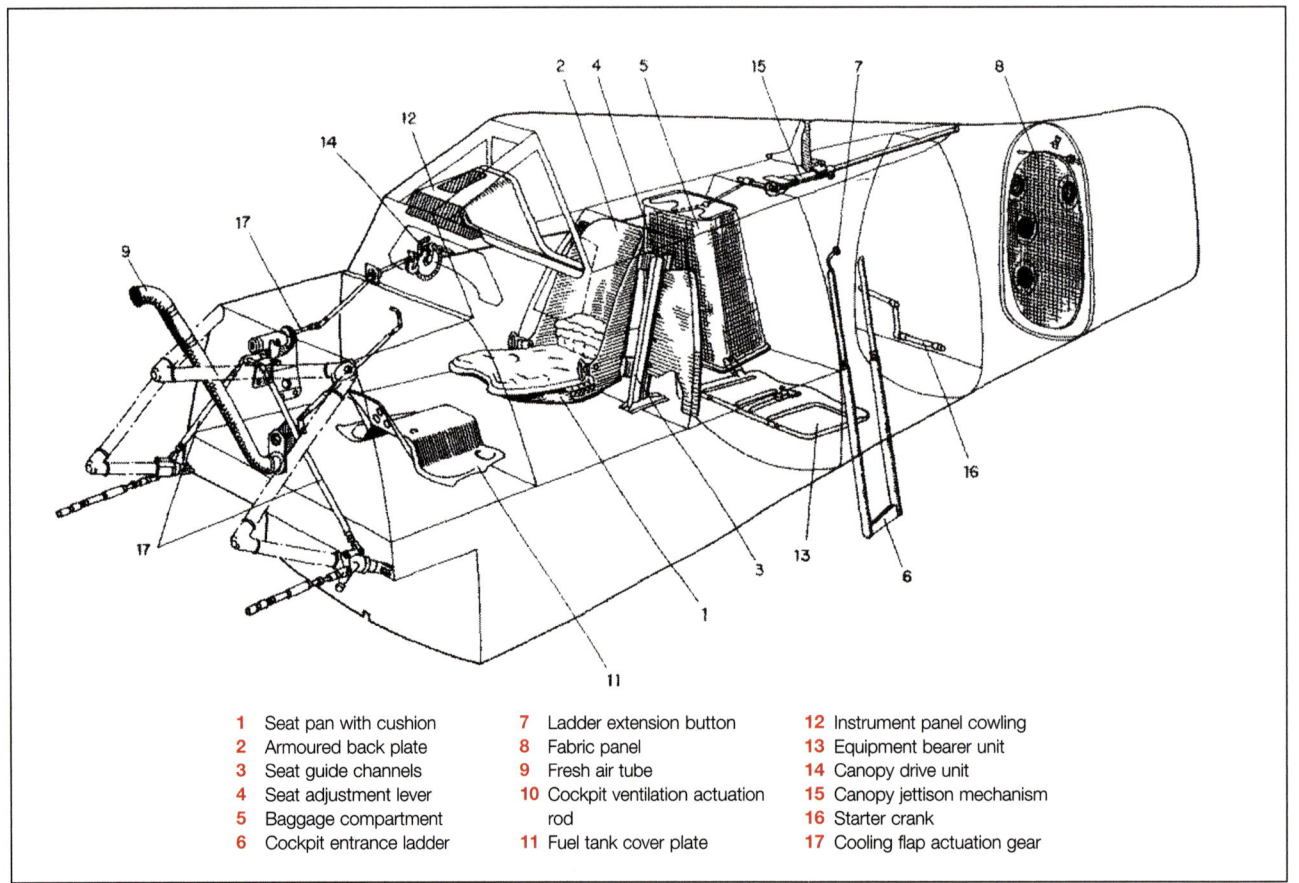

| | |
|---|---|
| 1 Canopy | 4 Fuselage side panels |
| 2 Wing root fillet | 5 Fuselage armament door |
| 3 Wing root armament door | |

| | | | |
|---|---|---|---|
| 1 | Seat pan with cushion | 7 Ladder extension button | 12 Instrument panel cowling |
| 2 | Armoured back plate | 8 Fabric panel | 13 Equipment bearer unit |
| 3 | Seat guide channels | 9 Fresh air tube | 14 Canopy drive unit |
| 4 | Seat adjustment lever | 10 Cockpit ventilation actuation rod | 15 Canopy jettison mechanism |
| 5 | Baggage compartment | 11 Fuel tank cover plate | 16 Starter crank |
| 6 | Cockpit entrance ladder | | 17 Cooling flap actuation gear |

62

FOCKE-WULF FW190 MANUAL

from these fittings; the top pair are U-sections and serve as tracks for the cockpit canopy to travel in. The two lower longerons support the alloy sheet which, riveted to them, forms the cockpit floor and the top of the fuel tank bay. Between the two longerons on each side, a top hat section stringer helps stiffen the top part of the fuselage. Bulkhead 5 contains the rear wing spar to fuselage attachment fitting. A detachable alloy panel forms the base of the fuel tank bay containing the two tanks; the panel is detachable by removing 28 screws.

The fuselage rear section, attached to the forward section at bulkhead 8 by a double row of rivets, consists of bulkheads 9 to 14, these being notched for longerons and stringers to pass through with alloy skin flush-riveted to the structure to complete the semi-monocoque assembly. The two upper longerons are spliced into those from the front fuselage and run past bulkhead 11. A channel-shaped top longeron extends between bulkheads 8 and 11. Stringers are rolled edge, Z-section except at the lower sides when they are formed from heavier U-section material. The lower parts of the bulkheads are shaped specially to accommodate oxygen bottles, radio and other equipment. An equipment access panel is built into the left side, hinged at the top. The flat top decking comprises two skin panels riveted to form a U-channel, which acts as a guide for the centre roller of the cockpit canopy. At bulkhead 12 a sealed cellulose acetate sheet prevents engine exhaust gas from being sucked back into the cockpit. The sheet contains rubber grommets to permit flying control rods and cables to pass through. At bulkhead 13, a tube running through the fuselage allows a lifting bar to be inserted. Bulkhead 14 is of heavier flanged construction to allow the tail unit to be bolted on.

## Cockpit

Positioned behind the engine and above the fuselage fuel tanks, the pilot's cockpit is generally well designed, incorporating the novel features of side consoles housing switches, circuit breakers, indicators and additional instruments. Main flight instruments are grouped in front of the pilot on two panels one above the other. Instrument fit and arrangement varied considerably between different marks, and so a typical fit of the most common mark, the A-8, is described here.

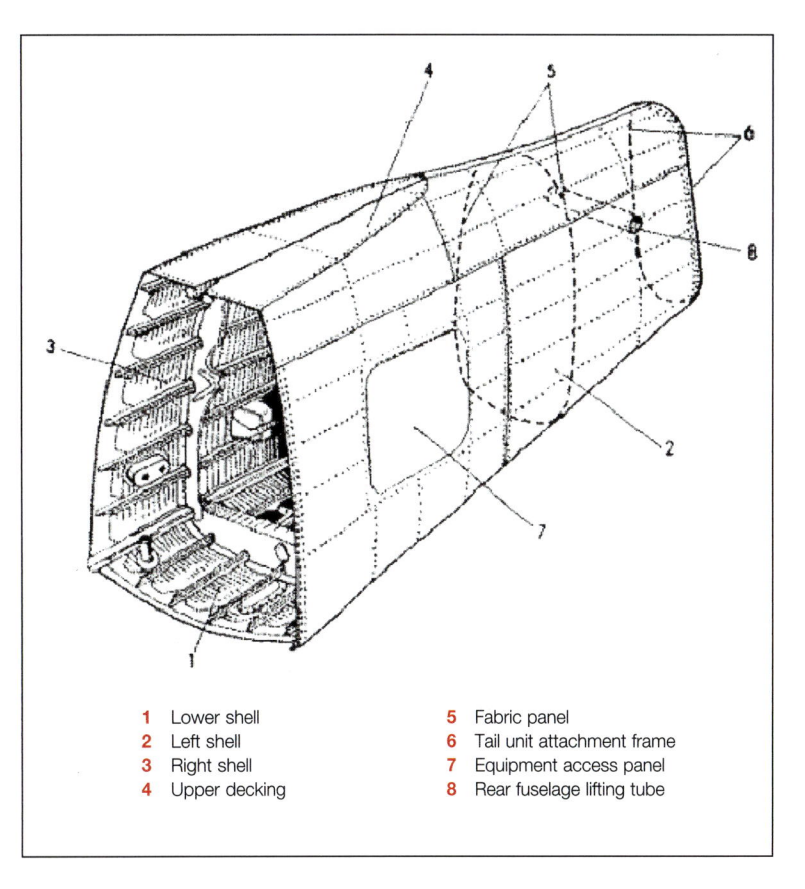

The pilot sits in a semi-reclining armoured seat, adjustable up and down and designed for a back-pack parachute. There is an armoured headrest at the top of the seat. In front of him, beneath the armoured windscreen, immediately below the cockpit combing is located the panel containing the ammunition counters for the weapons and their safety switches. Offset to the right of the centre line is the Revi gunsight, and on the right the panel houses the radio homing indicator. Under this is the main instrument panel containing the flight instruments, which are from left to right: altimeter, airspeed indicator, artificial horizon, vertical speed indicator, repeater compass, supercharger pressure gauge and engine tachometer. Beneath the main panel is the auxiliary panel, a load-bearing member of the cockpit and housing engine instruments: the fuel and oil pressure gauge (combined), oil temperature gauge, fuel contents gauge and the propeller pitch indicator. Other controls on the upper left side of the auxiliary

| 1 | Lower shell | 5 | Fabric panel |
| 2 | Left shell | 6 | Tail unit attachment frame |
| 3 | Right shell | 7 | Equipment access panel |
| 4 | Upper decking | 8 | Rear fuselage lifting tube |

**ABOVE** The rear fuselage structure extends between frames 9 and 14. The panel in the side gives access to some of the radio equipment, oxygen bottles and the aft fuselage tank. *(D. (Luft) T.2190 A-8)*

**OPPOSITE** Cockpit of Fw190 D-13. This varied in detail compared with the radial-engined aircraft. The power lever was gated and the electric pitch control for the propeller was omitted in Jumo-powered aircraft, as was the pitch indicator instrument. In its place a MW50 pressure gauge was fitted together with a switch to activate the boost. This model also featured changes to the layout of the consoles, which later were incorporated into the Ta152 design. *(Brian M. Silcox)*

**ABOVE AND BELOW** Two views of the cockpit of an early A series show the neat installation of instruments and the use of side consoles to house switches and indicators. The power lever is shown in the left console just behind the stick. *(Aviation-images.com)*

1 Ammunition counter with breech blockage indicators
2 Revi gunsight
3 AFN 2 radio homing indicator
4 Airspeed indicator
5 Artificial horizon
6 Vertical speed indicator
7 Remote compass indicator
8 Supercharger pressure gauge
9 Altimeter
10 Tachometer
11 Fuel and oil pressure gauge
12 Coolant temperature gauge
13 Oil temperature gauge
14 MW50 pressure gauge
15 Fuel contents gauge
16 Fuel warning lights
17 Fuel contents display switch
18 Ventilation knob
19 Emergency undercarriage release handle
20 Fuel tank selector lever
21 Switches for FuG25 IFF set
22 Clock
23 Undercarriage and flap indicator lights
24 Magneto switch
25 MW50 switch
26 Tailplane trim switch
27 Trim position indicator
28 Electrical emergency circuit breaker
29 Power lever, gated positions Aus – off, Anlassen – engine start, Steigen – climb, Start – take-off
30 Flaps and undercarriage buttons
31 FuG16ZY frequency selector switch
32 Fine-tuning control
33 Volume control
34 Headset socket
35 Rudder pedals
36 Control stick
37 Bomb arming and fusing panel
38 Oxygen blinker indicator
39 Oxygen pressure gauge
40 Oxygen shut-off valve
41 Cockpit light dimmer
42 Inboard circuit breakers
43 Outboard circuit breakers
44 Starter handle
45 Canopy cranking handle
46 Emergency canopy release

**65**

ANATOMY OF THE FW190 A-8

panel consist of a jettison handle for the under fuselage stores, with below it a lever running in a vertical slot, which is the fuel tank selector, and immediately to its left a red painted handle that serves as the emergency release for the undercarriage. A small sub-panel at the base of the left panel controls the IFF radio set. Other controls in this area are an engine start lever for setting the Kommandogerät to the starting position and a knob for lifting the starter motor brushes. On the opposite side of the cockpit, the right sub-panel houses the oxygen pressure gauge and flow indicator along with the flare pistol discharge tube.

Controls on the left side console consist of the instrument lighting dimmer rheostat and the power control lever (throttle), running in a slot close to the left side wall. The yellow painted handle contains a thumb switch, which is used to select the propeller pitch when manual control is selected. Other controls comprise the emergency electrical circuit breaker, the magneto selector switch, undercarriage and flap position indicator, propeller manual/automatic control selector, tailplane trim switch and incidence indicator gauge, and selector switches to lower and raise the undercarriage and to set the flap position. Further aft are controls for the FuG radio equipment and the fuel primer pump, while low down on the console, just ahead of the front of the pilot's seat, a large knob adjusts the throttle friction.

A clock is built into the right side console, and circuit breakers for the following: Revi gunsight, artificial horizon, generator, and one for each of the two fuel pumps; a tray alongside contains signal flares and the starter engagement handle is protected by a hinged cover. Further aft is located a small panel containing circuit breakers for the weapons. On the right sidewall of the cockpit, a large wheel with a handle actuates the canopy opening and closing mechanism, and just behind, a lever operates the emergency canopy jettison charge.

The floor-mounted control stick, type KG13B, holds the wing cannon firing button at the top of the stick, protected by a hinged safety guard, the bomb release button is located just above the handgrip on the left-hand side, and below the handgrip on the forward face is the radio press-to-talk button.

On versions fitted with additional armaments a fusing and armament panel is attached to the bottom of the auxiliary panel. This would contain some but not all of the following features, dependent on the armament fit of the particular version: two switches for the W.Gr21 air-to-air mortar system, the left being the safety switch and the right the launch switch; below is the bomb fusing panel with a five-position rotary selector switch that allows the pilot to choose to drop bombs with or without fusing when flying level or when in a dive; and at the base is a panel for controlling the fuselage mounted camera, allowing continuous film or individual frames to be exposed.

## Empennage

The tail unit consists of the vertical stabiliser, which is constructed of horizontal ribs, and a diagonal spar covered by left and right aluminium skin panels. These panels extend from the underside of the tail to the top rib just below the rounded tail tip. The diagonal spar takes the tailwheel loads on the ground and the fin, rudder and elevator loads in the air. The spar also carries the fittings for the tailwheel drag yoke, the tailplane and the tailwheel

**BELOW** The tail unit is constructed as a sub-assembly complete with control surfaces.
*(D. (Luft) T.2190 A-8)*

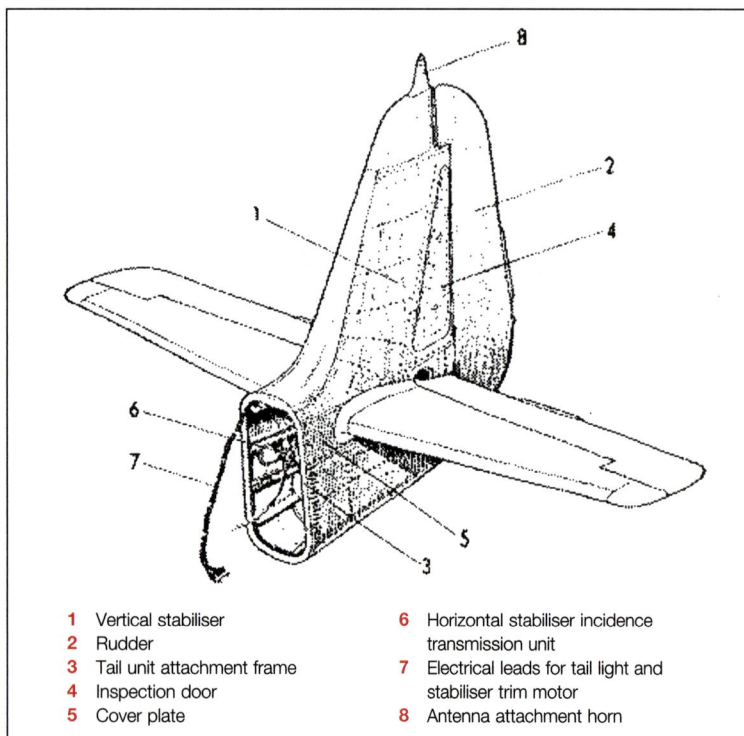

1 Vertical stabiliser
2 Rudder
3 Tail unit attachment frame
4 Inspection door
5 Cover plate
6 Horizontal stabiliser incidence transmission unit
7 Electrical leads for tail light and stabiliser trim motor
8 Antenna attachment horn

retraction cable pulleys. The panels are riveted to the ribs and to the leading edge of the fin, which is then covered with a capping strip. A triangular-shaped inspection cover is built into the left skin panel giving access to the tailwheel.

The rudder is attached to the vertical stabiliser in three places by pivot bearings, and moved by an arm bolted to the centre attachment point. Rudder construction is from a stamped light alloy spar, ribs and a trailing edge. The leading edge comprises aluminium skin flush-riveted to the spar, and the rest of the unit is fabric covered. The tip of the rudder contains a horn balance and the unit is mass balanced. A ground-adjustable trim tab on the trailing edge allows for lateral trim adjustments.

The tailplane, a trapezoid shape with a symmetrical aerofoil section, is built from two halves which are bolted together at the centre line. Constructed around a single aluminium spar, the upper and lower shells are riveted together with leading edges and tips screwed on. The tailplane passes through the tail unit, and is connected to the diagonal spar by a pivoting mount. On the leading edge, an electric motor housed in the tail contains a drive spindle that adjusts the incidence angle of the tailplane between +4° and −1° to act as the trim adjustment. The motor, operated by the pilot from the trim switch on the left side console, runs at 14,000rpm through a 533:1 reduction gear train that takes 20 seconds to move the tailplane leading edge over its full range of adjustment. Red reference markings on the tail unit indicate the '0', '+' and '−' positions. A relay unit also housed in the tail beneath the motor is attached to the tailplane through a stress frame and push-rod. Movement of the tailplane operates a lever on the relay which sends an electrical signal to the pilot's indicator unit in the cockpit. The relay unit also switches off the power to the motor at the limits of tailplane movement.

The elevators are two identical half units, constructed in a similar way to the rudder, with aluminium ribs, spar and trailing edge and fabric covering. The two halves are joined by connecting flanges at the spar ends inside the tail unit and each half pivots from the horizontal tailplane by three bearings. Both are aerodynamically and mass balanced. The right elevator is fitted with a ground-adjustable trim tab.

**LEFT** In D-series aircraft, a fuselage extension piece was placed ahead of the tail, housing relocated oxygen cylinders. *(GossHawk Unlimited Inc.)*

**LEFT** The fuselage extension plug being fitted between the fuselage and tail. *(GossHawk Unlimited Inc.)*

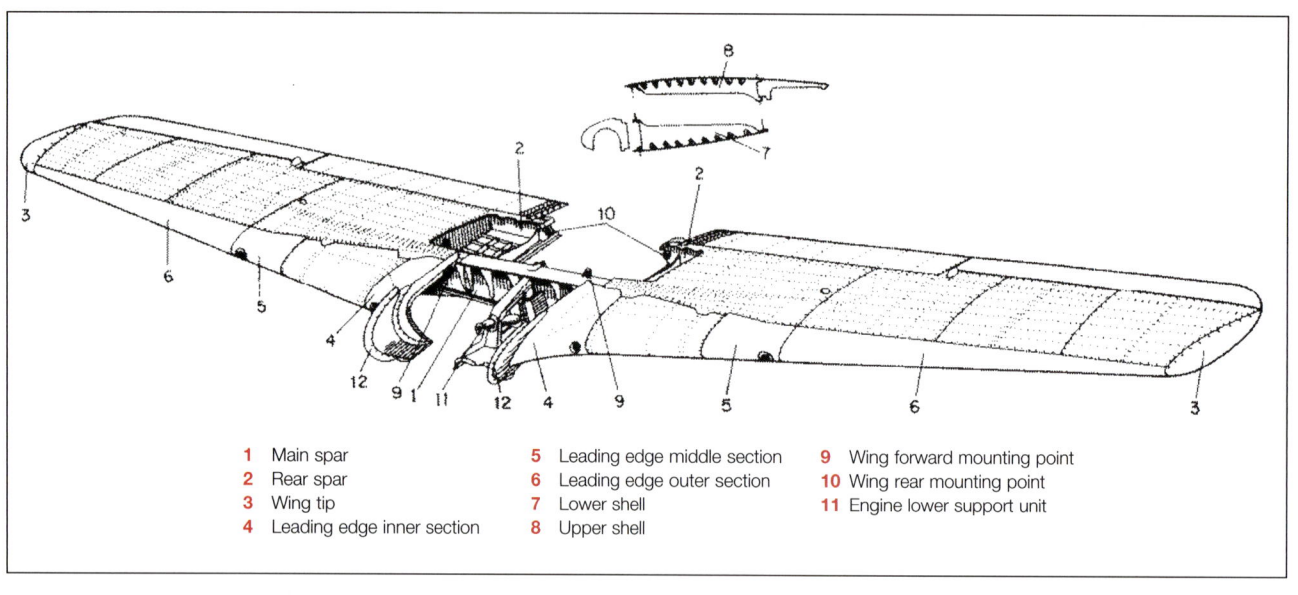

| 1 | Main spar | 5 | Leading edge middle section | 9 | Wing forward mounting point |
| 2 | Rear spar | 6 | Leading edge outer section | 10 | Wing rear mounting point |
| 3 | Wing tip | 7 | Lower shell | 11 | Engine lower support unit |
| 4 | Leading edge inner section | 8 | Upper shell | | |

ABOVE Complete wing assembly showing the carry-through front spar, the attachment points for the rear spars and the lower engine bearer. *(D. (Luft) T.2190 A-8)*

# Wing

The one-piece cantilever wing is of all-metal monocoque construction, the main structural members consisting of a continuous main spar which attaches below bulkhead 1 on the fuselage and a rear spar which does not carry through the fuselage but attaches on either side at bulkhead 5. The tapering main spar is built up in the centre from triple webbed I-beam construction, and on the centre line it is reinforced by a vertical channel member, the end of which forms the forging for the lower engine mount. The spar is some 425mm deep at this point, taking as it does the weight of the lower and side engine mounts, the attachment points of the wing to the fuselage, four 20mm cannon and the main undercarriage. At the side engine mounts, the spar is bent forward 14° to allow the main wheels room to retract into the wing; the spar bends back again outboard of the undercarriage legs. The triple web

RIGHT The main spar is attached to the lower wing skin and built as a sub-assembly complete with ribs and stingers, shown here during the rebuild of the D-13 model. *(GossHawk Unlimited Inc.)*

BELOW The rear spar is built into the upper wing skin, and the two sub-assemblies are then riveted together. *(GossHawk Unlimited Inc.)*

construction continues to a point beyond the inboard cannon ports where it then becomes double web and, finally, a single web I-beam member from the outboard cannon ports, to the tip. The rear spar is also of tapering I-beam construction, of double web build from the fuselage fittings for some 813mm and then of single web out to the tip. It carries the attachment points for the flaps and ailerons. On each side, there are five stamped aluminium ribs running between the spars which are riveted to both upper and lower skins. These form torque boxes at the cannon ports and the undercarriage fittings. Remaining ribs are of 'floating' design, being attached to either the upper or lower skin. Longitudinal Z-section stringers are flush-riveted to the aluminium skins, the stringers passing through cut-outs in the ribs. In the factory, a wing section is constructed of the upper skin together with the rear spar, complete with stringers and ribs, which is attached as a unit to the bottom skin with its stringers and ribs and the front spar. The skin above the flaps is another sub-assembly, secured to the rear spar by ten contoured ribs, with a single stringer running lengthways. The wing leading edge, constructed of four pieces, two from the fuselage to the undercarriage attachment point, contains five contoured ribs and stringers which are fastened to the spar by screws. Two outboard sections contain conventional D-type nose ribs and are also fixed by screws to the spar.

Wing flaps are of split design and of all-metal single spar construction, hinged in three places from the rear wing spar. An actuating arm at the centre hinge moves the flap, each one powered by an electric motor unit operating a drive spindle through a worm gear housing. An adjustable push-rod attaches the drive spindle to the flap; its other end is connected to the flap central attachment fitting. The two motors are synchronised to ensure balanced flap operation. Motors are operated by the pilot's pushbuttons in the left side console; three buttons control the three positions of the flaps, 0°, 15° for take-off and 60° for landing. Indication of the flap position is given by the two middle lamps of the six-lamp indicator unit, red indicating 'In' and green 'Out', with no indication of the take-off position. There is a graduated indicator scale showing the position of each flap through a small window in the upper skin which can be seen from the cockpit. The two flaps are interchangeable.

Ailerons are constructed in the same way as the other flying surfaces, with an aluminium spar, leading edge and ribs and a surface covering of fabric. Each has a built-in horn balance, mass balance and a ground adjustable trim tab on the trailing edge. Hinged by ball bearings at three positions with the actuator arm on the inboard hinge, the ailerons are of Frise design, allowing the leading edge of the up-going aileron to extend below the wing surface, reducing the effect of adverse yaw in the roll.

## Main undercarriage

The main undercarriage legs retract inwards into the underside of the wing and fuselage. When retracted the undercarriage is fully covered by leg fairing doors and hinged inboard wheel doors which move up with the legs. However, in the case of many later models, when the aircraft is fitted with the under-fuselage ETC501 rack these doors are omitted and extension pieces that are attached to the bottom of the leg fairings cover most of the wheel when in the retracted position.

The legs consist of oleo shock struts pivoted at the top to the main spar by a tapered mounting assembly. The two halves of the shock strut are connected by an anti-

**ABOVE** The wing leading edge is screwed to the two wing shells once they are assembled. *(GossHawk Unlimited Inc.)*

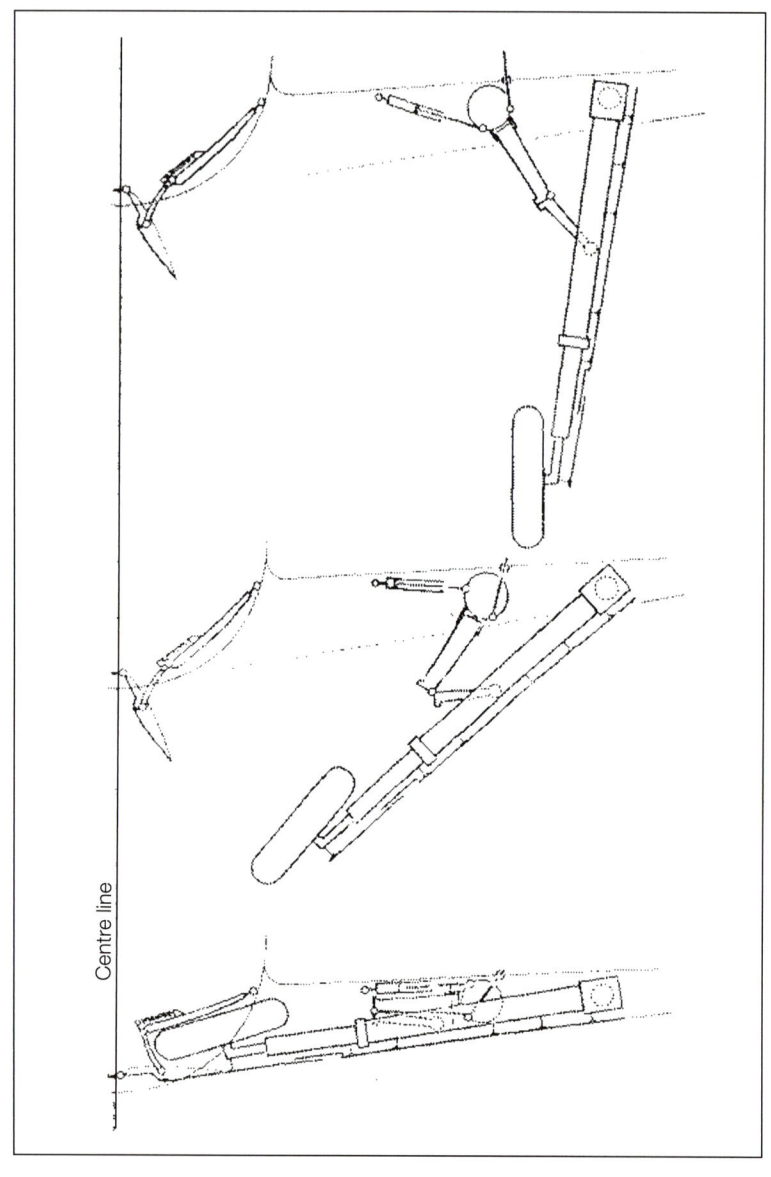

**ABOVE** Retraction sequence of main undercarriage leg. The electrical motor mounted on the spar rotates the drum which in turn causes the radius rod to fold at the hinge, drawing the leg into the wing. *(D. (Luft) T.2190 A-8)*

torque scissor link, and halfway up the leg a hinged radius rod connects to the retraction unit on the spar. The lower half of the shock strut contains the cantilever axle on which is mounted the hub and tyre measuring 700 × 175mm. Hydraulic drum brakes actuated from the pilot's rudder pedals allow separate braking on each mainwheel.

Retraction and extension is accomplished by individual electric motors, attached behind the spar in each wheel bay. Bolted to the motor is a geared rotating drum unit, forward of the spar. The motor operates at 14,000rpm and drives the rotating drum through a centrifugal clutch and reduction gearing of 10,491:1. During the retraction sequence the drum rotates, and as it does so, turns the upper part of the radius rod, causing the lower part to fold at the hinge and in turn pull up the leg into the wheel bay. When each leg reaches the fully up position, a hook on a locking unit engages with the leg, firmly holding it in place. A sealed air jack mounted between the spar and the rotating drum unit is compressed during the retraction cycle and aids undercarriage extension both normally and during emergency lowering. A mechanical indicator rod, connected to the rotating drum, pokes through a hole in the wing to confirm if each leg is fully locked down.

The full sequence of retraction takes place when the pilot presses the button marked 'Ein', which is covered by a red guard in the cockpit. This releases the hooks on the locking unit and starts the electric motors, which begin to retract the legs. As the main tyres move up they make contact with a plate on the upper strut holding the inboard wheel doors (when fitted). This

**LEFT** The up-lock mechanism which holds the retracted leg in position, seen here on a Flug Werk replica. *(Graeme Douglas courtesy of GossHawk Unlimited Inc.)*

**RIGHT** The tailwheel unit on Flug Werk machines is an original unit from a cache found in Germany. *(Graeme Douglas courtesy of GossHawk Unlimited Inc.)*

causes the strut to fold at its joint and closes the door behind the wheels; a spring latch holds the door against the main leg fairing. The leg moves further into the well and lugs on the leg contact the locking unit hooks, causing them to move up and hold the legs in place. This simultaneously shuts off the drive motors. Red lights on the indicator unit in the cockpit confirm retraction of each leg. The mechanical indicator rod is flush with the top surface of the wing when the legs are retracted.

To extend the undercarriage, the pilot presses the button marked 'Aus', which releases the hooks in the locking units and starts the electric motors turning in the opposite direction to lower the legs. As the main tyres release pressure on the inboard wheel door strut, a strut spring forces the doors open and the legs lower, and when fully down, a microswitch on each radius rod shuts off power to the motor and illuminates green lights in the cockpit. The mechanical indicator protrudes through the wing, indicating safe extension of each leg when a white band at the base becomes visible.

## Tailwheel

The tailwheel unit comprises a shock strut, a mounting arm, forked wheel housing holding the hub and tyre assembly and a drag yoke. The tyre is either 350 × 135mm or 380 × 150mm. The unit can rotate 360° for taxiing and can be locked for take-off by full backward movement of the control stick. Simultaneous retraction with the main undercarriage is achieved by a cable linked to the starboard

**RIGHT** The tailwheel components showing the mechanism for retracting the wheel. The large spring (12) pulls the assembly down to the lowered, locked position. When the cable (11) is tensioned, it releases the lock and pulls the assembly up the guide channel against the spring assembly. *(D. (Luft) T.2190 A-8)*

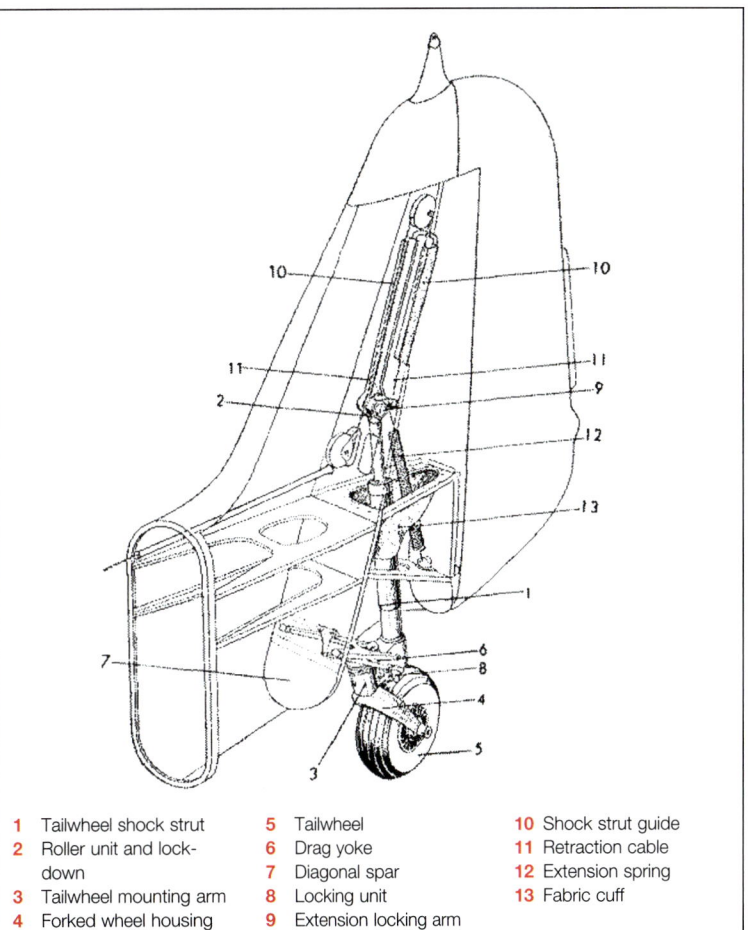

| 1 | Tailwheel shock strut | 5 | Tailwheel | 10 | Shock strut guide |
| 2 | Roller unit and lock-down | 6 | Drag yoke | 11 | Retraction cable |
| 3 | Tailwheel mounting arm | 7 | Diagonal spar | 12 | Extension spring |
| 4 | Forked wheel housing | 8 | Locking unit | 13 | Fabric cuff |
|   |                       | 9 | Extension locking arm |    |                   |

ABOVE **Also on the Flug Werk replica, identical to the original is the cable attached to the starboard undercarriage leg which pulls the tailwheel up as the main leg retracts.** *(Graeme Douglas courtesy of GossHawk Unlimited Inc.)*

main undercarriage leg which is routed back through the fuselage to the tailwheel down-lock. As the main leg moves up, the cable pulls the tailwheel down-lock out of a recess in a channel, allowing the assembly to slide up into the vertical stabiliser against the tension of a heavy-duty spring. The tailwheel is held in the retracted position only by the tension of the cable. When the main legs are lowered, the cable tension is released, allowing the spring to draw the assembly down the guide and the down-lock to engage in the guide recess.

## Flight controls

The three primary flight controls, the rudder, elevators and ailerons, are operated mechanically through a series of bellcranks, cables and/or push-rods. The operation of the tailplane and flaps is by electric motor as described previously.

The control circuits of the rudder and elevators contain differential bellcranks in which the control forces about the neutral position are reduced to a minimum. Large control movements of the stick or rudder pedals at the neutral position will cause a relatively small control surface movement. This difference progressively decreases as the control surface deflection increases. In later Fw190 aircraft the rudder differential bellcrank was replaced by a non-differential type.

## Elevator

Elevator control is actioned by fore and aft movement of the stick, which is transmitted to a torsion rod leading to the starboard side of the fuselage. The movement is then transmitted via a push-rod to a bellcrank at bulkhead 8, and from there, using two pairs of cables, to the differential unit under the tailplane. Output of this unit is by push-rods and bellcrank to the elevator horn.

BELOW **The elevator flight control circuit is via a combination of push-rods and cables.** *(D. (Luft) T.2190 A-8)*

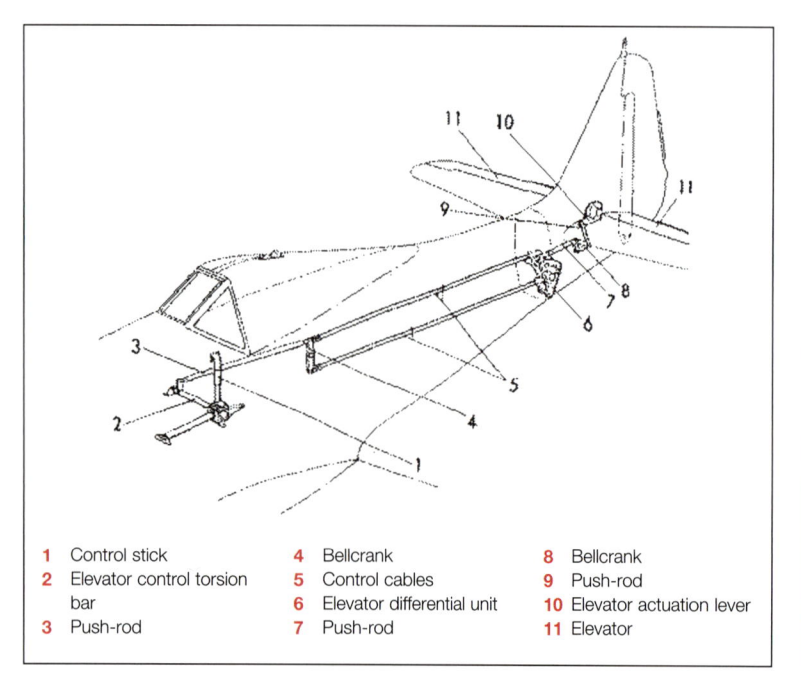

| 1 | Control stick | 4 | Bellcrank | 8 | Bellcrank |
| --- | --- | --- | --- | --- | --- |
| 2 | Elevator control torsion bar | 5 | Control cables | 9 | Push-rod |
| 3 | Push-rod | 6 | Elevator differential unit | 10 | Elevator actuation lever |
|  |  | 7 | Push-rod | 11 | Elevator |

BELOW **An elevator differential bellcrank unit minimises control stick movements around the neutral position.** *(D. (Luft) T.2190 A-8)*

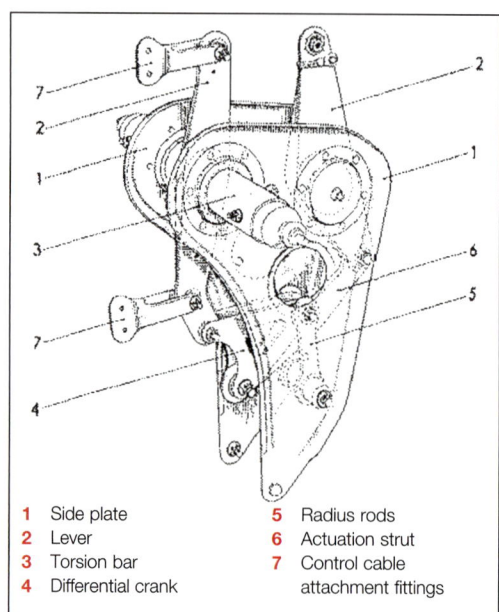

| 1 | Side plate | 5 | Radius rods |
| --- | --- | --- | --- |
| 2 | Lever | 6 | Actuation strut |
| 3 | Torsion bar | 7 | Control cable attachment fittings |
| 4 | Differential crank |  |  |

**RIGHT For rudder control, the pedals operate adjustable rods, which in turn move cables to the rudder via a bellcrank.** *(D. (Luft) T.2190 A-8)*

## Rudder

Rudder pedals can be adjusted in the cockpit by the grips to alter the length of the push-rods. Pedal movement is transmitted by flexible rods to the differential unit in the rear fuselage at bulkhead 14. Cables inside the vertical fin then connect the unit to the rudder attachment points. Both elevator and rudder movement are limited by stops in the differential bellcranks.

| | | | | | |
|---|---|---|---|---|---|
| 1 | EC-pedal unit | 4 | DUZ-flexible rods | 6 | Control cables |
| 2 | Rudder pedal arm | 5 | Rudder differential unit | 7 | Rudder |
| 3 | Adjustable push-rod | | | 8 | Adjustable grip |

## Ailerons

Aileron movement is achieved without the use of cables by push-rods and bellcranks alone. Left and right movement of the stick is transmitted forwards by a rod operating a bellcrank on the front spar and then directed outboard on both wings via push-rods before bellcranks and rods redirect transmission to the rear spar bellcranks, and then outboard once more to the aileron operating bellcranks. Deflection of the ailerons is limited by stops in the control stick base.

**RIGHT Looking back into the tail, this view shows the rudder bellcrank at the top and the elevator bellcrank below.** *(Rusty Gautreaux via Klaus Plasa)*

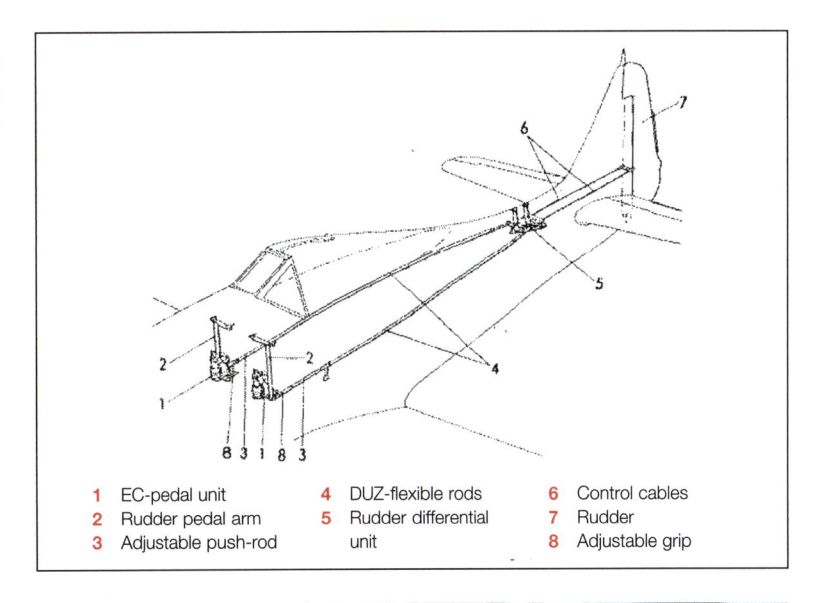

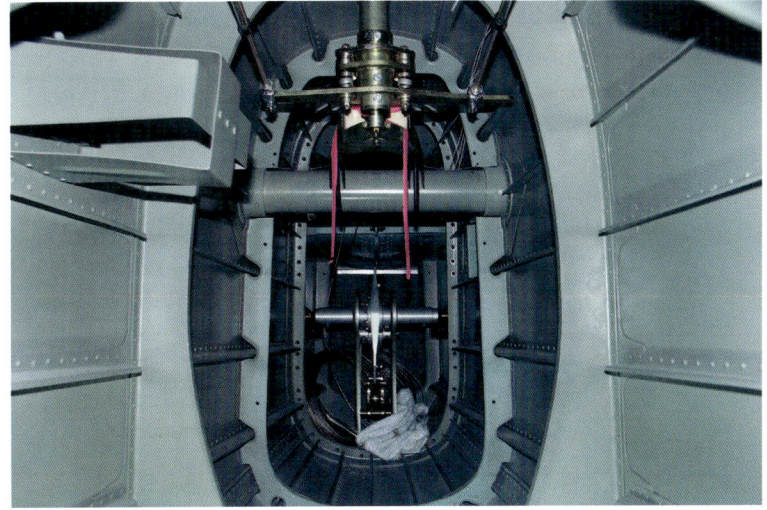

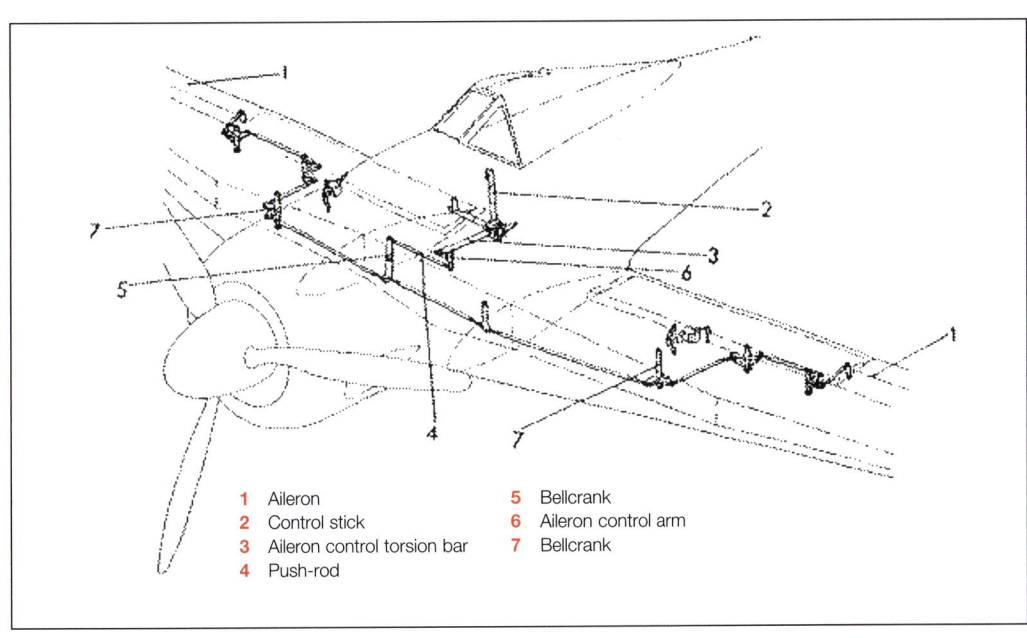

| | | | |
|---|---|---|---|
| 1 | Aileron | 5 | Bellcrank |
| 2 | Control stick | 6 | Aileron control arm |
| 3 | Aileron control torsion bar | 7 | Bellcrank |
| 4 | Push-rod | | |

**LEFT A complex series of push-rods and bellcranks transmit stick movements to the ailerons.** *(D. (Luft) T.2190 A-8)*

ANATOMY OF THE FW190 A-8

# Systems

## Fuel

Fuselage fuel is contained in two self-sealing fuselage tanks under the cockpit. The tanks are secured by fabric straps tensioned by adjustable bolts and are separated by a vertical bulkhead. The forward tank holds 232l and the rear 293l; both tanks contain immersed electric pumps controlled by circuit breakers in the cockpit. Additionally, a mechanical fuel pump is installed at the rear of the engine. An electrical fuel contents gauge in the cockpit is switchable between the two tanks, and low level indicator lights warn when the front tank is down to 90–100l (red light – return to base warning) and the rear tank is down to 10l (white light – tank switch-over warning). Tanks are filled through separate filler points on the right side of the fuselage, vent lines are incorporated and type C3 (96 octane) fuel is required. Fuel is pumped from the tanks by the electric pumps via filters on the forward firewall to the engine-driven pump. A gauge in the cockpit indicates fuel pressure.

When fitted, an under-fuselage drop tank holding 300l of fuel is connected to the ETC 501 rack and plumbed into the rear fuselage tank line. A pump incorporated into the stores rack feeds fuel from the drop tank to the rear tank once the fuel level has dropped below 240l in the rear tank. To assist in pressurising the drop tank, a bleed line from the supercharger is fed to the tank. The drop tank can be jettisoned by pulling a handle marked 'Bomben' in the cockpit, which severs the connection of the fuel and pressure lines at special rubber-sleeved separation points.

An additional auxiliary fuel tank is often fitted behind the cockpit at the rear of bulkhead 8 secured by two straps. This can be used either for fuel or for the nitrous oxide boost system (GM1). Tank capacity is 115l, and it is filled through a filling point on the left side of the fuselage. A pump unit at the top of the tank, and

**RIGHT** Fuselage fuel system comprising two internal tanks and a 300l drop tank. The two cockpit tanks have submersed electrical pumps and the drop tank has a pump incorporated in the ETC 501 rack. An engine-driven pump (item 15) is also fitted.
*(D. (Luft) T.2190 A-8)*

1 Forward fuel tank
2 Rear fuel tank
3 Fuel filler point
4 Filler line
5 Overflow line
6 Ventilation line
7 Spill line
8 Fuel pump unit
9 Fuel line (pump to fuel valve)
10 Fuel valve
11 Fuel line (fuel valve to filter)
12 Fuel filter
13 Fuel line (filter to fuel pump)
14 Fuel line separation points
15 Engine fuel pump
16 Fuel line (fuel pump to fuel injection pump)
17 Fuel injection pump
18 Bosch de-aerator
19 Fuel return flow line (de-aerator to fuel pump)
20 Ventilation line (de-aerator to forward fuel tank)
21 Fuel pressure measuring line
22 Fuel pressure gauge
23 Air pressure line (supercharger to drop tank)
24 Excess pressure valve
25 Reverse pressure valve
26 Under-fuselage drop tank
27 EP-1E fuel pump
28 Fuel line (drop tank to rear fuel tank)
29 ETC 501
30 Spacer bars
31 Fuel pump spill line
32 Fuel line to cold-start mixing lever
33 Fuel feed lines connecting line
34 Cut-off valve
35 Instrument panel bulkhead
36 Fuel transfer limit switch
37 Rear tank fuel pump]

operated from the cockpit, feeds the rear tank in the same way that the drop tank operates, via a fuel transfer limit switch in the rear tank which operates the auxiliary tank pump once the rear tank level has dropped below 240l. Later aircraft had a non-self-sealing tank with a supercharger air pressure fuel jettison system.

A small primer tank of 3l is contained in the rear fuselage main tank, and is used to prime the engine for starting. It is filled through a filler point beneath a sliding cover on the left side of the fuselage, and an electric pump sends fuel from the tank to the induction air pipes via a hand pump in the cockpit. The fuel is dispersed in an atomised state to all of the cylinders.

## Oil

Engine oil is contained in the 55l ring-shaped oil tank in the nose; immediately ahead of the tank is the oil cooler, both units being surrounded by armour-plated rings. Between the cooler and tank, a gap of about 10mm allows air to exit from the oil cooler. Cooling air passes across the surfaces of the cooler matrix after first being forced into the nacelle by the engine-driven fan. It flows through the matrix from back to front before exiting into the slipstream through the slot between the cooler and tank. A combined filler nozzle and measuring probe for the tank is situated on the left side of the nose beneath the cowling. While the oil temperature remains below 65°C, to speed up the supply of warm oil

**LEFT** An oil filter assembly is attached to the rear right mounting ring. *(Graeme Douglas)*

**BELOW** The oil system with the oil pump shown bottom right and the path of the reverse air flow through the cooler matrix shown at the top left. *(D. (Luft) T.2190 A-8)*

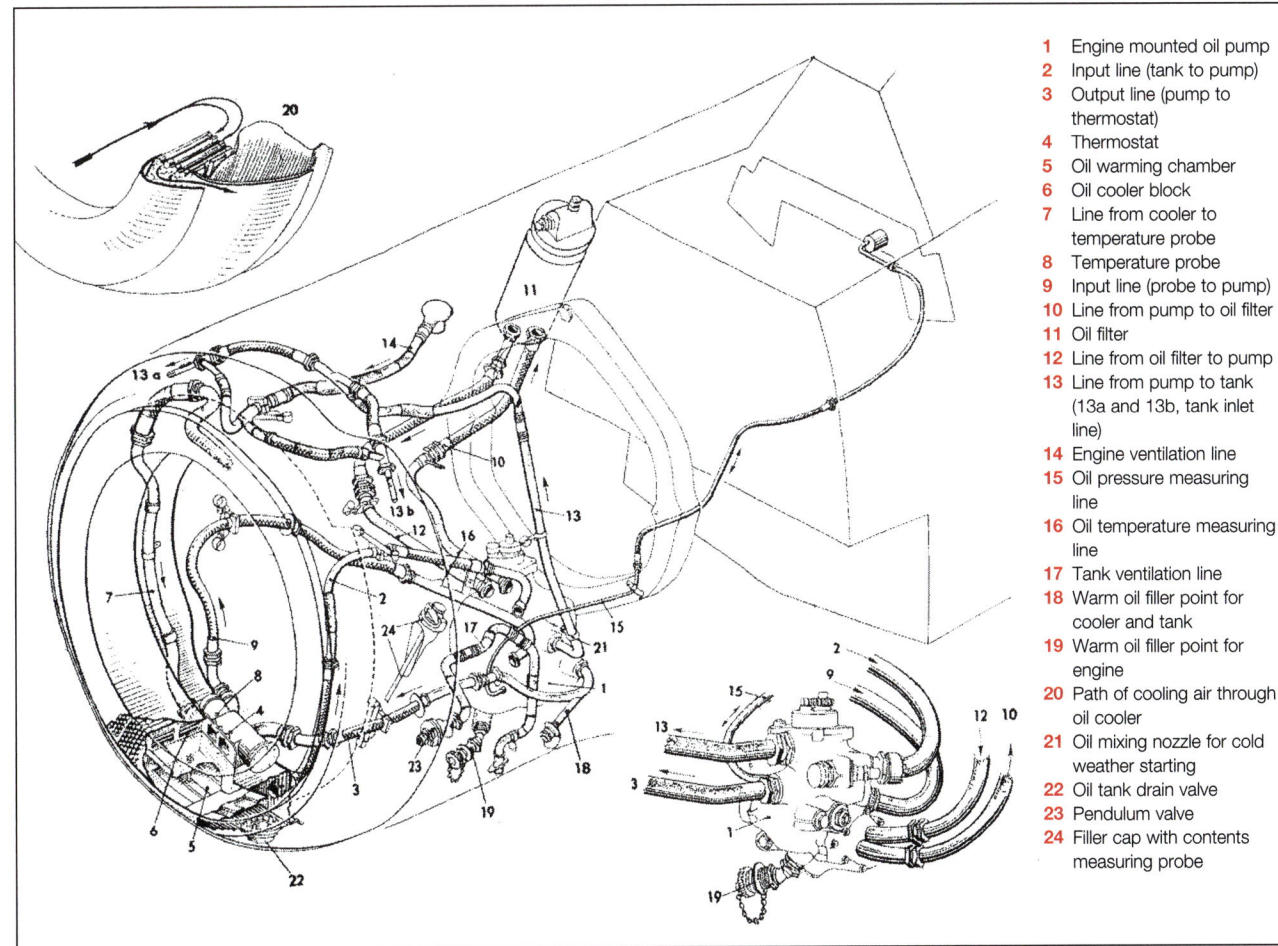

1. Engine mounted oil pump
2. Input line (tank to pump)
3. Output line (pump to thermostat)
4. Thermostat
5. Oil warming chamber
6. Oil cooler block
7. Line from cooler to temperature probe
8. Temperature probe
9. Input line (probe to pump)
10. Line from pump to oil filter
11. Oil filter
12. Line from oil filter to pump
13. Line from pump to tank (13a and 13b, tank inlet line)
14. Engine ventilation line
15. Oil pressure measuring line
16. Oil temperature measuring line
17. Tank ventilation line
18. Warm oil filler point for cooler and tank
19. Warm oil filler point for engine
20. Path of cooling air through oil cooler
21. Oil mixing nozzle for cold weather starting
22. Oil tank drain valve
23. Pendulum valve
24. Filler cap with contents measuring probe

to the engine, oil is directed through a warming chamber built into the bottom of the tank. Above this temperature, the thermostat opens and directs the oil through the cooler matrix. An oil filter container is positioned on the upper rear right side of the engine mounting ring. Oil temperature and pressure are displayed in the cockpit on gauges on the auxiliary instrument panel. Provision for pre-oiling during low temperature operations is provided by two filler points beneath the engine in the nacelle. One filler point allows warm oil to be forced up into the oil cooler and tank, and the other allows the engine to be filled with pre-warmed oil. Additionally, for cold weather starting, an oil dilution system in the form of an output line from the Maihak fuel pump sends fuel via a mixing nozzle to the engine oil.

### Propeller control

A VDM constant-speed propeller of 3.3m diameter is fitted to all BMW-engined models. Pitch control is normally hydraulically operated through the Kommandogerät (engine control unit) and determined by the power lever setting and other engine parameters, but it can also be controlled manually by an electrical back-up system. To change to manual control the pilot operates the switch on the left side console; this allows adjustment of propeller pitch through the thumb switch on the end of the throttle lever, and movement up or down on this increases or decreases propeller rpm. The pitch change motor and the rpm governor are bolted to the left side of the reduction gear casing. Limit switches built into the hub restrict pitch changes to their allowable limits. Propeller pitch is indicated to the pilot by a mechanically driven gauge in the auxiliary instrument panel which resembles a clock face, the hands pointing to various positions about 12 o'clock to represent various pitch angles.

### Electrical

The main electrical system consists of a 24v battery behind the pilot's seat with a ground plug to allow connection of an external battery. A 2kw engine-driven generator augments the battery power when the engine is running. All major circuits are protected by circuit breakers which act as switches to activate the circuits. Wiring harnesses are taken to the right side of the fuselage and fed to a main junction box in the aft fuselage from where various circuits are distributed.

Systems powered by electricity are:
- Main undercarriage extension and retraction
- Flaps extension and retraction
- Manual propeller pitch adjustment
- Tailplane trim adjustment
- Engine starting
- Instrumentation
- Radio and navigation equipment
- Autopilot system
- Fuel pumps
- Weapon arming and firing
- Ammunition counters
- Bomb and stores release
- Revi gunsight.

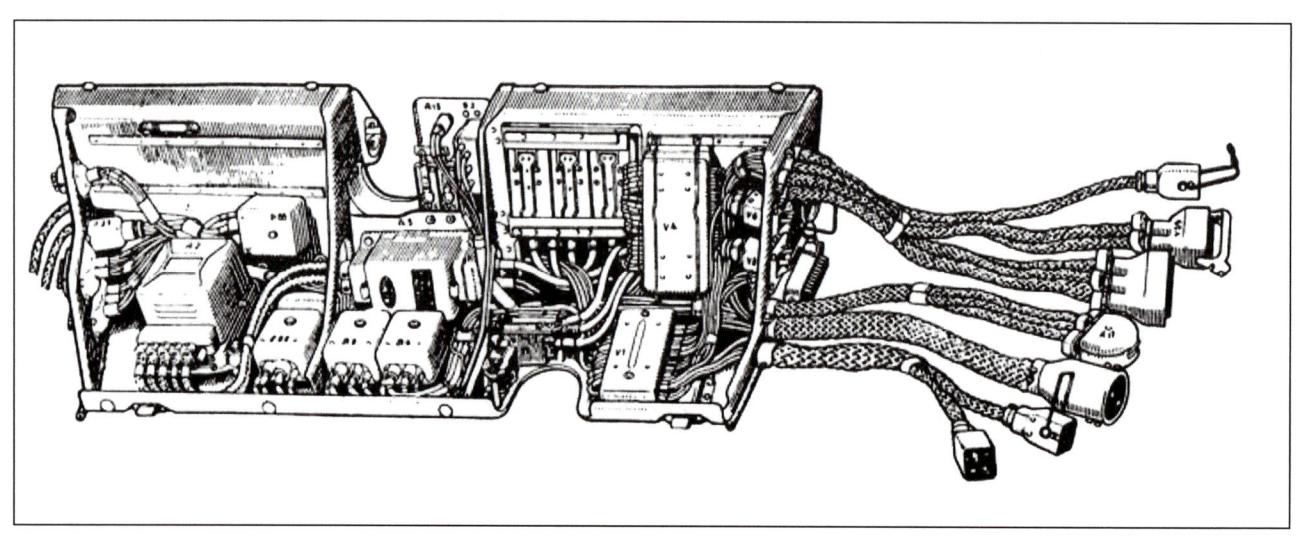

**BELOW** Left-hand console electrical switch modules in the cockpit are connected via seven individually shaped plugs for each circuit to avoid wrong connections. Quality and build was noticeably better than British and American designs of the period. (D. (Luft) T.2190 A-8)

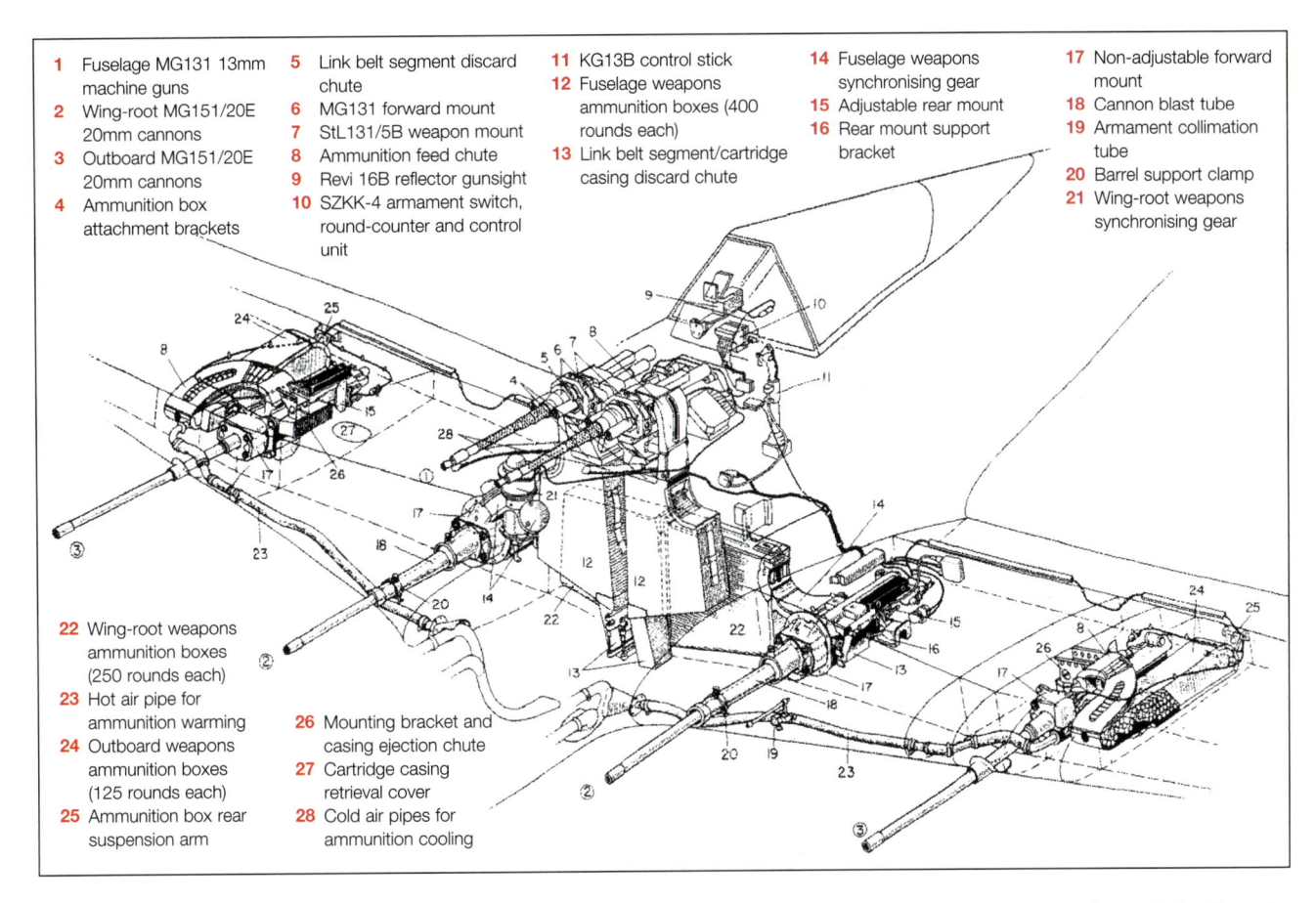

| | | | | |
|---|---|---|---|---|
| 1 Fuselage MG131 13mm machine guns | 5 Link belt segment discard chute | 11 KG13B control stick | 14 Fuselage weapons synchronising gear | 17 Non-adjustable forward mount |
| 2 Wing-root MG151/20E 20mm cannons | 6 MG131 forward mount | 12 Fuselage weapons ammunition boxes (400 rounds each) | 15 Adjustable rear mount | 18 Cannon blast tube |
| 3 Outboard MG151/20E 20mm cannons | 7 StL131/5B weapon mount | 13 Link belt segment/cartridge casing discard chute | 16 Rear mount support bracket | 19 Armament collimation tube |
| 4 Ammunition box attachment brackets | 8 Ammunition feed chute | | | 20 Barrel support clamp |
| | 9 Revi 16B reflector gunsight | | | 21 Wing-root weapons synchronising gear |
| | 10 SZKK-4 armament switch, round-counter and control unit | | | |
| 22 Wing-root weapons ammunition boxes (250 rounds each) | 26 Mounting bracket and casing ejection chute | | | |
| 23 Hot air pipe for ammunition warming | 27 Cartridge casing retrieval cover | | | |
| 24 Outboard weapons ammunition boxes (125 rounds each) | 28 Cold air pipes for ammunition cooling | | | |
| 25 Ammunition box rear suspension arm | | | | |

## Armament systems

Many alternative armament variants can be fitted to the aircraft, either as a factory kit (Umrüst-Bausatz) or as a field modification kit (Rüstsatz) but the standard A-8 armament installation is discussed here.

Weapons are arranged in three groups:

- Two MG131 machine guns in the upper fuselage cowling, with 400 rounds per gun.
- Two MG151/20E cannon, one in each wing root, with 250 rounds per gun.
- Two MG151/20E cannon, one in each wing outboard of the propeller arc, with 125 rounds per gun.

The fuselage and wing-root weapons are synchronised to fire through the propeller arc and the outboard cannon are unsynchronised.

Fuselage guns are mounted in adjustable weapon mounts type StL131/5b that are fixed to carrier brackets, which in turn are attached to bulkhead 1 and the windscreen mounting frame. The front of the mount is

**ABOVE** Diagram showing layout of standard armament for an A-8, although outboard weapons were often omitted. Note how if these MG151/20 were fitted, they were positioned on their sides. *(D. (Luft) T.2190 A-8)*

**BELOW** The weapons carried by the D-13 are three 20mm cannon. The one on the left is that used to fire through the propeller spinner and is equipped with an electrical gun cocking box and firing solenoid. *(GossHawk Unlimited Inc.)*

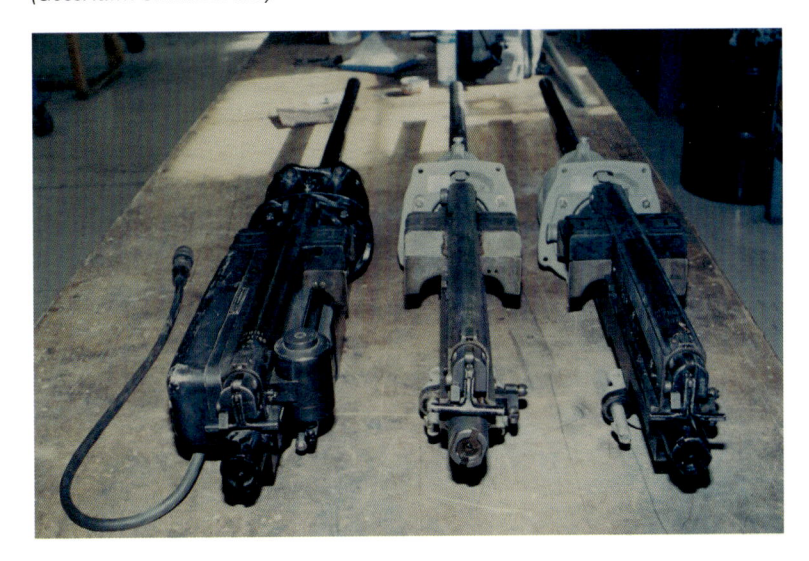

**ABOVE The D-13 carried no guns in the top weapons bay, so this area was used to house the ammunition for the Motorkanone. Ammunition from the box is fed via a chute to the gun below.** *(GossHawk Unlimited Inc.)*

fixed and contains a recoil fitting, while the rear is adjustable to allow the weapons to be harmonised to a range of 400m. Beneath the weapons, ahead of the main spar and bulkhead 1, two boxes hold the ammunition, which is loaded through a hinged door on the side of the box. Because of their close proximity to the engine, the boxes and ammunition are cooled by air from the nacelle ducted by two pipes into the top of each ammunition box. Ammunition is fed to the outboard side of each gun through feed chutes. Empty cartridge cases are ejected directly beneath each gun and disintegrated belt links out of the inboard side of both gun breeches. Ejection guides and an internal chute in each box allow the empty cartridge cases and belt links to fall through openings beneath the fuselage. A panel hinged at the windscreen base covers the fuselage guns. When released, it folds back over the windscreen to give access to the guns. The ammunition boxes can be removed through the wheel well openings.

The inboard wing cannon are mounted in type StL151/2b weapon mounts, the front one being attached to the main spar and the rear to a fitting between centre ribs 1 and 3. Each cannon is accessed through a wing root door on the upper surface of the wing. The door hinges inboard. As with the fuselage weapons, the forward mount provides the recoil mechanism and the rear allows adjustment of the weapons, the wing guns being harmonised to a range of 550m. The cannon barrel has a blast tube fitted over it inside the wing, and an adjustable clamp steadies the barrel inside the tube. Ammunition boxes are housed in the fuselage behind the wing spar, accessible through two hinged doors in the fuselage bottom. Belted ammunition is fed to the inboard side of each cannon through feed chutes. Empty cases are ejected below the weapon and belt links expelled out of the outboard side, all of these being ejected out of the wing through a chute screwed to the wing lower skin.

**RIGHT An early series aircraft is jacked up into flying position for weapon firing tests. The boxes beneath the wings are to catch spent cases and links. This aircraft does not have outboard cannon fitted.** *(Airbus photo archive, Bremen)*

Outboard wing cannon are fitted in similar mounts, type StL151/11, the forward support of which is attached to a bracket, which in turn is fixed to the wing lower shell between ribs 7 and 8. Adjustment is accomplished by the rear support, attached to rib 7 by a bracket. To facilitate ammunition feed, the cannon are positioned on their sides. Weapons can be removed from their mounts without affecting their adjustment. Ammunition boxes are positioned next to the cannon between ribs 8 and 9. In contrast to the ammunition for the fuselage guns, that for the outboard cannon is heated by hot air ducted from the exhausts from engine cylinders numbers five and ten and fed to the front of each box. At the front of the box two rollers help guide the ammunition before it is fed through a curved feed chute and then into a lead-in section and into the breech of the gun. Cartridge cases are ejected into the wing space between ribs 6 and 7. A spring steel barrier built into the chute prevents cases from returning to the breech and causing a jam. Cases are removed manually after flight through a small access panel in the lower wing. Links are ejected through a chute that is riveted to the weapons bay access door out of the wing's lower surface. The doors also give access to the weapons and ammunition boxes.

Synchronisation of the fuselage and inboard wing-mounted weapons is controlled by a mechanically driven unit at the top rear of the engine which sends electrical signals to the type EA firing unit of each gun, only permitting the gun to fire when clear of a propeller blade. Two electrical circuits control the cocking of the weapons, which are switched on by the pilot using the SZKK-4 box on the instrument panel. Switch I controls the fuselage and inboard weapons and switch II operates the outboard weapons, it being important to leave at least a three-second gap between switching the two circuits to avoid overloading the battery. Two buttons on the control stick fire the weapons in their respective groups. The SZKK-4 box also provides evidence of the rounds fired for the four cannon and indication lights to show a breech blockage of any of the six weapons. Weapons are aimed by the Revi 16B optical gunsight, which is mounted to the windscreen frame offset to the right in the cockpit. The shallow angle of the front windscreen ensures that the distracting reflection of the sighting image is not visible to the pilot. Electrical power is supplied via a circuit breaker.

## ETC 501 stores rack

With the advent of the A-8 model, the ETC 501 had to be moved forward by 200mm to allow room for access to the fuel tank in the rear fuselage. The ETC comprises the rack itself, the carrier which mounts it to the fuselage and an aerodynamic fairing. The rack can hold a bomb of up to 500kg or, with an ER-4 adaptor unit, four bombs each with a maximum weight of 50kg. In place of bombs, a 300l fuel tank can be installed, providing sway brace arms are fitted to the rack. As release is electrical for both bombs and tank, a type 500/XII release unit is fitted into the ETC 501. Power for the release circuit is provided by the circuit breaker on the

**ABOVE** Mechanical synchronising mechanism on top of the BMW engine prevented the electrical circuits firing the guns when a propeller blade was in the weapon's path. *(Graeme Douglas)*

**LEFT** Weapons are switched on at the SZKK-4 unit on the instrument panel. In this example (a D-9) the outboard weapons are MK108 cannon. Rounds remaining for wing cannon are shown in the vertical indicators and breech block warning lights are at the top of each column. Fuselage guns have no counters, only blockage lights. *(Graeme Douglas)*

**RIGHT** What appears to be an experimental early stores rack fitted with the 300l drop tank. The background in this photo has been airbrushed out by the censor. *(Airbus photo archive, Bremen)*

**BELOW** The armament and fusing panel has two switches at the top for the 21cm mortar, a rotary switch to allow a bomb to be dropped with a delay before exploding (mv) or without a delay (ov) in either a dive (Sturz) or in level flight (Wagerecht). The bottom panel controls the strike camera. *(Graeme Douglas)*

right-hand side console; the release circuit is controlled by the bomb fusing selection box in the armament panel in the cockpit, the rotary selector switch of which serves as the main switch of the release unit. A button on the left side of the control stick hand grip serves to release the load. Four lights above the selection box illuminate when stores have been released.

Emergency stores release can be activated by pulling the lever in the cockpit with a force of at least 30kg. The handle connects to a cable release, which releases all stores held by the rack.

## Special weapons

A variety of special weapons were used on the aircraft, of which perhaps the most unusual were upward firing cannon derived from the Schräge Musik project. This was a scheme to use upward firing cannon in night fighters against British heavy bombers. The fighters flew beneath their prey before firing into the unprotected underside of the bomber. A day-fighter version of this, which fired automatically, was developed, in which three MK103 cannon were mounted in the rear fuselage of the Fw190. The weapons were mounted in line pointing upwards and slightly out from the fuselage with a 2° angle of spread. The weapons were designed to fire when the fighter passed under the shadow of a bomber flying in daylight. A photo-electric cell, sensing the drop in ambient light, operated the firing mechanism of the cannon. Forty F-8 aircraft from JG10 were fitted with this system in order to test it in trials. It is thought that it went into limited combat use against day-flying American bombers.

Another weapon which was experimented with but not used operationally by the Fw190 was air-to-air rocket systems mounted on rails attached to underwing ETC 501 racks. Air-to-ground Panzerblitz, anti-tank rockets, were more successful. They were used on the Eastern Front from December 1944 onwards against Soviet tanks. The rockets were mounted on racks carrying 12 to 14 rockets and were capable of penetrating 180mm tank armour.

## Emergency power systems

Various systems were developed throughout the Fw190 A, F and G series to give a short-term engine power boost to improve performance. The original system, Erhöhte Notleistung (increased emergency performance), developed for fighter-bomber variants (F and G series), was a modification that used a bleed

**ABOVE** A 250kg bomb is loaded on to the ETC 501 stores rack of an Fw190 G-3. *(Bundesarchiv Bild 101I-496-3463-25A/photo Gehm)*

**BELOW** Close-up of the ETC 501 rack fitted to the underside of the A-8 belonging to the RAF Museum. This example is fitted with sway brace bars used when a 300l drop tank is installed. *(Andy Robinson)*

**RIGHT Emergency boost system consists of an instrument-mounted button (9) which controls a bleed valve mounted on the decking (3); this allows air to bleed into the supercharger airline, overriding the normal boost control and giving a short-term power increase.**
(D. (Luft) T.2190 A-8)

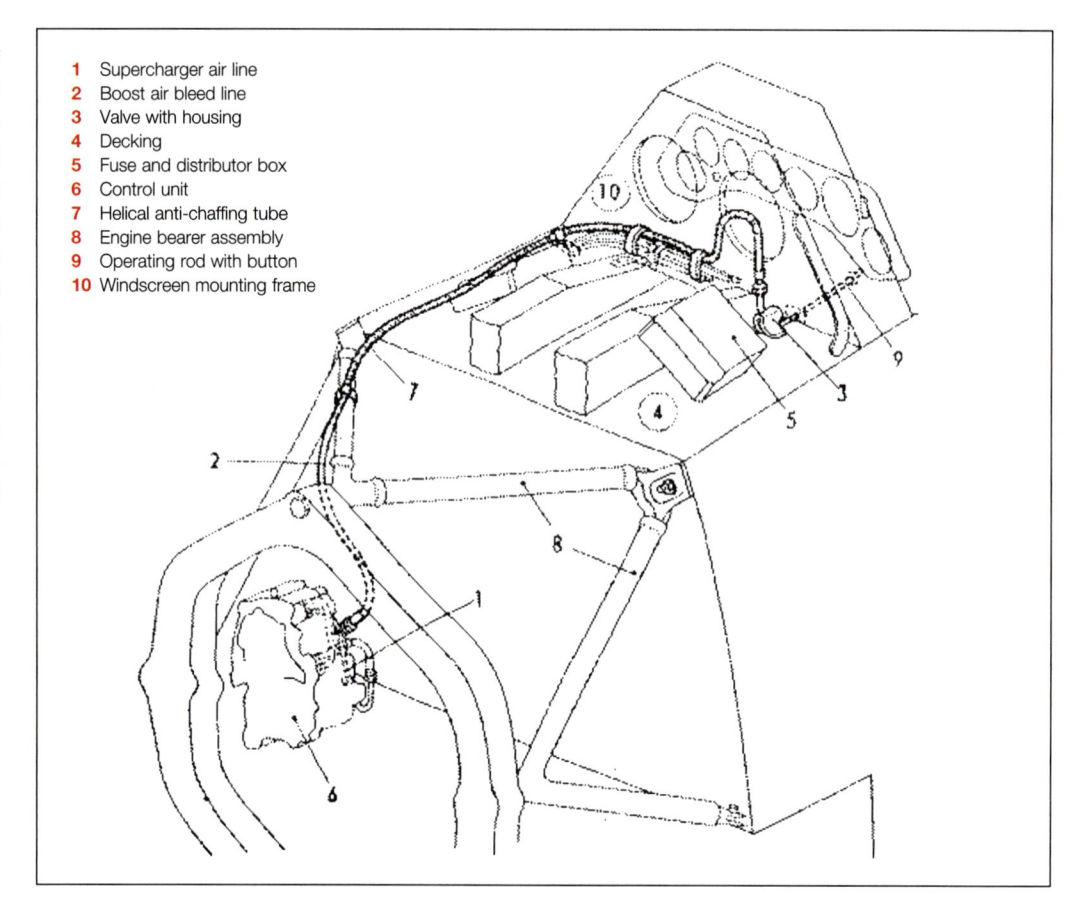

1. Supercharger air line
2. Boost air bleed line
3. Valve with housing
4. Decking
5. Fuse and distributor box
6. Control unit
7. Helical anti-chaffing tube
8. Engine bearer assembly
9. Operating rod with button
10. Windscreen mounting frame

from the supercharger pressure line to increase boost pressure at maximum rpm in low gear from 1.42 to 1.58ata and in high gear from 1.42 to 1.65ata, providing a short-term power boost at altitudes below 1,000m. The boost was controlled by a button on the left of the main instrument panel linked to a control valve, and the extra fuel required was sprayed directly into the supercharger. Aircraft fitted with this system were identified by a small yellow ring painted on the rear left corner of the fuselage armament panel. During 1944, a newer emergency boost system for take-off and emergency power was developed, controlled by inserting a pilot-operated stop cock in the pressure line of the boost regulator, with the effect of overriding the supercharger boost pressure regulator to allow a short-term boost of supercharger power to similar levels as the earlier system, which translated to between 22 and 25kph increase in speed. However, as with the older system, a time limit of 10 minutes' continuous use was placed on the system to prevent engine overheating. During production of the A-8 series, provision was made for the installation of an auxiliary fuselage tank. This could be simply an extra fuel tank of 115l to increase range, or it could be replaced by a non-self-sealing tank of either 115l or 140l for methanol-water injection (MW50) or an 85l tank for nitrous oxide injection (GM1). Methanol-water injection allowed a power increase of around 15 per cent from ground level up to maximum altitude. It worked primarily by producing an anti-detonant effect along with a secondary effect charge cooling. The use of GM1, which introduced extra oxygen into the fuel mixture, was not normally recommended as it only gave a worthwhile power boost at altitudes above 8,000m, and below this, the additional weight of the equipment reduced climb performance. Coupled to this was the increased risk of intake icing. It was planned that the MW50 system would eventually become the standard boost system for the BMW801 engine, but this was clearly at the expense of range if the fuselage tank could no longer be used for fuel. In the event, the MW50 system seems not to have been utilised in combat aircraft, probably because when tested it gave rise to small cylinder head cracks. Instead, in early 1945 orders were given that limited time emergency power for fighter variants (A series) could be achieved by a simple manifold pressure boost to 1.8ata, giving an equivalent power boost to around 2,400ps.

## Engine installation

As a result of a requirement by the RLM, BMW had to supply not only 'bare' engines for the Fw190 but also entire power units containing not just the engine cowlings, oil cooler and mounting ring but also complete exhaust systems, rear-mounted auxiliary components and wiring and control cables – in fact they had to supply everything back to the firewall on the airframe. Because of this, there were delays in the delivery of new engines to the Luftwaffe. These complete 'power eggs' received a 'T' suffix to the engine designation. The A-8 model had its 801 D-2 engines replaced during production with the BMW801 TU, itself a stop-gap measure while development continued on the planned replacements, the TS or TH. The TU contained some parts from development of the TS/TH series, allowing it to run at higher boost pressures, and was fully interchangeable with the 801 D-2. The new engines featured a thicker and heavier nose armour ring that helped to offset the rearward centre of gravity that arose as a result of fitting the fuselage fuel tank and equipment such as the Patin drive motor in the rear fuselage.

## Radio and autopilot installation

The radio system installed in most A-8 series is the FuG16ZY, which replaces the earlier FuG16Z, the major difference being the addition of range measuring circuitry. The set has to be relocated when the auxiliary tank is installed from bulkhead 8 to a position behind the pilot's seat. An access door in the side of the right fuselage allows the equipment to be serviced.

For versions of the A-8 designated as bad weather fighters, a PKS12 Patin directional control system is installed. The unit is a single axis autopilot controlling the rudder to facilitate coordinated turns in poor visibility or at night. The pilot can engage the system by selecting one of two turn rates, 1° or 2°/sec on a control stick mounted switch. When engaged, the system operates the rudder through a drive motor to steer the aircraft to a preselected heading on the repeater compass. The ailerons and elevators are operated in the normal manner.

## Oxygen system

Pilot oxygen is stored in three light steel spherical bottles. The bottles have a capacity of 2l each and are located in the equipment bay in the rear fuselage behind the fuselage auxiliary tank. Two of the bottles are opposite the equipment bay hatch and the third is below the hatch opening. The bottles are isolated from one another by the installation of

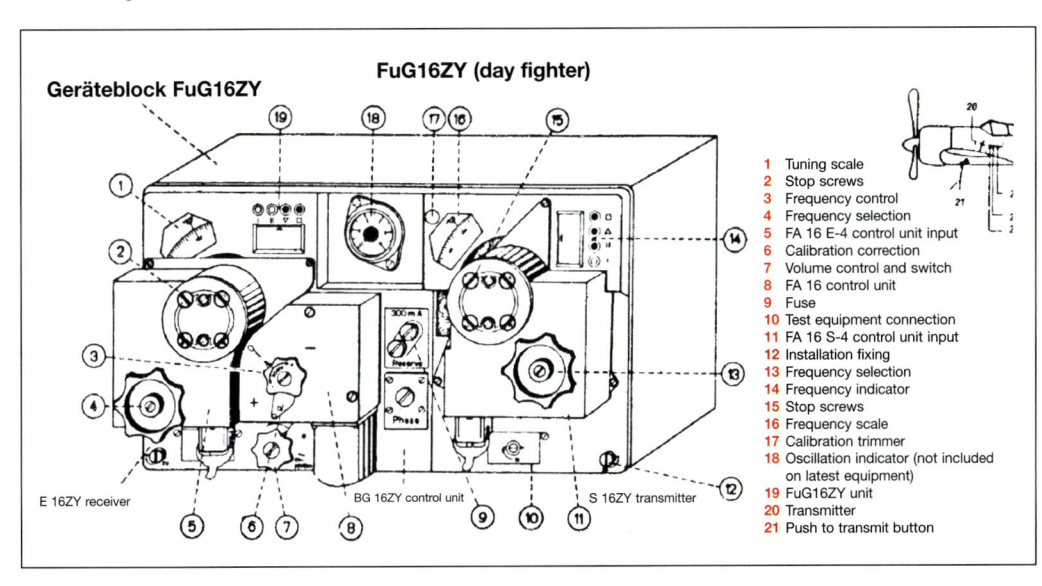

**FuG16ZY (day fighter)**

Geräteblock FuG16ZY

1 Tuning scale
2 Stop screws
3 Frequency control
4 Frequency selection
5 FA 16 E-4 control unit input
6 Calibration correction
7 Volume control and switch
8 FA 16 control unit
9 Fuse
10 Test equipment connection
11 FA 16 S-4 control unit input
12 Installation fixing
13 Frequency selection
14 Frequency indicator
15 Stop screws
16 Frequency scale
17 Calibration trimmer
18 Oscillation indicator (not included on latest equipment)
19 FuG16ZY unit
20 Transmitter
21 Push to transmit button

E 16ZY receiver    BG 16ZY control unit    S 16ZY transmitter

**LEFT** Standard radio installation in the A-8 comprising two systems: the FuG16ZY, which is a VHF transceiver set for R/T communications that can also be used for ground fixes and D/F homing; and the FuG25a IFF set, designed to identify the fighter as friendly to German radar. *(D. (Luft) T.2190 A-8)*

**ABOVE** The FuG16ZY installed in the hatch on the starboard side of the fuselage, below the cockpit. *(GossHawk Unlimited Inc.)*

**BELOW** The small 'Robot' camera sometimes fitted in the wing of ground attack versions, triggered by a switch on the pilot's power control lever. *(D. (Luft) T.2190 A-8)*

1. Shutter release
2. Camera forward fixing point
3. Camera base plate
4. Platform forward attachment point
5. Adjustable platform
6. 'Robot' camera
7. Film advance spring

four non-return valves, separating the bottles into two discrete systems as a safety measure. Another non-return valve is installed between the external filler connection and the first oxygen bottle. The regulator unit is behind and to the right of the pilot's seat, and a button in the centre of the unit to activate emergency oxygen can be operated by the pilot's elbow. The pressure gauge, flow indicator gauge and flow valve are on the lower right auxiliary instrument panel. When the flow valve is opened, oxygen flows firstly via the high-pressure lines to the regulator, where its pressure is reduced and it is mixed with ambient air to provide a demand supply of breathable air and oxygen to the pilot. The bottles have a working pressure of 150atü.

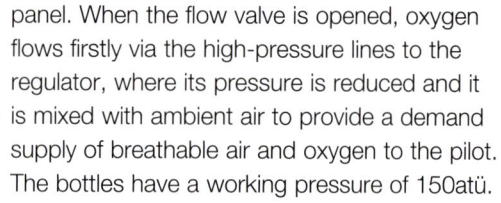

## Camera systems

On the A-8 series, a 16mm cine camera is fitted to record images when the aircraft weapons are fired. The type BSK 16 camera is installed looking out of a port in the left wing. The port is protected by a glass window and the camera is mounted on an adjustable platform; it is powered by an internal electric motor. Depressing the firing button for the fuselage and inboard wing weapons activates the camera or it can be operated by a button on the power control lever. A film roll of 15m long is fitted and each activation by the firing button is limited to 3.75m per run, equating to about 50sec of film.

On F- and G-series aircraft, a 'Robot' model II still camera is fitted instead of the cine camera in the same location. Triggered by a button on the power control lever and taking images 24mm × 24mm, the film is advanced a frame at a time by a pre-wound spring mechanism on top of the camera which operates whenever the shutter is released. The 'Robot' camera can be retrofitted in place of the BSK in A-series aircraft, but without a connection to the weapons.

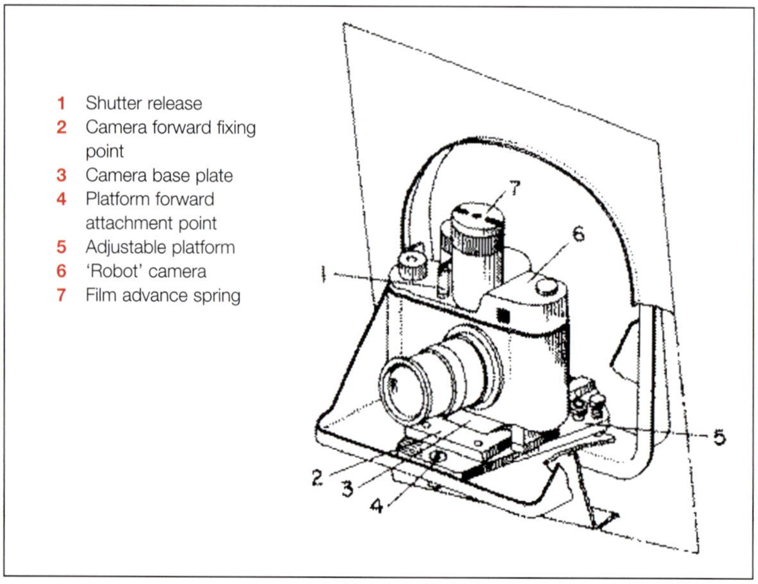

## Emergency equipment

A first-aid kit is carried and installed between bulkheads 9 and 10 on the right side of the rear fuselage, accessible from outside.

Stowed in the right side console is a flare gun together with flares. It can be inserted through a tube in the right side of the cockpit for firing. The pilot has a parachute and a dinghy pack.

In order to clean oil from the three front windscreen panels, a bleed from the fuel pressure gauge is fed to a stopcock below the main instrument panel. Opening this allows fuel into spray tubes containing small holes. The fuel is blown rearwards in the slipstream, keeping the front screen and two side panels clean.

# TECHNICAL SPECIFICATIONS

## FOCKE-WULF Fw190 A-8

### Dimensions, weights and performance

| | |
|---|---|
| Wingspan | 10.50m |
| Length | 8.95m |
| Height | 3.95m |
| Undercarriage track | 3.50m |
| Wing area | 18.30sq m |
| Empty weight | 3,062kg |
| Max take-off weight | 4,864kg |
| Max fuel load | 939l including drop tank. Type C3, 96 octane |
| Oil capacity | 55l |
| Performance | Max speed at sea level 571km/h, at 6,300m 656km/h with GM-1 |
| Engine | BMW801 D-2 or TU |
| Armament (standard) | 2 × MG131 13mm machine guns in fuselage upper cowling |
| | 2 × MG151/20E 20mm cannon in wing roots |
| | 2 × MG151/20E 20mm cannon in outboard wings (not always fitted) |
| Propeller | VDM wooden blades, constant speed, 3.3m diameter |

## FOCKE-WULF Fw190 D-9

### Dimensions, weights and performance

| | |
|---|---|
| Wingspan | 10.50m |
| Length | 10.24m |
| Height | 3.36m |
| Undercarriage track | 3.50m |
| Wing area | 18.30sq m |
| Empty weight | 3,490kg |
| Max take-off weight | 4,900kg including auxiliary fuel tank and 500kg bomb |
| Max fuel load | 935l including drop tank. Type B7, 90 octane |
| Oil capacity | 60l |
| Performance | Max speed at sea level 545km/h, at 6,600m 650kmh without boost |
| Engine | Junkers Jumo 213 A |
| Armament (standard) | 2 × MG131 13mm machine guns in fuselage upper cowling |
| | 2 × MG151/20E 20mm cannon in wing roots |
| Propeller | Junkers VS 111 wooden blades, constant speed, 3.5m diameter |

## FOCKE-WULF Ta152 H-1

### Dimensions and weights

| | |
|---|---|
| Wingspan | 14.82m (with rounded wingtips) |
| Length | 10.82m |
| Height | 3.36m |
| Undercarriage track | 3.95m |
| Wing area | 23.5sq m |
| Empty weight | 4,030kg |
| Max take-off weight | 5,217kg |
| Max fuel load | 1,280l including 300l drop tank. Type B4, 87 octane |
| Oil capacity | 62l |
| Performance | Max speed at sea level 563km/h*, at 12,400m 752km/h** |
| Engine | Junkers Jumo 213 E-1 |
| Armament (standard) | 1 × MK108 30mm engine-mounted cannon |
| | 2 × MG151/20E 20mm cannon in wing roots |
| Propeller | Junkers VS 9 wooden blades, constant speed, 3.6m diameter |

Note: * denotes speed obtained with MW50 boost  ** denotes speed obtained with GM-1 boost

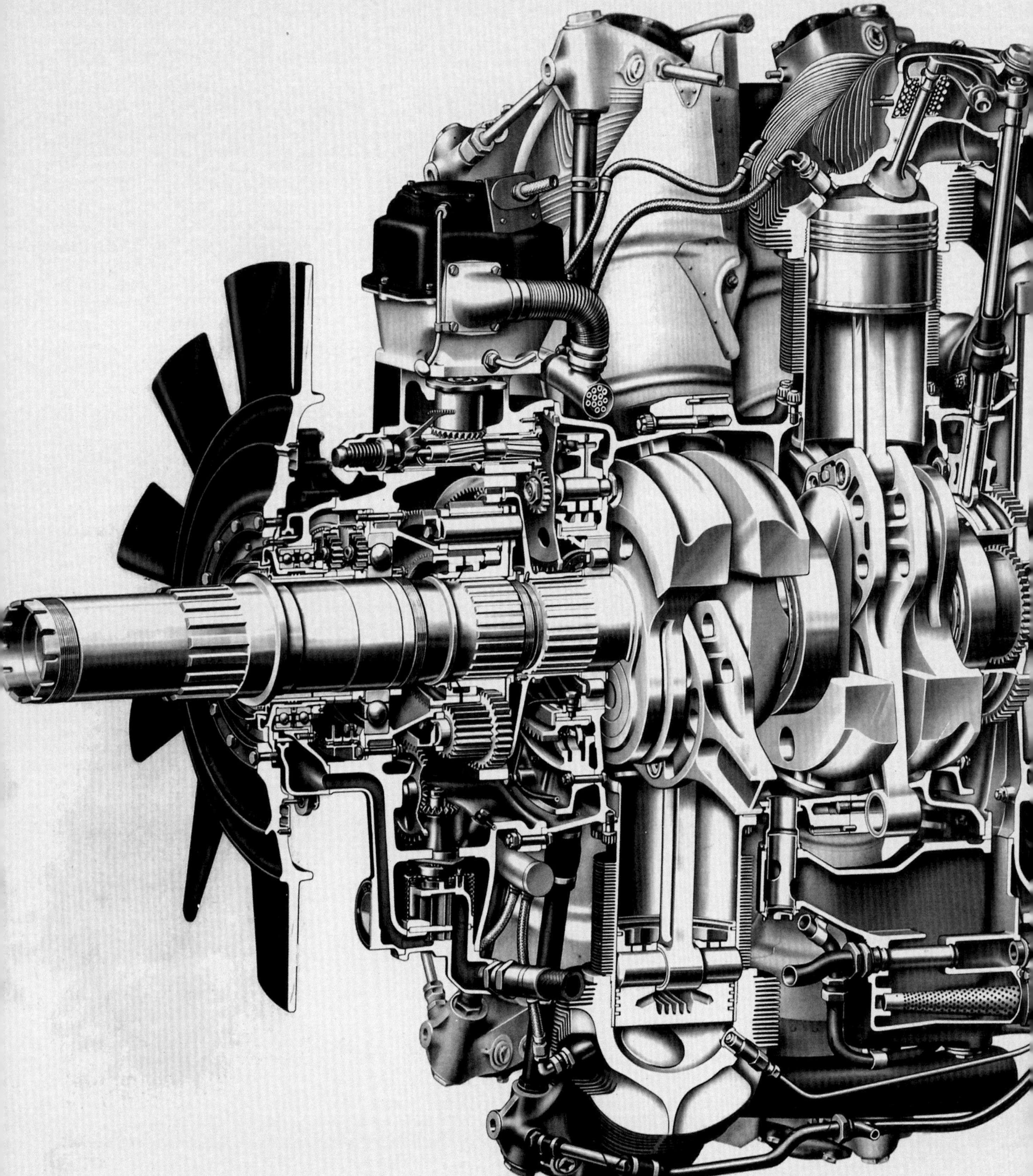

*Chapter Four*

# Power for the Fw190 and Ta152

**Two very different engines powered the production models of the Fw190 and Ta152, and both proved to be excellent power plants for their respective roles. The BMW was a rugged, reliable engine best suited for low- to medium-altitude versions, while the Jumo excelled in high-altitude interception aircraft.**

**OPPOSITE** Cutaway drawing of the BMW801 14-cylinder radial engine, showing the close spacing of the two rows of cylinders and the two master rods in the lower cylinders.
*(BMW Classic Archive)*

# BMW801 radial engine

**(Powering the A, F and G series)**

The radial-engined versions of Focke-Wulf's famous fighter were all equipped with a BMW power unit. In the first two prototypes this was the BMW139, and in all subsequent models it was the BMW801. The genesis of this partnership is a rather complex story of takeovers, competing designs and German engineering excellence overcoming almost insurmountable technical problems. The history of the engine development of the Fw190 has often been stated incorrectly in accounts of the aircraft, but the true chain of events which led to the development of Germany's best air-cooled radial engine of the war is a fascinating one.

## Development history

The Bayerische Motoren Werke AG traced its roots back to the First World War, when it produced in-line aero engines. Following the Treaty of Versailles, the company was prohibited from manufacturing aero engines and instead switched production to motorcycles and brake units for railway carriages and in the late 1920s to automobile production. Following the National Socialists' rise to power in 1933 when Germany began to rearm, orders for armaments and military equipment expanded rapidly, allowing the company to increase the size of its main Munich-based plant. The company produced a range of successful aero engine designs, including the BMW132 radial, which powered the Junkers Ju52 transport. This was based on the nine-cylinder, licence-built American Pratt and Whitney Hornet engine. In 1936 the RLM funded the development of a new and larger radial engine design, the BMW139. A competitor firm, Brandenburgische Motorenwerke GmbH (Bramo) of Berlin, also produced a design to the same specification, the Bramo 329. The BMW engine used components and materials from the 132 in the design of the 14-cylinder 139, and this engine was to power the first two prototypes of the Fw190; but it was most certainly not built as an 18-cylinder, 2-row version of the 132 as is often mistakenly stated. In 1939 BMW bought the Bramo company, and in a rationalisation of its aircraft engine manufacturing business renamed it the BMW Flugmotoren-Werke GmbH. Development of both the 139 and 329 ceased, and instead elements of both designs were combined into a brand new engine which was being developed, the BMW801.

Work on the new design, a 14-cylinder, 2-row, air-cooled radial of almost exactly the same displacement as the old BMW139, began in October 1938. By adopting a 'square' engine in which the diameter of the piston is the same as the stroke (156mm), the BMW team under the direction of Dipl.-Ing. Martin Duckstein and Helmuth Sachse produced an engine with a reduced crankshaft throw, enabling them to reduce the dimensions of the crankcase. They also designed the crankshaft to run on a single-row ball race in the centre journal, reducing the length of the shaft and permitting the cylinder rows to be closely spaced, which in turn allowed overall engine length to be saved. The development time agreed with the RLM was very short, and the first test bench run, during which it produced some 1,370ps, was in May 1939. It was released for series production in December of the same year. Early engines had significant problems, mainly because of the very short development period but also because of changing military requirements. Between January 1939 and January 1941, some 11,000 changes were made to the design. It was hardly surprising that the Fw190, equipped with the pre-production 801 C-0 version of the engine, which was notoriously unreliable, was plagued with problems which took some time to resolve. By 1942 a reliable version, the 801 D-2, had been developed. This went on to power the many Fw190s and also several other Luftwaffe types, including the Dornier Do 217 and some versions of the Junkers Ju88. Many versions of the 801 were produced, including complete 'power egg' assemblies which included pre-installation of items such as the engine bearers, oil coolers and the engine covers in order to speed up engine changes in the field; these units were given either a 'T' or an 'M' suffix. Another series of 'bare' engines, the S, introduced many minor changes to bearings and bushes along with a standardised boost system which increased power to 2,230ps but was otherwise very similar to the D-2 described below. All versions featured a mechanically driven supercharger, fuel injection and the innovative Kommandogerät, a hydraulic-mechanical unit positioned at the rear of the engine that was designed to automatically control settings for fuel mixture strength, boost pressure, propeller pitch, ignition timing and the switching of the supercharger speed control.

## Crankcase and crankshaft

The two rows of seven cylinders are staggered on a triple-split cast steel and machined crankcase. Early engines have a crankshaft constructed from four machined steel forgings, the front and rear cranks joined together by a special Hirth coupling containing an internal bush which is screwed into the threads on the ends of the two shafts and engages the serrations on the two halves of the coupling. The outer surface of the joint forms the bearing surface of the centre main bearing, a single-row ball race; the front and rear bearings are roller bearings. The four crankshaft webs contain integral counterweights and are drilled for lead filling for balancing. The two crankpins are offset 180°, and the master rods, of H-section steel construction one in each row, operate in cylinders eight and nine, with big end bearings of lead-bronze, and the six articulated rods have bronze-lined bearings. Later engines from 1944 onwards had a simpler, pressed together crankshaft that was supported by three roller bearings.

## Cylinders and pistons

The cylinder barrels are steel-lined with aluminium close finning and fitted with baffles and air ducts. At the base of the cylinder, the mounting flange is drilled for the 18 attaching studs on the crankcase. The cylinder heads of aluminium alloy construction are screwed and shrunk on to the cylinder. Two overhead valves per head are fitted; the exhaust valve stem is hollow and filled with sodium to aid cooling, valve seats are aluminium-

**ABOVE** A complete 'power egg' engine installation with oil tank and cooler is positioned in place to fit to an early series aircraft. Just below the four exhaust pipes can be seen one of the oval engine air intakes. *(Airbus photo archive, Bremen)*

**RIGHT** Detail of the baffles surrounding a cylinder head. The design of this was critical to ensure the flow of air around all cylinders and prevent overheating. The two spark plugs are installed in the front of the cylinder, and the black pipes connecting the rocker boxes allow oil to drain between boxes. *(Graeme Douglas)*

**ABOVE** Sectioned cylinder head showing the intake valve assembly. The fitting for the fuel injector nozzle is also sectioned. Also of note is how tightly the baffle wraps around the closely finned barrel. *(Graeme Douglas)*

bronze for the inlet and steel for the exhaust. The valve rockers are fully enclosed, running on needle roller bearings, and are pressure lubricated; a connecting tube joins the rocker boxes on each cylinder. The aluminium-alloy pistons employ three compression rings and an oil control ring above the piston pin, and another compression ring at the base of the piston skirt.

### Valve gear

Two four-lobe cam rings (one for the inlet and one for the exhaust) open and close the valves for each row of cylinders, the rear row of cylinders having its cam rings and push-rods at the rear, and the front row has the corresponding gear at the front of the row. Cam gears are driven from the crankshaft in the same direction as the crank via an epicyclic gear train with a reduction ratio of 1:8. The cam lobes operate roller-ended tappets actuating the push-rods contained in tubes connecting the crankcase and the rocker boxes.

### Reduction gear

Inside the aluminium-alloy reduction gear casing, forward of the front cam ring, a large steel drum containing the spur gears of the reduction drive is driven from the crankshaft. The propeller shaft is supported by a lead-bronze bushing in the nose of the crankshaft and a thrust race in the nose of the gear casing. The internal epicyclic gears rotate the propeller drive shaft at 0.54 × crankshaft speed. At the forward end of this drum a large-diameter spur gear drives a small gear on a shaft running forward. This in turn, via another pair of gears, drives a floating sleeve concentric with the crankshaft to which the 12-blade, magnesium-alloy cooling fan is attached. The fan is geared up to turn at 1.72 × crankshaft speed, this being equivalent to about 3.18 × the propeller speed. From the same gear,

**LEFT** Units mounted at the front of the engine:
1. Twin magneto housing
2. Engine speed governor controlling propeller pitch (hydraulic)
3. Electric motor for propeller pitch control
4. Pitch adjustment unit for electrical adjustment
5. Twelve-bladed cooling fan.

*(Graeme Douglas)*

drive is taken to power the twin Bosch-type ZM14 magnetos which are mounted on the top of the reduction gear casing.

## Supercharger and accessory drive

An aluminium alloy supercharger delivery casing is connected to the rear crankcase, and at the rear of this a magnesium-alloy intake casing is attached, long bolts passing through both casings securing them to the crankcase. The supercharger impellor, machined from an aluminium forging, consists of 24 blades; alternate blades have a curled centre section to direct air from the centre to the outside of the impellor. The impellor has a two-speed drive, delivered through a main drive gear and two hydraulic clutch mechanisms. Low gear is 5.31 × crankshaft speed and high gear 8.31 × crankshaft speed, the change being made automatically by the Kommandogerät. The rear casting is magnesium alloy and carries the flanges for mounting the starter motor, generator, vacuum pump, fuel delivery pump, fuel injection pump and the Kommandogerät.

## Fuel injection system

The cylindrically shaped fuel injection pump, built by the Deckel Company, was the first of its type to be designed in a radial format for a production engine. The pump consists of 14 chambers each containing a plunger; these are moved up and down by a spring-loaded roller which in turn is operated by three cams running on a cam ring at a 1:6 reduction of crankshaft speed. The other end of the plunger is fitted with a spur gear which in turn rotates the pump plunger to regulate fuel flow. The

**BELOW** Rear of the engine showing accessories:
1 Electrical generator
2 Inertia starter
3 Kommandogerät (engine control device)
4 Fuel de-aerator unit (attached to injection pump behind)
5 Engine driven fuel pump
6 Reduction gearbox for manual starting
7 Engine mounting ring containing oil supply for Kommandogerät.
*(Graeme Douglas)*

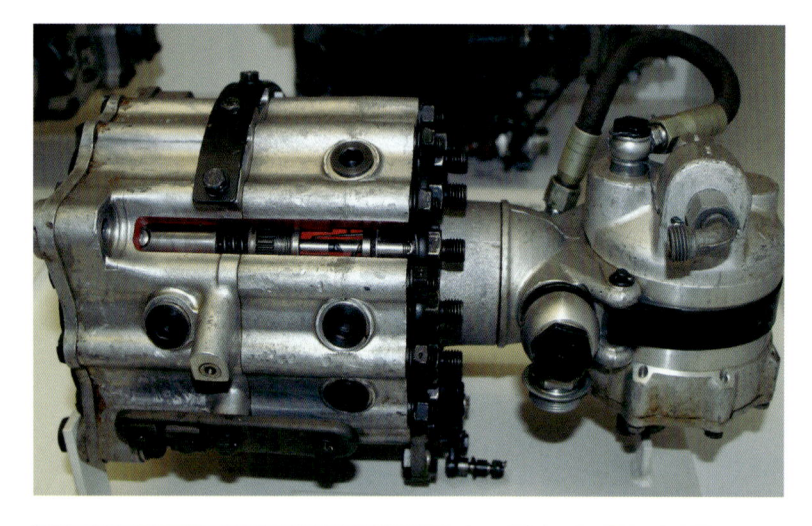

**LEFT** The intricate fuel injection pump with one of the 14 chambers sectioned to show the cam-operated plunger. As the plunger moves up and down the chamber the helical-cut grooves move in and out of alignment with transfer ports, forcing fuel out of the outlet on the right. The drive gear meshes with those in each of the other chambers to adjust the fuel flow. The unit at the right is the de-aerator. *(Graeme Douglas)*

space enclosed by the pumps contains a domed de-aerator unit. Fuel supplied by the delivery pump is fed to the pump plungers through a circumferential gallery in the rear of the pump body. Air is bled off through various galleries to the de-aerator unit and fuel quantity is controlled by the intermeshing gears of the plunger bodies, which also mesh with a common ring gear. A control shaft connected to the Kommandogerät rotates the whole assembly of gears which in turn rotates the pump plungers in their bores. This changes the alignment of the helically cut grooves in the plungers in relation to the cut-off ports, therefore adjusting fuel quantity for various throttle settings. Each pump unit contains a non-return valve. The injector nozzles, connected to the injection pump by high-pressure delivery pipes, are positioned between the valves in the cylinder heads. The body of each of the injectors contains a small fuel filter.

**ABOVE** The pump in place at the rear of the engine. Each of the outlets is connected to a high-pressure pipe which is connected to an injector in each cylinder. *(Graeme Douglas)*

**RIGHT** The oil pump body contains two pressure pumps and is at the bottom rear of the engine just above the exhaust pipes from the lower cylinders. *(Graeme Douglas)*

**RIGHT** Instructions for draining sludge from the oil system and cleaning the filter together with the correct order for refilling the system are displayed on the filter housing at the rear of the engine. *(Graeme Douglas)*

## Engine lubrication

The engine is lubricated by a total of two pressure pumps and four scavenge pumps. The oil pump body is located at the lower rear of the engine, driven from a gear train from the accessory drive. One pressure pump delivers oil at 12 atmospheres, this pressure being maintained by a spring-loaded relief valve, the output being sent to the oil cooler. The other pump is regulated by a temperature compensating control valve to maintain around 7 atmospheres when the oil is hot. The output of this pump passes through a filter and thence to the engine to deliver oil to the larger major components. A pressure-reducing valve lowers the pressure for the valve gear lubrication, and oil drains to the lower rocker boxes where it is scavenged by one of the four scavenge pumps and returned to the oil tank. Likewise, two pumps scavenge oil from the propeller reduction gear, fan drive gear and front cam gear drive. Drainage of the centre crankcase, supercharger casing and accessory drives along with the crankcase breather is all accomplished by a fourth pump.

## Kommandogerät (control device)

In order to minimise the workload of the pilot, especially when in combat, the BMW801 is fitted with an ingenious hydraulically boosted mechanical computer which detects changes in atmospheric pressure, charge temperature and manifold pressure (boost). These inputs are then used to automatically control a number of engine parameters: engine RPM, ignition spark timing, fuel mixture, manifold pressure and the switch-over for the supercharger gear change. In the cockpit is a single 'power control lever', not a throttle in the conventional sense, through which the pilot sets the power required and allows the Kommandogerät to adjust engine parameters to maintain engine power over a range of different flight conditions.

In contrast, Allied aircraft had separate controls for the throttle, mixture, propeller and

### ENGINE SPECIFICATION – BMW801 D-2

| | |
|---|---|
| Type | Two-row static air-cooled radial |
| Number of cylinders | 14; number 14 is the top vertical cylinder. |
| Firing order | 1, 10, 5, 14, 9, 4, 13, 8, 3, 12, 7, 2, 11, 6. No. 1 is the next clockwise cylinder on from no. 14 (from rear of engine) |
| Bore/stroke | 156mm/156mm |
| Displacement | 41.8L |
| Compression ratio | 7.22:1 |
| Supercharger speed ratio | 5.31:1 (low blower), 8.31:1 (high blower) |
| Take-off and emergency rating | 1,730ps at 2,700rpm at 1.42ata |
| Maximum cruise | 1,370ps at 2,300rpm at 1.2ata |
| Rotation of crankshaft and propeller | Clockwise viewed from rear |
| Propeller reduction | 0.54:1 |
| Dry weight including engine mounts | 1,250kg |
| Length | 2,006mm |
| Diameter | 1,290mm |
| **Accessories** | |
| Magnetos | 2 × Bosch ZM14 CR10 |
| Fuel injection | 1 × Deckel injection pump, Maihak fuel supply pump |
| Starter | 1 × Bosch inertia electric starter plus provision for hand starter crank |
| Generator | 1 × Bosch 2kw |
| Control unit | 1 × BMW Kommandogerät |
| Vacuum pump | 1 × Askania |

**RIGHT** The Kommandogerät is positioned at the rear right of the BMW801 engine. It is a complex series of hydraulic servos, mechanical drives and evacuated capsules which together automatically adjust a number of engine parameters in response to the pilot's power lever setting. Hoses connect it to its own oil supply contained in the black engine mount ring.
*(Graeme Douglas)*

1. Supercharger switch-over unit
2. Supercharger regulator
3. Cover over drive gears for ignition timing adjustment
4. Duz cable to magneto
5. Injection pump regulator
6. Measuring manifold
7. Cap over mixture limiting screw
8. Linkage for power lever in cockpit

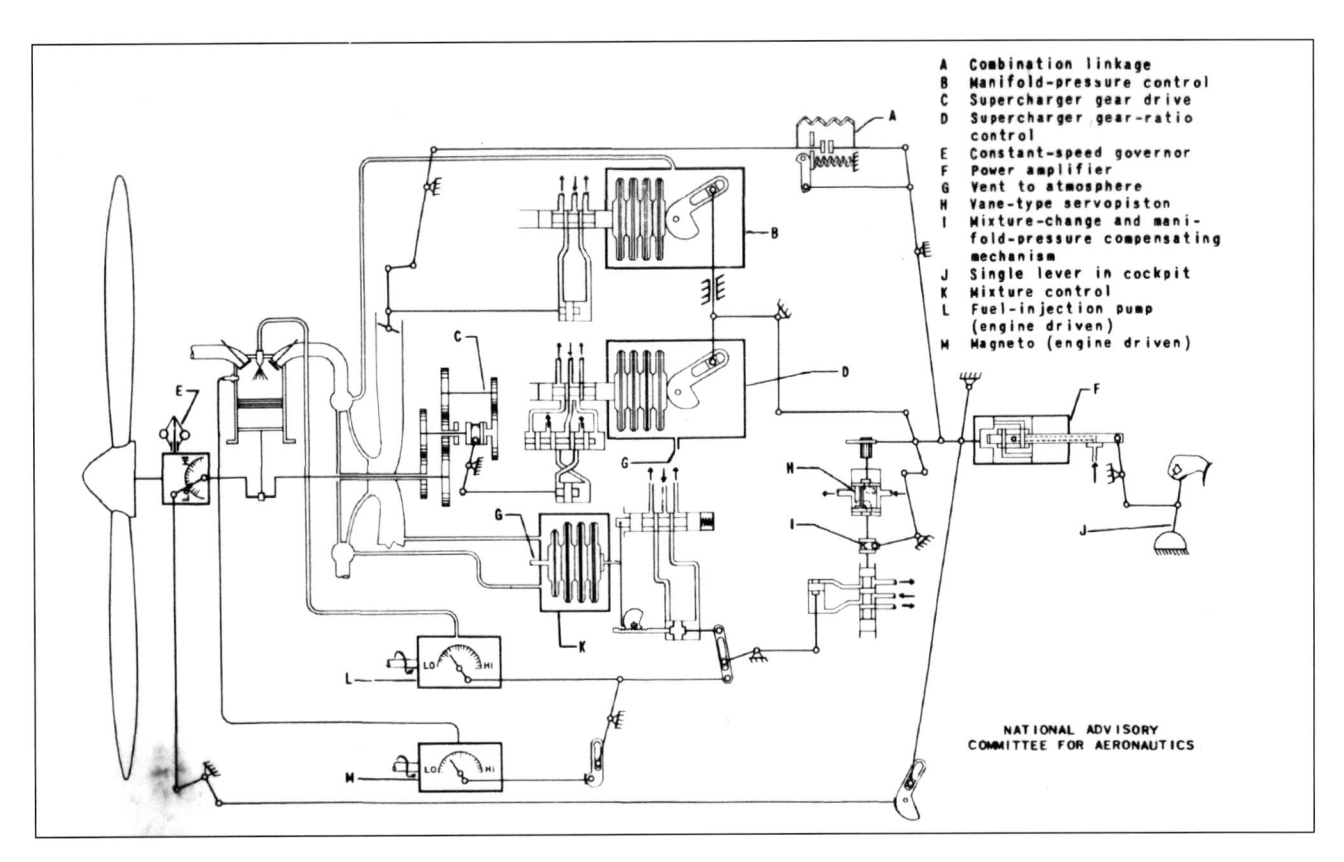

```
A  Combination linkage
B  Manifold-pressure control
C  Supercharger gear drive
D  Supercharger gear-ratio
   control
E  Constant-speed governor
F  Power amplifier
G  Vent to atmosphere
H  Vane-type servopiston
I  Mixture-change and mani-
   fold-pressure compensating
   mechanism
J  Single lever in cockpit
K  Mixture control
L  Fuel-injection pump
   (engine driven)
M  Magneto (engine driven)

NATIONAL ADVISORY
COMMITTEE FOR AERONAUTICS
```

supercharger (or turbo supercharger), all of which required readjustment at various altitudes and flight conditions; and because one control affected the others, any change would require resetting all the others, thus leading to potential distraction especially when in combat.

The pilot's power lever in the cockpit is connected to the Kommandogerät via a hydraulic amplifier which overcomes the friction of the internal mechanisms of the device. Only in the starting and idle cut-off positions is the lever directly linked through to the mechanism. The amplified movement of the lever is transmitted to a camshaft pinion, which in turn rotates the camshaft; this positions a series of cams and gears on the camshaft to various set-points which are used to determine reference positions for the various adjustable engine parameters. Adjustments are accomplished by hydraulic servo units responding to movements of evacuated capsules that are sensitive to temperature and pressure changes. The hydraulic pressure actuates servo pistons, which in turn move mechanical linkages to operate the mechanism required. The device automatically readjusts any of the other parameters in order to restore equilibrium in the system.

In order to limit the speed of the engine in a steep dive, which falls outside the control parameters of the Kommandogerät, a dive lever is provided in the cockpit to override the set-point position determined by the cam. Failure of the unit will still allow the engine to be controlled, as the power lever maintains a limited mechanical control over the throttle valve position and the various servos will seek positions within the normal cruise regime of the engine. Emergency propeller pitch is provided by a separate electric pitch control, operated by a switch on the end of the power lever handle.

The Kommandogerät has its own hydraulic oil supply contained in the hexagonal-shaped tubular engine mount ring and pressure and scavenge pumps control the flow of oil to and from the servo units at a working pressure of around 8 atmospheres.

The use of the Kommandogerät, although it did not perform as well as an experienced pilot, freed the pilot of many tasks that could distract him in combat. It was a successful, albeit complex, device at the forefront of 1940s technology, which today's aircraft and automotive designs emulate and miniaturise using digital electronics.

**ABOVE** A functional schematic that helps to explain the interconnections and linkages between components in the Kommandogerät. The unit was tested by the Americans during the war. They produced a detailed report of its functioning and acknowledged the advantage of a system with a single power lever for the pilot. It is curious that the system was never widely adopted by the Allies post-war. *(NACA report 19930093290 via NASA)*

## Junkers Jumo 213

**(Powering the D series and the Ta152 H)**

As good an engine as the BMW801 undoubtedly was, its weakness was its lack of high-altitude performance, something that was especially needed to attack high-flying American daylight bombers engaged in raids over Germany. Focke-Wulf tried a number of different engines in experimental prototype airframes and found that the Junkers V-12 engine offered the best performance when married to the Fw190 airframe. This gave rise to the successful D series and finally the ultimate expression of Kurt Tank's creation, the formidable Ta152 H fighter.

### History and development

The Junkers Motorenwerk (Jumo), separate since 1923 from the parent Junkers aircraft manufacturing company, was solely concerned with manufacturing aircraft engines. It led the way in Germany's production of aircraft diesel engines and built a number of successful petrol engines during the 1930s. The first of this family of engines, the Jumo 210, of 20l displacement, first ran in October 1932, and although a solid design it developed a maximum power of only around 710ps and was therefore soon overtaken by the rapid development of engine and airframe design during the 1930s. It was superseded in 1937 by the much larger Jumo 211, and it was from this unit that the very successful 213 was derived.

These engines all shared a layout common to most German in-line designs of the period: that of an inverted V-12 with fully automatic mixture control (later versions had fuel injection). The early examples of the 211 engine had a non-pressurised cooling system which was inefficient at removing heat and therefore required a large amount of cooling water to be pumped around the engine; this in turn resulted in a bulkier, heavier power plant. Junkers set about a redesign in 1938 with a pressurised cooling system, strengthened crankshaft and improved supercharger. These changes allowed the use of higher power settings, but the engine

**BELOW** A preserved Jumo 213 engine displayed in the Deutsches Museum, Munich, retains the original alloy mounts used in the Fw190 D and the Ta152 series. *(Graeme Douglas)*

reached the end of its development producing around 1,520ps at 2,700rpm. However, the improvements continued, and under the direction of Dr Ing. August Lichte it evolved into the Jumo 213. The two engines shared the same bore and stroke of 150 × 165mm and a displacement of 35l, but with a redesigned engine block of smaller external dimensions and with further increases in boost pressures from the transversely mounted supercharger. Engine mounting points were placed in the same positions as on Junkers' competitor engine, the Daimler-Benz DB603.

Tested in 1940, the Jumo 213 A delivered about 1,750ps at 3,250rpm, but this improvement came at a price. The early experimental aircraft suffered from severe vibration problems between the airframe and engine, making the aircraft almost impossible to fly. It was found that the problem was due to crankshaft resonance in the continuous speed range. Staff at the Luftwaffe test centre at Rechlin discovered that the firing order of the cylinders was imposing uneven loadings on the crankpins, causing them to become overstressed. What had worked well on the slower-running, lower-powered 210 and 211 engines was now proving a problem with the 213 at higher speed. Research showed that there were too many torque reversals per cycle of the crankshaft. The problem was finally cured by changing the firing order so that the crank was systematically loaded and then unloaded.

Once these early problems were solved, the Jumo developed into one of Germany's best piston engines of the war, the 213 E and F versions, with their two-stage, three-speed superchargers which developed up to 2,150ps with MW50 or GM1 nitrous oxide injection. They had full-pressure altitudes of 9,800m, giving the Jumo a superior high-altitude performance to that of the much-vaunted Daimler-Benz DB603.

Installed as a 'power egg' complete with all cowlings, fittings and mounts, the 213 powered not only the Fw190 D series and Ta152 H but also the Ta154, Junkers Ju188 and Heinkel He219. It was not, as is sometimes claimed, designed as a bomber engine, and its first test flight in fact took place in an Fw190 test aircraft.

**BELOW** This ghost view of the Jumo 213 gives a good idea of the layout of all major shafts and drives within the engine. The supercharger drive is on the right through a cross-shaft.
*(Handbook for Jumo 213 A-1 and C-0)*

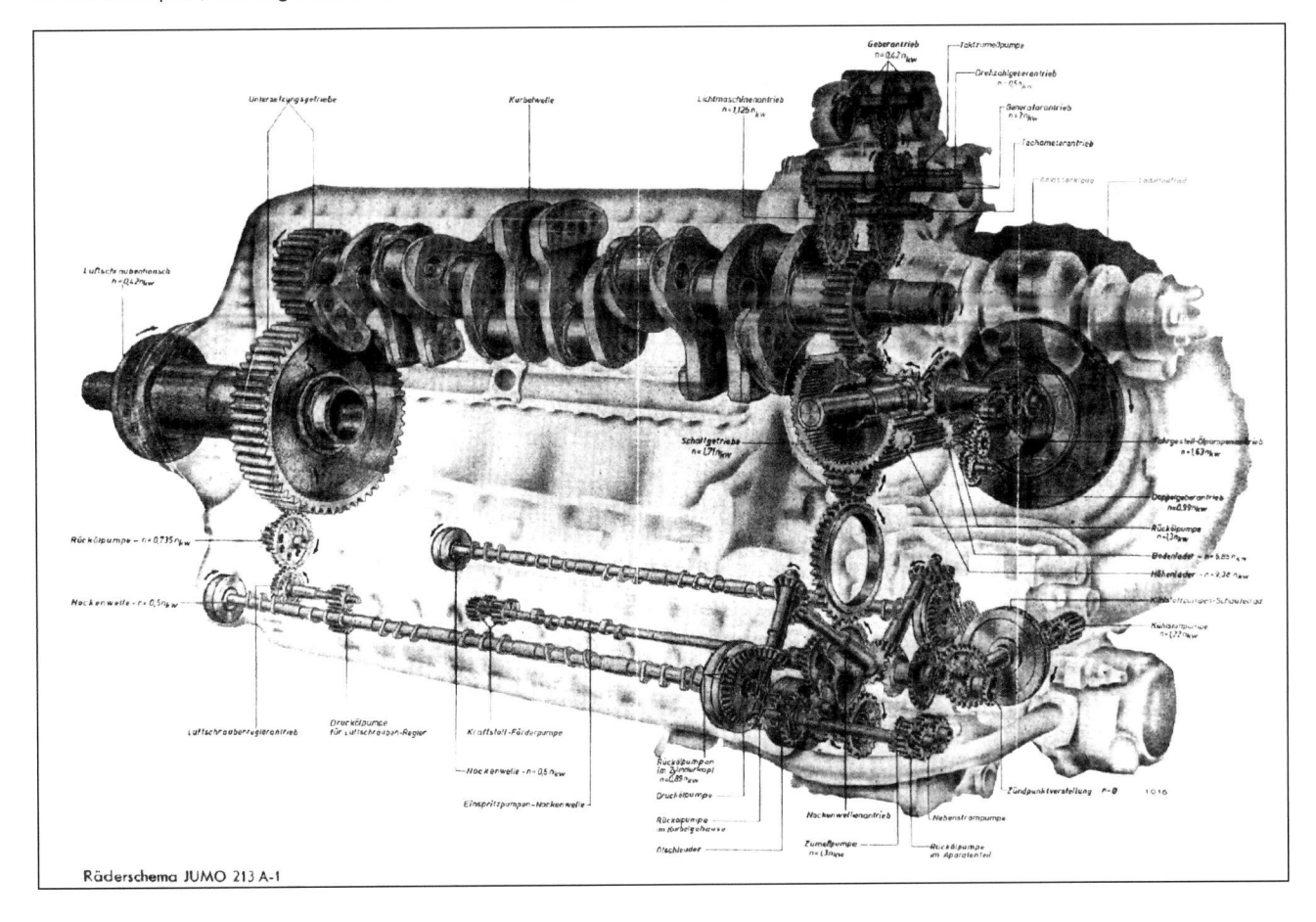

**RIGHT** An installation drawing of the Jumo 213 E fitted to the Ta152 series; the installation is very neat with the annular radiator contained in the forward cowling. *(Airbus photo archive, Bremen)*

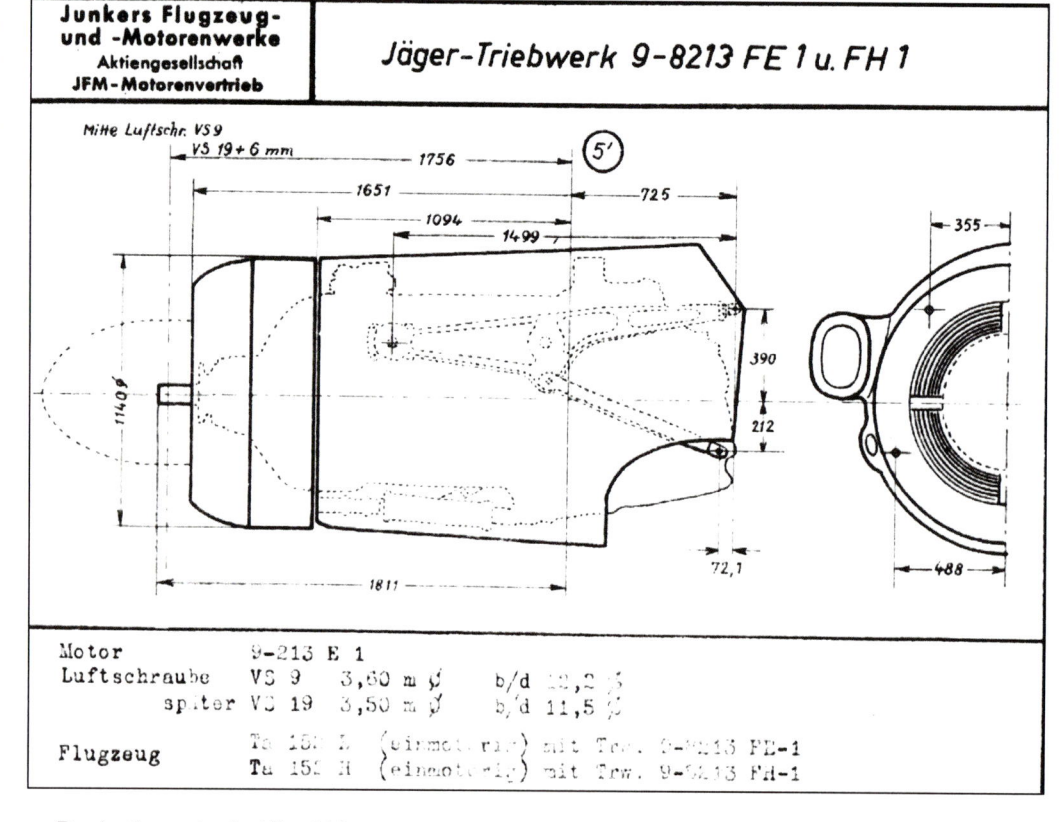

**BELOW** From the parts manual for the 213, the six-throw crankshaft, complete with adjustable counter-balance weights that are added to each crank web to reduce engine vibration. *(Parts Manual for Jumo 213 A)*

Production output of the 213 was very slow to build up because of Junkers' primary commitment to produce the 211 engine in large numbers to satisfy the needs of the German bomber force and because Allied bombing repeatedly disrupted production. It was only by 1944 that the engine was being produced in useful quantities. In total only around 9,000 examples were manufactured between 1942 and the end of the war.

## Crankcase

The crankcase and cylinder blocks are cast in one piece along with the reduction gear housing. Long studs on the blocks serve to hold down the cylinder heads, and the crankcase top cover is bolted to the top of the housing to form an oil-tight seal. A front cover over the reduction gear serves a similar purpose. The crankcase is reinforced and stiffened by five vertical transverse walls and cross tie-rods; within each wall, a crankshaft main bearing is housed. On each side of the crankcase, five cast fittings provide alternative mounting points for engine mounts. Four cast lugs at the top of the housing serve as hoisting eyes for transporting the engine. The space between the cylinder blocks is designed for fitting a central weapon firing through the hollow propeller shaft.

## Crankshaft

The crankshaft comprises three pairs of crankpins, each pair offset by 120° with dynamic counterweights fitted to the crank webs for balancing. The crank is supported by seven plain bearings and a roller bearing at the front. The crankpins and main journals have oil passages and the crank webs are drilled to transmit oil to all crankshaft bearings.

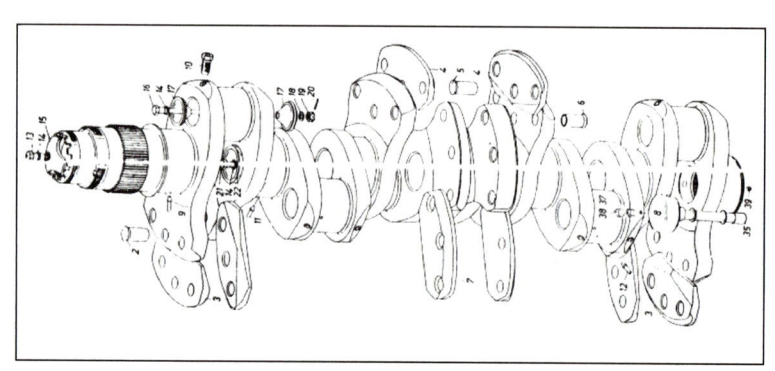

Between the front roller bearing and the first plain bearing, the reduction spur gear is mounted on serrations on the end of the crank

by two conical rings. At the other end, a spur gear attached to the end of the crank drives the gears in the accessory casing.

## Connecting rods and pistons

The main connecting rod on each crankpin is forked with the straight auxiliary rod between the fork, and the two main rod caps are held by four bolts and the auxiliary rod by two bolts. These serve to clamp the two halves of the big end plain bearing to the crankpin. The small end of the connecting rod contains a sleeve for the piston pin (gudgeon pin).

The light-alloy pistons carry six rings, three compression rings nearest to the crown and then an oil control ring and two more oil control rings on the other side of the piston pin. The floating piston pin is secured by a mushroom-headed plug at each end.

## Cylinder heads

The two removable heads each contain a single camshaft, running in seven bearings and driven by bevel gears at half crankshaft speed from the accessory gear drive train at the rear of the engine. Immediately above the camshaft is a single rocker shaft on which are mounted the

**ABOVE** With the cover removed, the six crankpins can be seen together with the seven main bearing caps and, at the left, the spur gear for the propeller reduction drive. *(GossHawk Unlimited Inc.)*

**LEFT** The Deutsches Museum also contains a display of the engine internal components. Here, the accessory drive train is shown from the crankshaft at the top, down through intermediate gears to the supercharger cross-shaft drive in the centre. Drive is transmitted downwards via two more gears to the bevel gear shafts driving the two camshafts. *(Graeme Douglas)*

99

POWER FOR THE FW190 AND TA152

**ABOVE** The camshaft cover is removed showing the bevel gear drive to the camshaft. A single outboard exhaust valve is operated by the middle of three cams. Behind, twin inlet valves are controlled by the outer cams. Operation is by roller cam followers and rockers pivoting from the shaft below the camshaft. All valves are fitted with dual coil springs. *(GossHawk Unlimited Inc.)*

**RIGHT** The reduction gear case has been removed from the engine; the large gear is for the propeller drive shaft. It is through this gear that the centrally mounted cannon fires. *(GossHawk Unlimited Inc.)*

**BELOW** Oil feed in the reduction gear case on a Jumo 213 C. In this model, the oil feed to the propeller pitch control mechanism does not pass through the hollow propeller shaft, allowing the use of a Motorkanone firing through the hollow shaft. *(Handbook for Jumo 213 A-1 and C-0)*

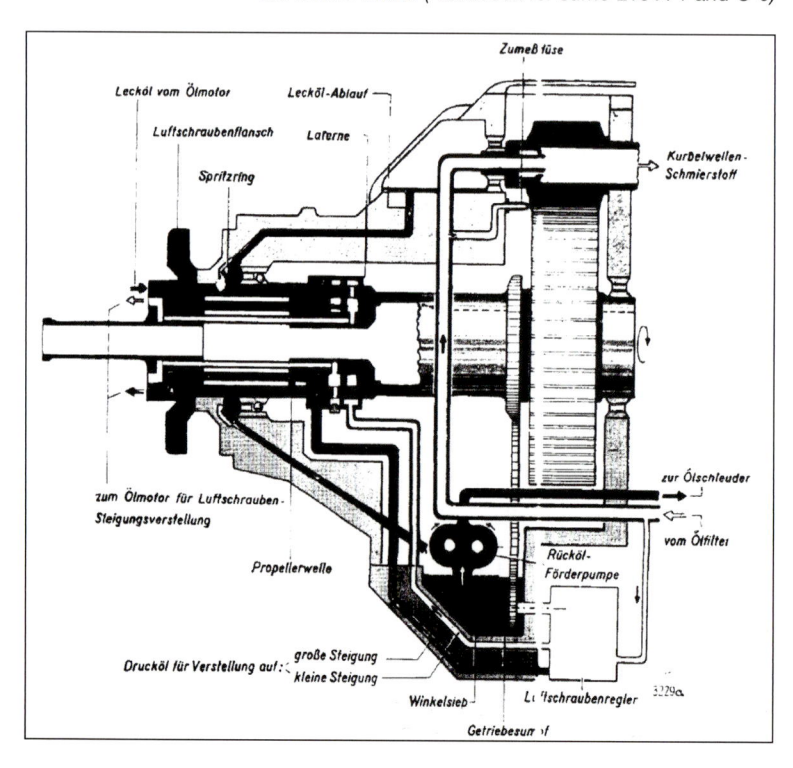

rocker arms for the two inlet and one exhaust valve per cylinder. Cam followers are roller bearings and all valves are fitted with dual coil springs. The exhaust valve is outboard and two spark plugs are screwed into the head on either side of it. On the inboard side of the head, the fuel injection nozzles are fitted between the two inlet valves. At the base of each head a light alloy cover acts as an oil sump, and scavenge pumps remove excess oil from this area.

## Reduction gear

The propeller speed is reduced by a pair of spur gears. The larger pinion on the propeller shaft is coupled to the shaft by a Hirth coupling. The shaft is supported by two roller bearings and a thrust bearing built into the reduction gear casing.

The propeller shaft is hollow. In the 213 A-1 engine fitted with Junkers propeller type VS111, two oil pipes for adjusting the pitch of the propeller are installed inside the shaft. In the case of the 213 C engine onwards, fitted with a VS9 propeller, in order to fit a Motorkanone some rearrangement is made to the supercharger drive and the oil pump along with the oil feed to the propeller. This is now fed via standpipes in the gear housing through passageways drilled in the outside of the hollow shaft through to the propeller adjusting mechanism.

A gear train from the propeller shaft drives the propeller pitch regulator (governor) and a scavenge pump inside the reduction gear cover.

## Supercharger

The mechanically driven supercharger is mounted at the rear right-hand side of the engine. Drive is taken from the rear of the crankshaft via a short cross-shaft to a bevel gear set and then, via a clutch unit, to the two-speed gear change unit, the output of which drives the supercharger unit.

## Cooling system

There are two cooling circuits on the Jumo 213. The main circuit, which circulates coolant to control the engine temperature, consists of the engine-driven pump, radiators and a heat exchanger. Coolant (50 parts water, 50 parts Glycol and 1.5% anti-corrosion oil) is contained in two interconnected header tanks, one on each side of the engine. It is circulated through the engine by the pump, with the heat from combustion being absorbed by the coolant and then dissipated into the airstream by passing it through two semicircular radiators in the front of the cowling. The coolant then passes through a heat exchanger beneath the engine, which serves as an oil cooler, before returning to the pump again to be recirculated. The secondary circuit has a separate pump unit within the body of the main coolant pump; this circulates coolant to the reservoir tank mounted on top of the engine, which is returned from the tank to the secondary pump. It is only in the pump body that the two circuits are allowed to mix.

The coolant system is designed to operate at a temperature of 100°C at all altitudes, and to achieve this, the opening of the annular gills is controlled automatically by a thermostat on the top of the crankcase. The system is pressurised: any steam that may be generated is separated in the pump and sent to the secondary circuit where it can condense in the reservoir tank. Excess pressure in the tank is controlled by a pressure relief valve, which also serves to maintain pressure at altitude by allowing evaporation of the coolant from the tank. The system contains about 26l of coolant and the main pump has a circulation capacity of between 12 and 14l/sec; the secondary system is rated at 0.7l/sec.

**LEFT** Supercharger unit on the starboard side of the engine; the circular intake is fed from the large cowling-mounted air duct. Below is the coolant pump, with the cover removed. *(Graeme Douglas)*

**BELOW** Cutaway drawing of the engine-driven coolant pump illustrating the inlets and outlets for the main circuit (Hauptstrom) and secondary circuit. *(Handbook for Jumo 213 A-1 and C-0)*

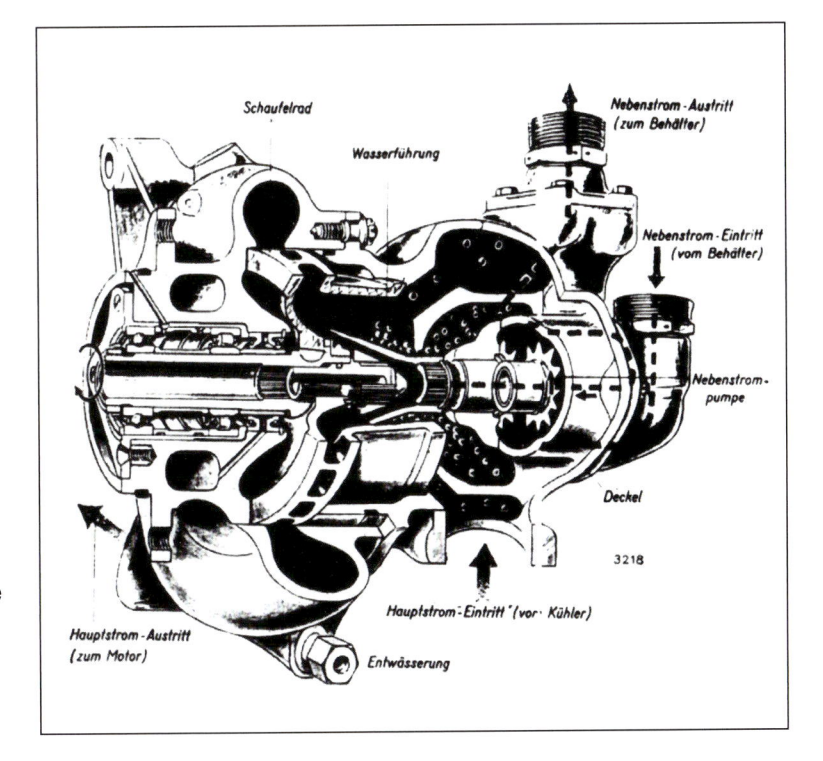

**RIGHT** A schematic of the coolant circuit illustrates the flow through the two semi-circular radiators (2). This illustrates a Jumo 213 E engine with a supercharger intercooler (6). *(Handbook for Jumo 213 A-1 and C-0)*

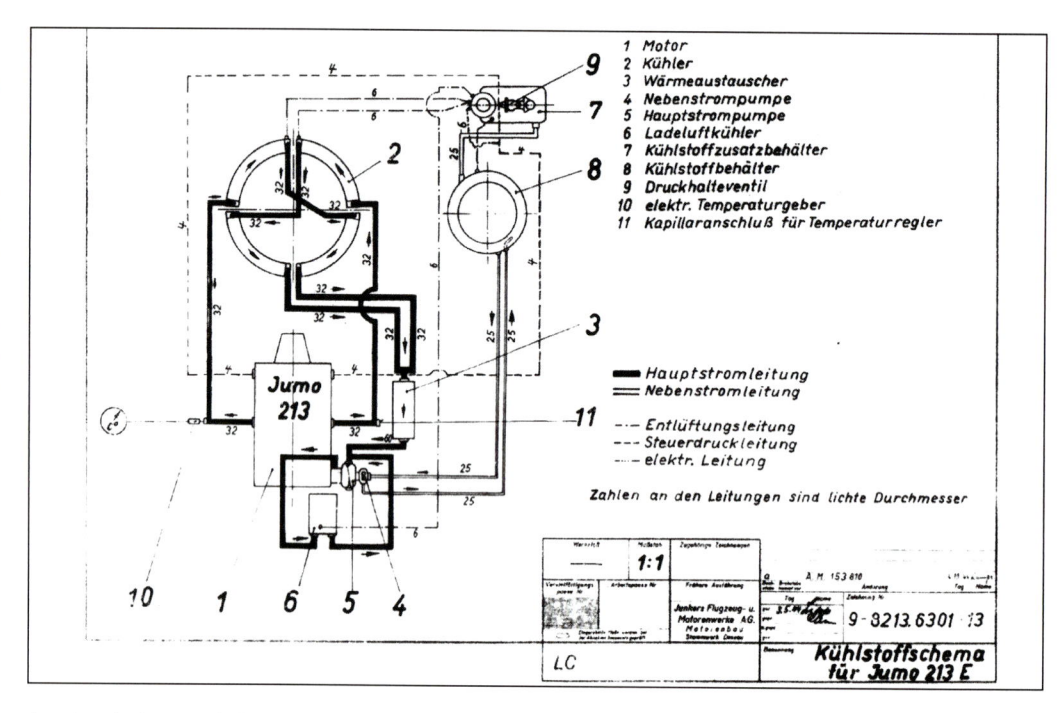

1. Motor
2. Kühler
3. Wärmeaustauscher
4. Nebenstrompumpe
5. Hauptstrompumpe
6. Ladeluftkühler
7. Kühlstoffzusatzbehälter
8. Kühlstoffbehälter
9. Druckhalteventil
10. elektr. Temperaturgeber
11. Kapillaranschluß für Temperaturregler

**BELOW** This oil circuit schematic shows the pressure circuit in solid black lines and the scavenge oil circuit in grey shading. *(Handbook for Jumo 213 A-1 and C-0)*

An electrical gauge is installed in the cockpit to monitor coolant temperature.

## Lubrication system

A pressure lubrication system with main and secondary circuits is employed. Two tanks on the left side of the engine contain oil. The main pressure pump delivers oil drawn from the lower tank. Pump pressure is regulated by a relief valve set to a maximum pressure of 7.5atü, while the oil passes through a filter containing closely spaced steel discs which trap and filter out impurities. The oil pathway splits into two sub-circuits. One is for the lubrication of the

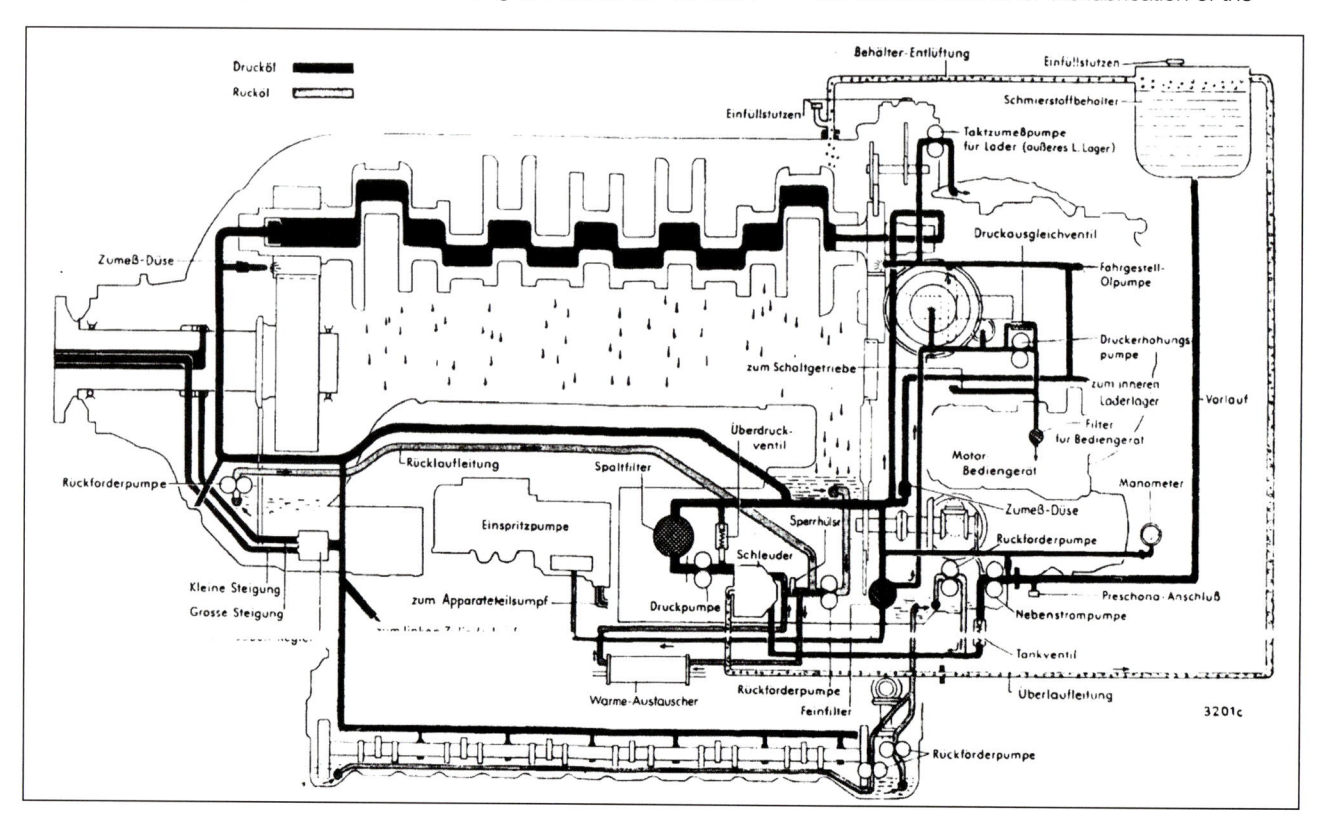

**RIGHT** At the rear of the engine, the engine control unit, Motorbediengerät (MBG) is mounted on the accessory casing. The black box below contains the twin magneto units and the supercharger output ducting feeds compressed air to the two banks of cylinders. *(Graeme Douglas)*

reduction gear via a metering nozzle along with the crankshaft main and big-end bearings. A second branch of this circuit splits off to the right and left cylinder heads to supply all moving parts via the hollow rocker shafts. A third branch of this first circuit supplies oil to the propeller governor system. The second sub-circuit splits into three branches: one is to the rear end of the crankshaft, another lubricates the auxiliary gear train and the supercharger, and the third directs oil to the fine mesh filters which in turn feed the fuel injection pump, engine control unit and supercharger gear switching unit.

Oil flung from the crankshaft lubricates the cylinder liners. Excess oil from a number of areas is removed by scavenge pumps. That from the bottom of the crankcase and reduction gear sumps, along with oil from the bottom of the auxiliary housing and the cylinder head sumps, is returned by scavenge pumps to a heat exchanger under the engine. The heat exchanger, rather than using air to remove excess heat from the oil, instead uses cooled engine coolant passing through pipework to lower the temperature of the returning oil. From here, the oil is fed to an oil spinner, designed to separate any air from the oil, before being returned to the pressure pump for circulating again around the engine.

The secondary circuit supplements the main circuit and makes good any oil losses in the system. A smaller secondary pump draws oil from the tank and delivers it to the oil spinner, where it is fed into the main circuit. Any surplus is fed back to the upper tank via a return line. The tank is vented through a line to the crankcase.

Oil circulation capacity at 3,000rpm is about 5,300kg/h in the main circuit and 2,100kg/h for the secondary circuit. Oil pressure should be around 4.5atü at 2,700rpm with an oil temperature of 110°C. Permissible consumption is 14.5l/h. In the cockpit, oil pressure and temperature gauges are provided.

### ENGINE SPECIFICATION – JUNKERS JUMO 213 A-1

| | |
|---|---|
| Type | Inverted V form, 12 cylinders, two banks offset 60° liquid cooled. |
| Firing order | 1, 10, 3, 8, 5, 7, 6, 9, 4, 11, 2, 12 (Rechlin order), cylinders numbered from propeller end 1–6, right bank, 7–12, left bank |
| Bore/stroke | 150mm/165mm |
| Displacement | 34.97l |
| Compression ratio | 6.5:1 |
| Supercharger speed ratio | 6.85:1 (low blower), 9.38:1 (high blower) |
| Take-off and emergency rating | 1,750ps at 3,250rpm at sea level |
| Maximum continuous | 1,330ps at 2,700rpm at sea level |
| Rotation of crankshaft | Anti-clockwise viewed from rear |
| Rotation of propeller | Clockwise from rear |
| Propeller reduction | 0.4166:1 |
| Dry weight | 1,350kg |
| Length | 2,437mm |
| Width | 776mm |
| Height | 1,154mm |
| **Accessories** | |
| Magnetos | 2 × Bosch ZM12 CR 8 |
| Fuel injection | 1 × Junkers injection pump, incorporating air bleed pump |
| Starter | 1 × Bosch inertia electric starter type AL/SGC24DR2 with hand start option |
| Generator | 1 × Bosch 2kw |
| Control unit | 1 × Junkers Bediengerät |

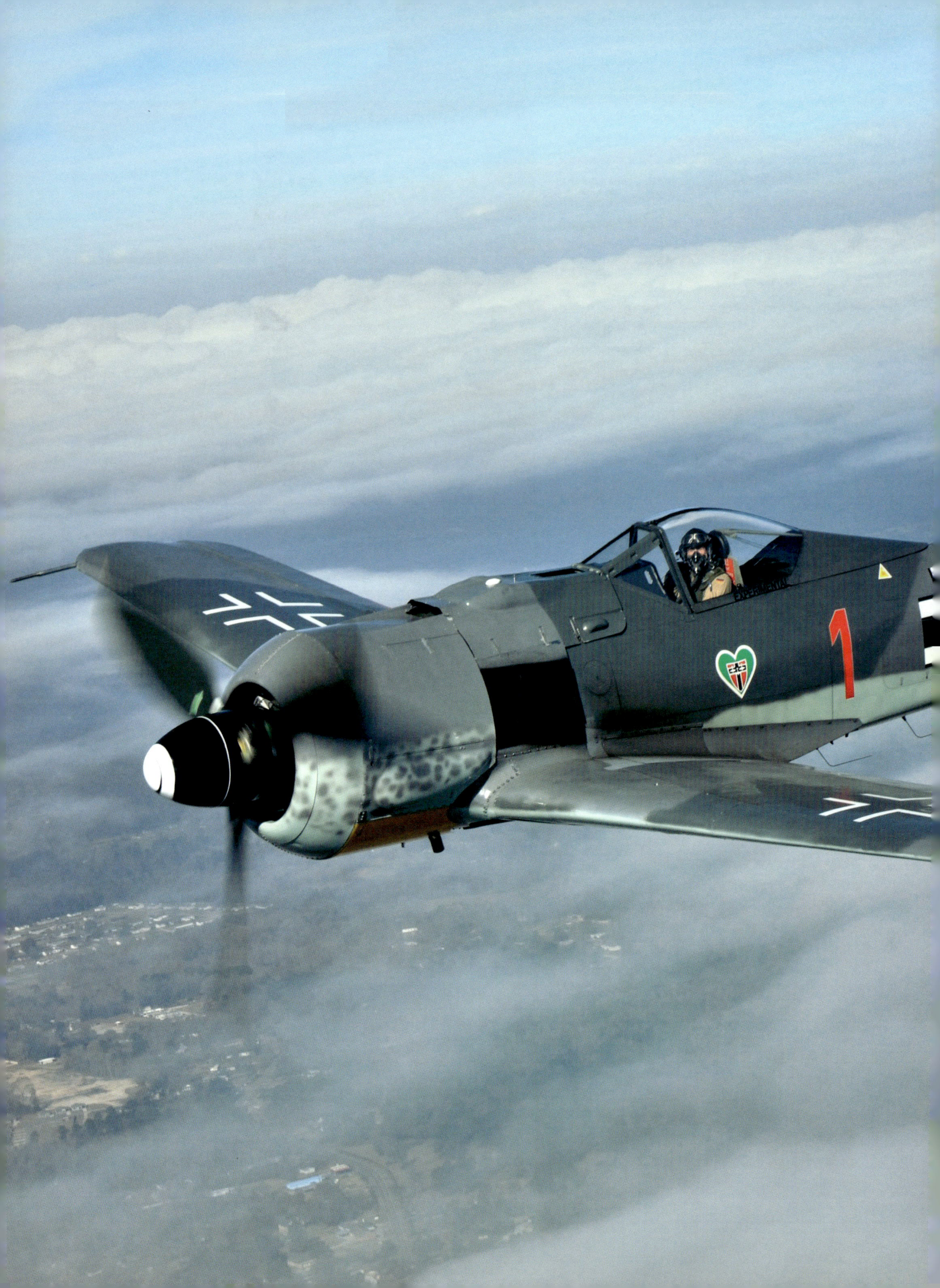

*Chapter Five*

# The Flug Werk replicas

Had it not been for Flug Werk, far fewer people around the world would have had the opportunity to see the shape of a Fw190 design in the skies. Thanks to this company, a squadron of full-sized replicas were produced, which are now owned and operated around the world.

**OPPOSITE** In the skies above Louisiana, Flug Werk Wk Nr 990004 looks the part and is the culmination of many thousands of hours' work and effort. It contains a few parts from an original airframe, but is in reality a Flug Werk new-build. *(Rusty Gautreaux via Klaus Plasa)*

In recent years the world's population of Fw190 aircraft has been bolstered by an unusual source. A company set up in Gammelsdorf, near Munich, in the mid-1990s, initially to manufacture and supply components for historic restoration projects, expanded its operation to encompass the manufacturer of complete new-build Fw190 airframes. Construction was subcontracted to Aerostar SA of Bocău, Romania. The new-build machines designated as FW190 A-8/N (FW for Flug Werk and N for 'Nachbau' meaning 'replica') were constructed where possible to original factory drawings. Naturally, small changes were made to meet current airworthiness requirements and where modern materials provided a safer or lighter option. However, no fibreglass or carbon fibre parts are used in construction but aluminium sheet metal of modern, higher technical specification is used. The new-builds are based on the Fw190 A-8 model but weigh far less than their original counterparts. In fact at a take-off weight of 3,550kg, they are almost 750kg lighter than the combat versions thanks to the substitution or deletion of steel armour plate used for pilot protection. Where it is visible, for example in the pilot's headrest, copies made from aluminium help to reduce weight, along with the deletion of all guns and bulky radio equipment. The same goes for changes to the wing structure as it is no longer required to hold heavy weaponry. Nevertheless, Flug Werk claims that the airframe is between 95 and 98% original. Most have been built as 'kits' and shipped to their owners with partially completed wing, fuselage and empennage; the owner is then responsible for fitting the engine and propeller and supplying electrical wiring, instrumentation, oxygen system and so on. It is still a huge amount of work for the owner to undertake, and most take several years to complete their Flug Werk replicas to their own particular specification. Flug Werk recommends the fitting of a Dongan HS-7, a Chinese licence-built copy of a Russian Shvetsov ASh-82 engine. The original BMW engine is almost unobtainable, and the ASh-82, as well as being almost exactly the right size and with a similar power output to the original, is a proven, reliable design with an ancestry that goes back to the 1940s as a re-engineered Soviet version of the American Wright Cyclone engine. The Dongan versions have an ample supply of spare parts, having been built well into the 1980s.

Mainwheel tyres supplied with the kits are those fitted to commercial Boeing 737 nosewheels, as these are plentiful, affordable and approximately the right size. The tailwheel units, however, are genuine overhauled Focke-Wulf units, discovered some years ago in a shelter in Germany. Each kit is supplied with one of these units, fitted with new seals.

Between 1997 and 2011, when production ceased, a total of 20 kits and one museum exhibit were produced and purchased by owners all over the world. In the near future more of these are likely to become airworthy to join the small number already flying (listed in Appendix 2). Of particular interest are two D-9 kits, one of which is supposed to be eventually re-engined with an original Junkers Jumo engine.

**BELOW** Some stages in the building of a Flug Werk kit are illustrated here, using various aircraft as examples. The complete kit arrives on a trailer.
*(Rusty Gautreaux via Klaus Plasa)*

**LEFT** The bare fuselage and wings have been mounted in wheeled jigs to facilitate work on them and for easy movement around the hangar.
*(Rusty Gautreaux via Klaus Plasa)*

**LEFT** Underside of the wing showing the undercarriage bays, main spar and the jig bracing strut between the rear spar attachment points. Access covers are for flight controls; no weapons bays are built into the replicas.
*(Rusty Gautreaux via Klaus Plasa)*

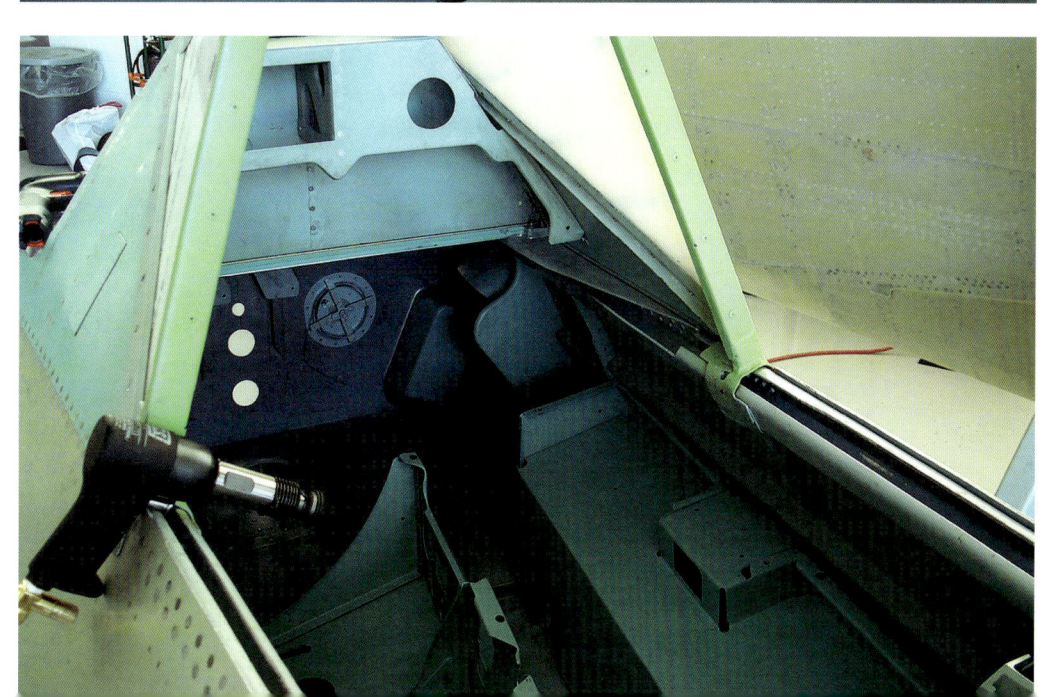

**LEFT** The bare cockpit as received from Flug Werk, ready to be equipped to the owner's specification. A large amount of work will be required to finish this.
*(Rusty Gautreaux via Klaus Plasa)*

**RIGHT** The ASh is a very similar size and is close to the power rating of the original BMW engine but is far more readily available. *(Graeme Douglas, courtesy GossHawk Unlimited Inc.)*

**BELOW** The ASh radial engine is mounted to the engine bearers. *(All photos Rusty Gautreaux via Klaus Plasa)*

**ABOVE** The ASh installed on the engine bearer frame and with cowlings fitted. Unlike the original, with air intakes at the engine sides, on the ASh the air intake is at the top with a cover installed. This requires an intake scoop to be fitted to the top cowling.

**LEFT** In order to join the wing to the fuselage, the front of the fuselage complete with engine is raised by forklift trucks and the wing assembly on wheeled trolleys placed underneath. With this aircraft, the owner has chosen to paint the airframe components separately before assembly.

**ABOVE** Wing spar attachment bolts are lined up with their respective fittings.

**ABOVE** With the wing securely attached, jacks are positioned under the aircraft in order to take the weight. The undercarriage legs have been secured up in the bays until the aircraft can be lifted high enough for the legs to fully extend.

**ABOVE LEFT** Jacks are raised and the legs are lowered.

**ABOVE** Undercarriage oleos are compressed in order that they can lock into the down position …

**LEFT** … allowing the aircraft to be fully supported on its undercarriage.

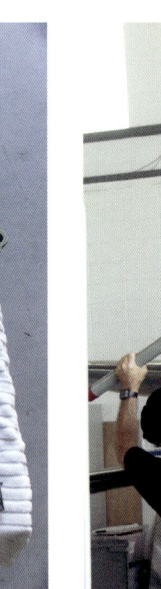

**ABOVE** Before installing the propeller, components of the hub assembly are laid out for inspection.

**ABOVE RIGHT** A trial fit of the hub to the propeller shaft is made minus the blades.

**RIGHT** Finally, the propeller assembly is installed on the shaft. Note the cooling fan behind the propeller and the ring oil cooler, although in the original BMW installation the cooler was contained in the cowling ring.

**BELOW** In the cockpit, the left-hand side console instruments and circuit breakers are wired.

**BELOW RIGHT** The console installed in the partially completed cockpit.

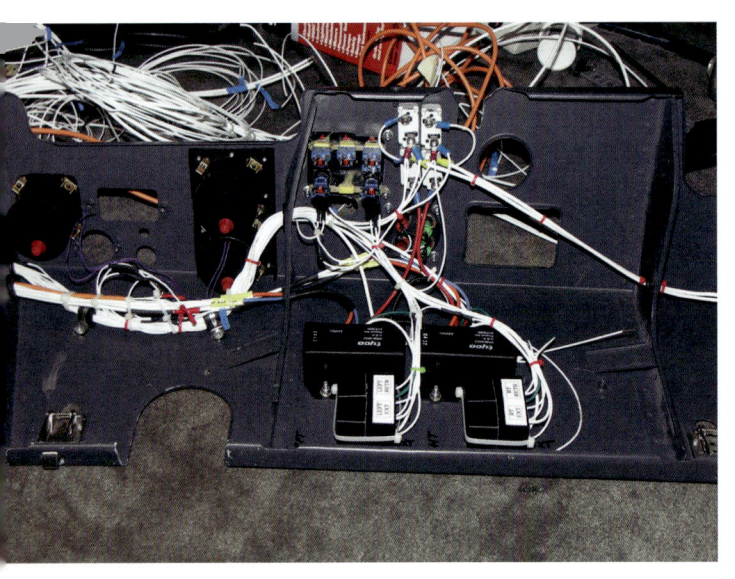

**ABOVE** The completed cockpit. Most of the instruments are new and American, including of course modern radios and GPS.

**RIGHT** Original switch fascia and indicator lights have been used for the undercarriage and flaps.

**ABOVE** This example in Germany was spray painted after the aircraft was completed, and therefore required much masking before the paint was applied.
*(All photos Frank Hohmann, Flug Werk)*

**ABOVE RIGHT** The first primer coat is applied.

**RIGHT** Before the mid-grey camouflage coat on the fuselage.

**BELOW** A darker grey finish on the upper surfaces.

**BELOW RIGHT** A blended demarcation between the two shades of grey and typical Luftwaffe 'blotched' finish is given to the fuselage sides.

**ABOVE** Finally, national insignia are applied, to be followed by unit markings.

**LEFT** After several years' work, the Flug Werk replica is ready for flight testing. Pilot Klaus Plasa straps on a parachute prior to the first flight. *(All photos Rusty Gautreaux via Klaus Plasa)*

**LEFT** Wearing an oxygen mask with built-in microphone helps to reduce cockpit noise breaking through radio transmissions.

THE FLUG WERK REPLICAS

**RIGHT** Engine start.

**BELOW** When taxiing, coarse use of the rudder is needed to steer the aircraft left and right in order to check that the area in front is clear.

**LEFT** With the tail raised for take-off the view ahead is improved. Note the use of the first stage of flap for take-off.

**BELOW** The Flug Werk replica is a distinctive shape in the skies above Baton Rouge, Louisiana, USA. Since this photograph was taken the aircraft has been sold and is now airworthy in Australia.

115

THE FLUG WERK REPLICAS

**ABOVE** Undercarriage down, preparing to land after the initial test flight.

**RIGHT** The end of a successful test flight. Engineer Rusty Gautreaux, pilot Klaus Plasa and owner Don Hanson are pleased with their efforts to bring another Flug Werk replica to airworthy status.

Although the Flug Werk replicas look like the original Focke-Wulf, there are some internal differences which Dave Goss from GossHawk Unlimited summarises:

*Basically, when you look at the replica, it looks Focke-Wulf, the fuselage and the wings are to scale. They use the same techniques, using half ribs in the wing, but when you look at the stringers for example, they are of a simpler design. Flug Werk, in order to keep the costs of the kit down, have modernised production techniques and so it does tend to wander away in the small detail. For me, though, the biggest difference in the wing is the cannon casting of the original which is not reproduced in the replicas ... and the blister that you found on the top of the wing for the cannon is missing. All Focke-Wulfs had that blister.*

Dave is full of admiration for Claus Colling and Flug Werk in their ability to produce 20-odd kits in today's tough commercial environment.

*It's amazing that two partners and a small group of people produced 20 World War Two fighters. It's insanity! Two of us bought all the tooling from them, I'm a minority partner in it, the wing fixtures, everything, but I couldn't afford to scratch build an aeroplane.*

In the Flug Werk kit completed by GossHawk, Dave Goss and his team have made efforts to keep the replica as authentic and practical as possible. The ASh engine initially came with an oil cooler situated in the now empty area of the fuselage decking ahead of the windscreen, which was the fuselage gun bay of the original aircraft. However, in order to add extra cooling, especially needed in the heat of the Arizona desert, a bespoke ring cooler was made to fit inside the cowling ahead of the engine. It is not the same as the original, but it is at least a nod to the original design concept. Additionally, a 12-bladed fan was added in the installation along with the correct size and shape of spinner.

## THE COST OF OWNERSHIP

With the production of the Flug Werk kits has come the chance for some people (albeit those with very deep pockets) to own an aircraft which is as close as it comes to a real Focke-Wulf. Although Flug Werk stopped producing kits some years ago, there are reported to be one or two still unsold. The prospective buyer can expect to pay around $750,000 for a kit including engine and propeller. But that is just the start of a project, of course. A kit will require a great deal of time for the owner to complete, and many, many parts to be purchased and fitted. The kits only comprise the basic bare airframe and the engine. Instruments, electrics and a host of other detailed parts will be required in order to complete the work to an airworthy standard. If the owner undertakes the bulk of the work himself, then he is committing to several years of labour. If he entrusts the work to a restoration facility, then the work will possibly be completed quicker, but clearly the professional labour involved will increase the final bill significantly. The question of how much it would cost to complete a kit is almost impossible to answer, as every owner will fit their aircraft out to their own particular specification. But as a very rough idea, perhaps half of the cost of the kit should be added to cover the build.

Of course another possibility for those who don't feel the need to build their own replica warbird is to purchase an example already built by someone else. At the time of writing, there is a Flug Werk replica offered for sale for an undisclosed figure (offers are invited). Given the figures quoted, then a prospective buyer must surely have to look at offering at least $1,250,000. This is a lot of money for an aircraft which, although to all appearances is a Focke-Wulf, is of course still a replica. The cost of the genuine article (the only original flying) is almost impossible to assess because it is unique.

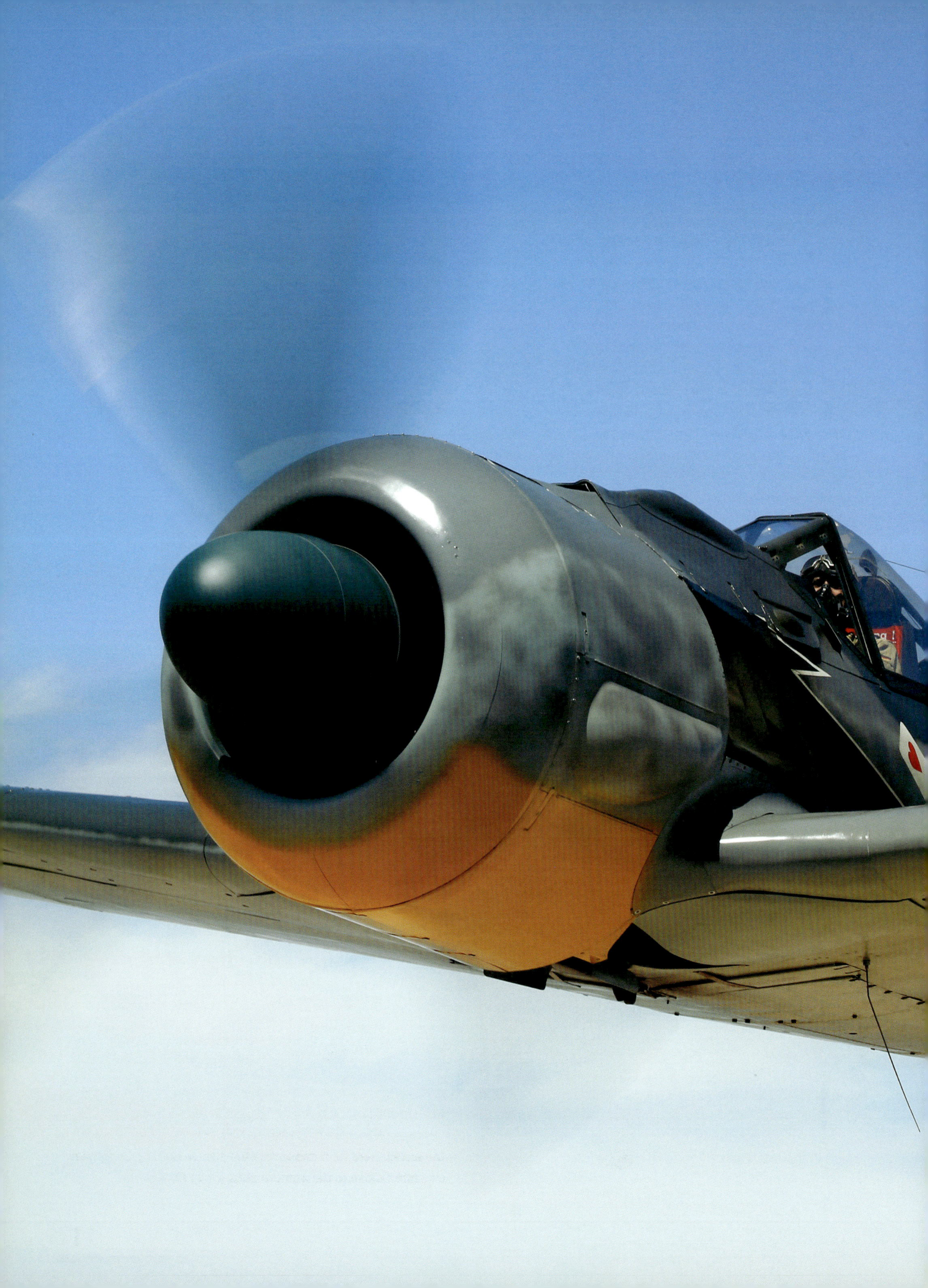

*Chapter Six*

# Flying the Fw190

Until a few years ago no pilot had flown a 190 since 1946. Then Flug Werk started to produce their replica aircraft, and as owners completed them they needed someone to test-fly their new replica warbirds. But where to find a pilot with experience on an aircraft that hadn't been operational since the Second World War? Fortunately there was an answer in the shape of Klaus Plasa, a pilot with vast experience of warbird flying, who has now done most of the test-flying for Flug Werk owners around the world.

**OPPOSITE** From the Arizona desert to snow-covered Germany, Klaus Plasa has flown Flug Werk replicas around the world. Here he manoeuvres the fighter built by GossHawk Unlimited close to the camera ship. *(Doug Fisher)*

**ABOVE** Not all test flights go to plan. In this case, faced with an erratic/uncontrollable running engine and a left undercarriage leg not lowering, Klaus selected 'gear up' and belly landed on a grass strip parallel to the runway. The wooden propeller blades snapped, and the cowling received a dent, as did the flaps. *(Klaus Plasa)*

Klaus is a Transall C-160 pilot with the Luftwaffe and graduate of the National Test Pilot School in the US; he also flies for Airbus Defence Group, part of the Airbus Group (formally EADS) as a regular display pilot for their Bf109 based at Manching airbase in southern Germany. Clearly his familiarity with the Bf109 made him a natural choice for the testing of the Luftwaffe's stablemate and he has gained a great deal of experience on the 190 since his first flight in 2006. Not all test flights go to plan; in fact it is the nature of the exercise that the test pilot's job is to find faults with the aircraft in flight in order that they can be later rectified on the ground. Klaus has suffered more than his fair share of engine failures and detached pieces of airframe over the years but continues to strap on his parachute with good humour and a smile, which disguises his dedicated professionalism to the difficult task at hand.

In his account he relates in his own inimitable style the trials and tribulations experienced when he first encountered the formidable FW190 for his initial test flight.

## Maiden flight

As I entered the hangar I was almost overwhelmed by its pure masculine appearance standing there somewhat forlorn in the corner with its wide, Pit bull like undercarriage: my first meeting face to face with the Focke-Wulf 190 A8N. The 'N' standing for Nachbau (replica) as Claus Colling and his small group of dedicated engineers lived the dream of recreating flying examples of this otherwise almost extinct species of the German fighter plane.

Since I had some previous experience on Mustangs, Corsairs and recently Messerschmitt Bf109s, Claus came forward with a proposition no one would ever turn down.

He said: 'I send you to the "National Test Pilot School" (NTPS) in Mojave, California, and in return you conduct the flight test program for me. What do you think?' There was no doubt in my mind; I jumped at the opportunity even though it would be quite some task ahead for any newly graduated test pilot.

That was in 2006 and the programme still continues today as the last in the line of the new-builds is still to be finished and needs to be 'broken in'.

Anyway, I started to prepare myself for my first and the aircraft's maiden flight, amongst other things, by reading all available pilot reports from both German and Allied sides.

They didn't reveal too much of how exactly this machine handles though. The German equivalent of the pilot's operating handbook says: 'Take-off and landing characteristics are normal.' Aha!

Having spent literally weeks in the workshop helping to add finishing touches to the ship

RIGHT **Klaus Plasa carrying out the pre-flight inspection on a FW190, in this case on the formerly US-registered N4190.** *(Rusty Gautreaux via Klaus Plasa)*

CENTRE **Cockpit checks prior to donning flying helmet.** *(Rusty Gautreaux via Klaus Plasa)*

did a great deal to boost my confidence in this machine. I am a firm believer that the better the pilot knows and understands what lies behind all those buttons and levers the safer it will be during operation, especially during possible tight moments. And these were about to come. ...

Any maiden flight is typically only a 10–15 minute local sortie, normally with the gear down to come in for a quick landing if so needed. The pilot will stay in the middle of the performance envelope and will carry out only a few very basic checks to prove the overall integrity of the aircraft.

Some aerodynamic and engine parameters such as oil and fuel pressure, cylinder head temperature and especially the oil temperature, as this airplane had an entirely new designed oil cooling system, will be noted. My basic slogan during maiden flights is: if the engine is happy, so is the pilot! Let's see!

The proper functionality of the VHF communication radio is often somewhat neglected if one looks at the entire task of building such a complex fighter plane. The ultra-loud cockpit environment usually makes it difficult to receive and transmit readable voice messages. This is one of the reasons that I now wear a mask during flight to muffle some of the noise from the microphone.

After addressing many small details I finally had no more excuses: time to fly!

With the briefings for the rescue personnel, tower controllers and Flug Werk engineers accomplished I prepared for my final pre-flight routine on this crisp, sunny, winter day.

RIGHT **The pilot wears an oxygen mask in case of carbon monoxide fumes leaking into the cockpit, but also to improve radio communications in the noisy environment during flight.** *(Rusty Gautreaux via Klaus Plasa)*

Cockpit preparation is straight forward:

Parachute strapped, seat and rudder pedals adjusted, seatbelt fastened, clip board stowed (there is no place to put it, really, so I stuff it between my leg and the right console). This cockpit is surprisingly tight even by Bf109 standards, as it tapers from bottom to top so much that I have to place my shoulders somewhat diagonally to allow the canopy to slide forward as I crank it closed with the coffee grinder handle on the right side of the cockpit; the handle being of a similar design to that on the Mustang, by the way.

But for start-up and taxi I leave it open. Starting the 14 cylinder direct injected Ash-82T engine is very simple and it never fails to start on the first attempt: Turn on one of the two electrical fuel pressure pumps, activate the primer solenoid until the ground crew signals some fuel pouring from the overflow, shout loudly 'CLEAR PROP!', push the starter T-handle IN to allow the inertia flywheel to wind up. (I think this is some Bendix/Eclipse patent that was taken over (i.e. stolen) by the Germans and eventually by the Russians.) When the whine of the flywheel sounds high pitched enough you pull the T-handle OUT to engage the starter to the crankshaft and – voilà! With the usual blue-white smoke engulfing the entire fuselage, the engine comes impressively loudly to life.

This is surely a spectacular moment for any bystander who usually steps back a few yards in sheer respect of this 'beast', holding fingers in their ears, while I need to check upcoming oil pressures. There are two pressure indicators for two oil pressure pumps working the front and the rear crankcase separately – and I adjust the throttle to about 1,000rpm or so.

Warm-up of the oil capacity of 80 and some odd litres will take a little while, but the good news is that I don't have to worry about any coolant temperature like on the temperamental DB605 engine (Bf109), possibly rising and exceeding the red line before the oil temp becomes 'green' at 40°C.

Taxiing is quite 'normal' indeed. It took us some engineering hours – even years – though to get the massive drum brakes right and some 190s have since been converted to disc brakes. To steer the four ton aircraft you mainly use differential braking as the tail wheel is fully swivelling. Moving in a straight line it locks straight automatically when the control stick is held aft of full forward – again similar to the Mustang's design – a feature that gave us a lot of headaches during the initial test phase because it sometimes either didn't lock (no flight that day!) or didn't unlock (giving me a hard time trying to leave the runway after landing).

Run-up is uneventful even though the brakes wouldn't hold much beyond 2,000rpm, but all

**BELOW** The subject of his maiden flight account, this is Klaus Plasa signalling 'chocks away' in D-FWJS at Manching airbase. *(Andreas Zeitler)*

parameters are well within margins so I execute the final 'Before-Take-Off-Check':

- Fuel tank on
- Mixture normal
- Prop full fine
- Flaps cracked to START
- Elevator trim set (⅔ nose down, I assume this to be correct for now)
- Flight controls free and full
- Harness tight
- Canopy closed
- Get clearance.

The Tower responds 'Focke-Wulf, wind 230° at 8kts, runway 25 Left, you are cleared for take-off!'

I line up, moving forwards a few yards to make sure the tail wheel has locked, and try to memorise this three-point attitude picture for the landing later.

Frankly, I think this is the very loneliest moment in any flight test as from now on it is just the two of us: my craft and me. No soul on earth being able to help from now on even though all eyes are focused on us!

Taking a deep breath I shake these thoughts off and smoothly apply power.

Smooth enough to be able to control the upcoming 'torque' but aggressive enough to shorten the period until the flight controls, namely the rudder, become effective enough for directional control. Passing about 1ata manifold pressure (MAP) I hesitate pushing the throttle further forward and cautiously lift the tail. Again cautiously enough to control the massive precession now caused by the 3.30m (10ft10in) diameter propeller as the tail comes up. Once the tail is 'flying', it is much easier to execute directional control with the rudder and I feed in 1.3ata take-off power with the throttle, quickly glancing across the engine instruments scattered all over the panel. Rpm, at 2,600, are OK. Lift-off. Airspeed not noted (next time, maybe?). During further acceleration I aim for 250 km/h, the maximum flap operation speed, to raise the flaps before reaching it.

My left hand leaves the throttle and feels for the laundry machine like push button on the left side console just next to the gear push buttons (remember to leave it down!).

There are three flap buttons, *EIN* (up), *START* (13° open for take-off) and *LANDUNG* (50° for landing).

I admit I can't find it without looking down, and while 'searching' I note a substantial loss of power! POWER?? MAP is down to below 1ata still dropping! My hand jumps back to the throttle, shoving it to about where it was. The damn thing crept aft even with the friction knob fully tightened! I need to add that to my little memorised check list. ...

**BELOW** Taking off at Manching. *(Andreas Zeitler)*

**ABOVE** Unusual 'selfie' taken from a remote wingtip camera of Klaus Plasa test-flying a Flug Werk replica in Germany. *(Klaus Plasa)*

I think the Tower tries to call me – can't hear him properly, and he should leave me alone for now anyway! – Aviate (aircraft OK?) – Navigate (need to turn left to stay close to the field) – Communicate (not now, please!)

And only now do I realise the massive crackling in my earphones rendering any usable reception over the radio useless.

Already passing 4,000ft, it is time for level-off as my assigned airspace reaches only up to 5,000ft while manoeuvring just south of the airfield. I reduce the power to about 1ata and toggle the rpm down to 2,000rpm to avoid overshooting the flap speed. This thumb operated rocker switch on the butt of the throttle lever comes in appreciatively handy because I don't need to let go of the throttle.

But for the flap button and the trim switch I do need to let go of it (even the tiniest little gimmick is operated electrically on this ship. Thank God it is Bosch and not Lucas!). Now I am prepared to reset the throttle every time I let go, but it keeps me annoyingly busy.

All right, you flaps, time to come up! Zzzap – now they are *EIN* with only a little pitch change and almost no need for trimming. But I notice that I still need to almost stand on the right rudder to keep the ball centred and also exercise some right aileron pressure on the stick (left wing heavy). Gill doors close. Oops – now that causes some pitch change!?! Time to make some notes on my little scratch pad before my personal ROM space is all used up!

I also make a quick note about the rather excessive low frequency vibration; either caused by the engine, the propeller, the airframe or more likely some combination of all of them. This appears to be a serious matter even today with all of these airplanes and may have caused some damage to the airframe (loose rivets) on this and other FWs. It also feels alarmingly uncomfortable!

I notice that the canopy rattled an inch or so open. I crank it closed with one hand while pushing the frame forward with the other.

'Look, Ma, no hands!', but the Focke-Wulf immediately rolls left almost on its back, so I catch the stick and 'finish' a left roll having lost some 800ft or so. This annoys me even more! Not that I wasn't anticipating it. But all this just adds to the high work load during this entire

**RIGHT** Flaps down for final approach. Klaus Plasa brings N190DK back in after a test flight. *(Doug Fisher)*

**ABOVE A three-point landing back at Casa Grande concludes another successful flight.** *(Doug Fisher)*

flight. Seemingly it keeps you preoccupied all the time preventing you from actually enjoying the flight!

About 12 minutes into the flight I observe the oil temperature still rising, ever so slowly but still moving towards its top limit while using only moderate power.

So I decide to come in for landing and call ATC without expecting any answer. Positioning myself for the overhead approach as briefed I adjust power and speed. Re-trim elevator. I feel for and select flaps *START*, my chosen final flap setting since I won't be using *LANDUNG* until such time as I have widened the flight envelope.

Turning downwind I mentally run my 'Approach Check List':

- Fuel: fullest tank (I select front tank, monitor fuel pressure being ready to switch back should it drop)
- Check gear down – two green (lights) two pins (on either wing)
- Flaps: set
- Prop: (coming to high RPM on finals)
- Clearance
- 'Tower, Focke-Wulf is manoeuvring to land runway 25 Left, gear down.'

No matter what he tried to crackle to me I continue my approach and make sure the runway and the approach sector are clear. I notice the high sink rate this thing builds up when I pull the power towards idle. I was expecting that and control the glide angle with power and the airspeed with pitch (220km/h feels just OK now).

A curved approach allows me to keep sight of the runway as long as possible while I recheck 'Gear – Flaps – Prop' and flip the switch for the gill doors open (should have done that earlier). Something hushed by on the left side of the fuselage … a smoke puff? A bird? Some aircraft part? Never mind, I recheck my speed, re-trim the elevator one last time and cross the fence at 200+km/h. Check the windsock! Start the round out … pull power further back, flare, power coming off now …flare … (uh??) … ffflaare … tou-touch! Directional control now, left rudder, right rudder…some brakes now. Brakes? Even pumping the brakes doesn't do much so my left hand reaches forward to the Mag switch just in case I lose control! But we finally slow down to bikers' pace and I relax a little, having used up much of the left side of the 137ft wide anti-skid runway and about 4,000ft length.

I crank the canopy open and cautiously continue taxiing using all of the weak brakes to the pre-briefed parking spot where a cheering crowd awaits me (more the airplane, I think, really).

Shutting the engine off is accomplished by pulling the non-original mixture lever all the way back into the 'cut-off' position and, once the prop has come to a stop and turning them off, I shout 'MAGS OFF!' to the audience.

An overwhelming amount of comments and questions, which I only distantly register over my temporary deafness, come floating up from all possible sides. 'Hey! Congratulations' … 'You made it!' … 'Nice victory roll!' … 'How fast is it' … and such. 'Tell us, how was it?' THE question to which answer they longed to hear in great anticipation!

125

FLYING THE FW190

**RIGHT** The engine panels are open for inspections after flight. Unlike panels on many British and American machines, these were designed to stay attached to the airframe, allowing for quicker replacement in an emergency. They also served as lightweight work platforms. *(Andreas Zeitler)*

I think for a moment. What can I say, knowing that they only saw a Focke-Wulf circling seemingly nonchalantly over their heads, hearing the deep drone of its powerful engine.

'Good!' I hear myself saying. 'Good? You old liar!' I think to myself.

After the crowd's dust has settled and during the post-flight discussion, I try to decipher my airborne notes. From a combination of vibration, cramped environment and stress they look like – well, not like my own handwriting.

Much will need to be addressed before further flight-testing. Oil cooling; throttle friction; canopy locking mechanism; radio equipment; tail wheel lock; brakes – just to mention a few items.

Frank, the chief engineer, rushes into the briefing booth in our hangar.

'Klaus, what have you done to the gill doors?' he asks. 'Why?' I reply, wondering what is wrong now. 'You lost one on the left side!'

Uh, that was the hush on finals! Consequently, 'gill doors' were added to the already long to-do-list.

So, what have we got at the end of the day?

Dreaming up, building and test flying a project like the Focke-Wulf – well, nobody said this is going to be an easy undertaking. Parts had to be modified, improved or replaced. Systems were reworked, redesigned or even discarded only to start at the drawing board again. After so many years I think we've come a long way since! But then again: what an achievement to produce a complex frontline fighter aircraft such as the Fw190 in so many different variants during those very dark wartime days!

And the rest of the story?

Deep inside I am extremely thankful and feel pride and honour to have the privilege to test fly these – eh – beautiful beasts. GOOD!

# Fw190 A-series pilots' operating instructions

This checklist and these procedures are based on an American Pilots' Operating Instruction book, compiled, it is safe to assume, for test pilots to be able to operate captured examples of the German fighter. Modern equipment aside, this contemporary document would enable a modern pilot to fly a restored Fw190.

## Pre-flight checks
- Forward circuit breakers:
- Generator – ON
- Battery – ON
- Starter – ON
- Pitot heat (if required) – ON
- Rear circuit breakers:
- All breakers – ON

- Magnetos – OFF
- Landing gear switch – DOWN
- Flaps switch – UP
- Stabiliser incidence – set to 0°
- Propeller operation – switch to MANUAL, set pitch to 12:00 on indicator
- Fuel quantity – check
- Fuel selector valve – both tanks ON
- Fuel booster pumps – check one at a time, pressure 0.3–0.4kg/cm$^2$
- Oxygen – ON
- Oxygen pressure – 150kg/cm$^2$
- Clock – set
- Altimeter – set.

## Engine start
- Propeller – turned several revolutions by hand
- Battery switch – OFF
- External power – connected
- Magnetos – ON both
- Power lever – ¼ open
- Rear booster pump – ON
- Prime – several short strokes
- Starter – ENERGISE, push handle down 10 to 20 seconds
- Starter – ENGAGE, pull handle up.

## After start and taxi checks
- Oil pressure – rising within 15sec, to 8–9kg/cm$^2$, if not, shut off engine
- Power setting – set to 1,100–1,200rpm
- Battery – ON, disconnect external power
- Oil temperature – when at 30°C, power to 1,400–1,500rpm
- Rear booster pump – OFF
- Engine fuel pump – test, switch to each tank for 1 minute, check pressure
- Rear booster pump – ON
- Magnetos – set rpm at 2,400rpm, maximum drop 50rpm
- Propeller – switch to AUTOMATIC, check manifold pressure and rpm
- Taxi – keep control stick forward in turns
- Brakes – check operation.

## Take-off checks
- Propeller – AUTOMATIC
- Fuel – selector on BOTH, rear booster pump ON
- Flaps – set to TAKE-OFF position (15°)
- Tailwheel lock – line up with runway, taxi forward, pull back control stick
- Power lever – open slowly to take-off setting
- Landing gear – UP as soon as airborne, check lights and wing indicators
- Flaps – UP
- Power – reduce after no more than three minutes.

## Approach and landing
- Airspeed – reduce to 300kph
- Propeller – AUTOMATIC
- Landing gear – DOWN, confirm with lights and wing indicators
- Flaps – fully DOWN
- Trim – as required
- Approach speeds – 185–195kph powered, 200–220kph glide
- After landing – use brakes sparingly, raise flaps at end of run.

## Emergency procedures
### Engine failure
- Airspeed – maintain at 300kph
- Power lever – to IDLE CUT-OFF
- Flaps – set to TAKE-OFF position
- Landing gear – UP unless landing on runway, then DOWN
- Fuel selector valve – CLOSE
- Ignition – Magnetos OFF
- Battery master – OFF.

### Landing gear failure
- Check – landing gear circuit breakers
- Landing gear switch – DOWN
- Release handle – pull to release up-locks, wheels drop under their own weight
- Indicator – check wing indicators show white strip visible.

| OPERATING LIMITATIONS AND SETTINGS | | | | | |
|---|---|---|---|---|---|
| | Manifold pressure (ata) | RPM | Rated Altitude (m) | Blower ratio | Max time (min) |
| Take-off | 1.35 | 2,450 | 600 | low | 3 |
| Climb and | 1.29 | 2,350 | 700 | low | 30 |
| Combat | | | 5,300 | high | 30 |
| Max cruise | 1.13 | 2,250 | 1.200 | low | – |
| | | | 5,300 | high | – |
| Max economy | 1.10 | 2,100 | 1,800 | low | – |
| | | | 5,400 | high | – |

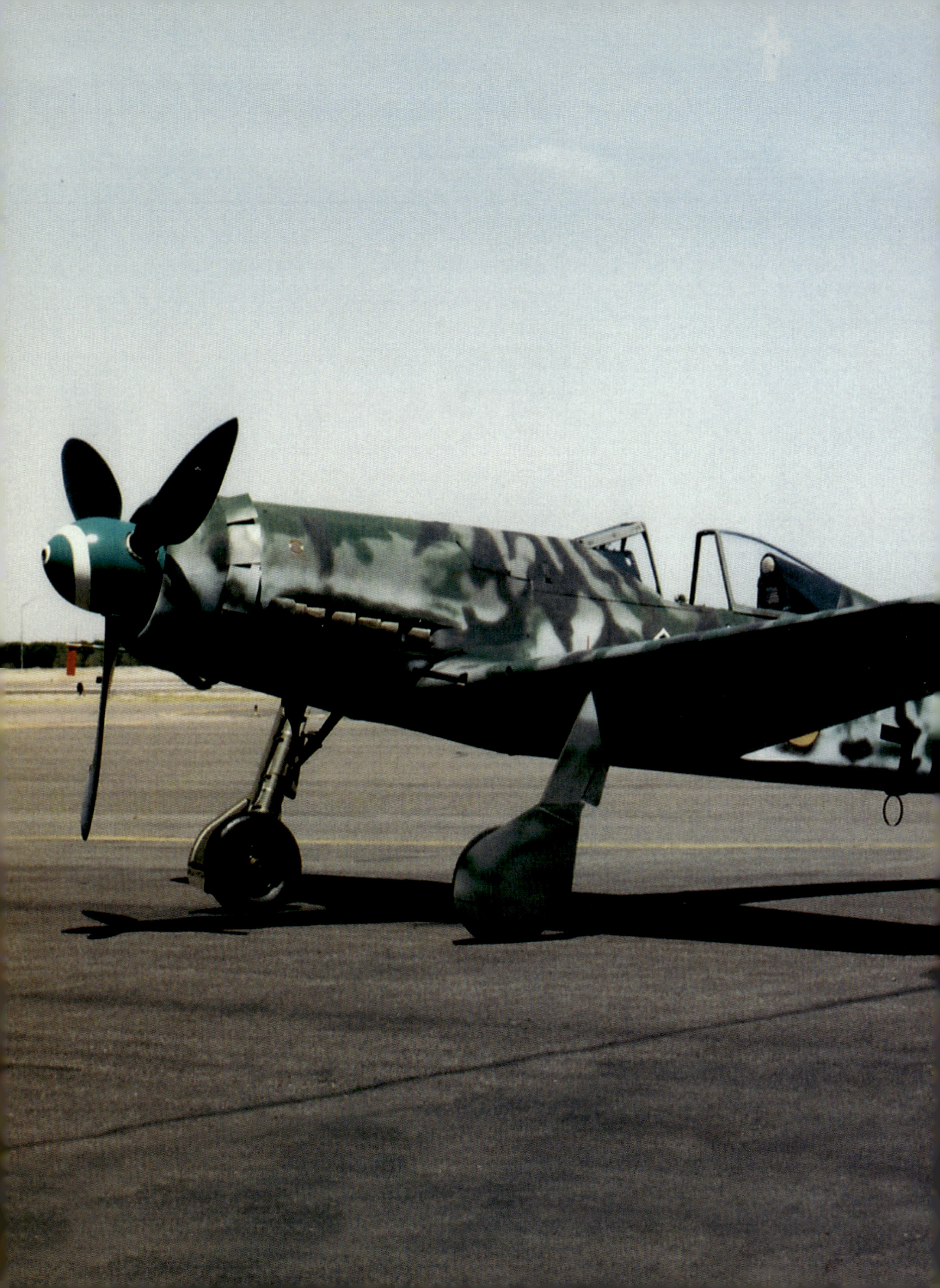

*Chapter Seven*

# The engineer's view

At the end of the war, the Fw190 disappeared very quickly. Unlike its Luftwaffe stablemate, the Bf109, which spawned licence-built versions through the 1950s, Fw190 production virtually ceased at the war's end. Only now are there moves afoot to restore some of these superb aircraft to both museum and airworthy status.

**OPPOSITE AND OVERLEAF** The beautifully restored Fw190 D-13/R11 'Yellow 10' in the Arizona sunshine. The aircraft carries the personal markings of Major Franz Götz, Kommodore of JG26, exactly as it was when he surrendered to the Allies in May 1945.

Compared to the proliferation of Spitfires, Hurricanes, Mustangs or Messerschmitt Bf109s (either original or in their Hispano Buchón guise), the number of preserved Fw190 airframes around the world is pitifully small – less than 30, of which several are wrecks or large component pieces only. The number of original airframes still flying is easy to calculate – just one, owned by the Flying Heritage Collection in Seattle. Where to go to find the expertise to rebuild an example to either static or flying condition? There is perhaps only one place with the necessary expertise and knowledge – GossHawk Unlimited Inc. in Arizona, USA. GossHawk, owned by Dave Goss, has built up a reputation as the one-stop shop concerning all things Focke-Wulf and Flug Werk related.

Had Dave Goss chosen a career unconnected to aviation, it would have been a surprise. He was born into an air force family: his father, trained as both a navigator and bombardier, was navigating in a B-17 during the Second World War when he was shot down, ending up as a POW. Dave enlisted into the US Army to serve as a gunner/crew chief on Bell Huey helicopters in Vietnam, followed by a tour in Germany as a helicopter mechanic. Returning to civilian life, Dave enrolled in further education courses that led to him gaining his A&P licence. On moving to Arizona, he became acquainted with the Champlin Fighter Museum in Mesa and went to work there as a mechanic in 1983. Dave's introduction to the German fighter began at this time, and he rose to become General Manager for Doug Champlin's aircraft collection, of which one of the prize exhibits was the extremely rare Fw190 D-13.

Forming GossHawk Unlimited in 1995, with just one employee, one of Dave's first commissions was the restoration of this unique Focke-Wulf D-13. The rebuild has been completed without compromise, with attention to detail and originality being the key driving forces, along with all systems being restored to a potentially airworthy condition. This was far from straightforward, as this particular long-nosed Focke-Wulf model was constructed in such small numbers (probably fewer than 30) that very little documentation exists. However, by using his meticulous eye for detail, Dave was able to confirm – to the surprise of many – that the D-13 had been on display for many years assembled with the wrong wing. The correct wing had been inadvertently fitted to the National Museum of the United States Air Force's D-9 example. Although, from the outside, the two wings appeared to fit, he found that the D-9 wing he had did not contain the cartridge case and link ejection chute for the nose-mounted cannon which was fitted to the D-13 but not to the D-9. Other clues surfaced as Dave examined the control runs for the ailerons. The D-13, because of the breech of the cannon projecting into the cockpit, had the take-off point for the aileron push-rods moved to the rear of the control stick, with the rods running along the rear spar instead of the front spar as in all preceding Focke-Wulf models. With this evidence, a wing swap was arranged, the USAF transporting the D-13 wing from Ohio to Arizona in a C-130 transport aircraft and taking the D-9 wing back in return. More anomalies surfaced as the restoration progressed. The cockpit floor was known to be original and yet contained no slots to locate the side console assemblies as were fitted to the D-9. Eventually, with reference to photographs of the airframe in a semi-derelict state, Dave was able to confirm that the side consoles for the D-13 were of a totally different, simpler design built in order to speed up production in the dying days of the war.

When the wings of the aircraft were taken apart, dozens of metal shims fell to the floor. The small pieces of aluminium had been placed there by factory workers at the time of construction to compensate for gaps between the ribs and the wing skin, which had possibly been caused by unskilled workers or hurried production practices. All the pieces were gathered up and replaced where they had come from.

In further efforts to reduce production times and conserve dwindling stocks of aluminium, the German factories resorted to constructing non-structural parts from wood. Items such as the wing flaps, access hatches and the fuselage fuel tank cover were often built from wood in the later stages of the war, and these have been faithfully reproduced in the D-13 rebuild.

The result of GossHawk's three-year restoration programme was completed in 2004 and is very probably one of the finest and most authentically restored Second World War aircraft. It is now owned by the Flying Heritage Collection (FHC).

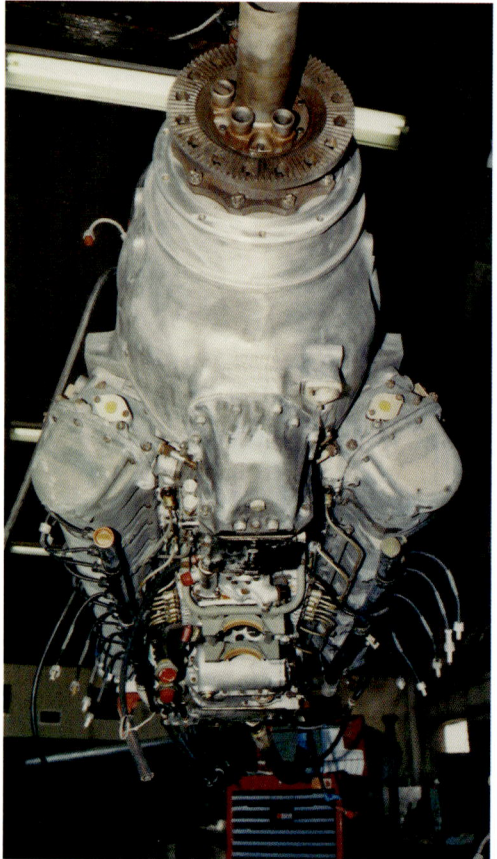

**ABOVE** The restoration of the long-nosed D-13 involved a complete strip-down of the airframe and engine. Just a few steps are shown here to summarise the work involved. Stripped of components, the fuselage is placed in a jig to give easier access to the underside. The circular hatch was fitted to later models with the extra fuselage tank behind the pilot. *(All photos GossHawk Unlimited Inc.)*

**LEFT** The Junkers Jumo engine has been removed for restoration.

**BELOW** The circular coolant radiator is made in two halves installed at the front of the cowling. It differs in detail from the radiator fitted to the Ta152.

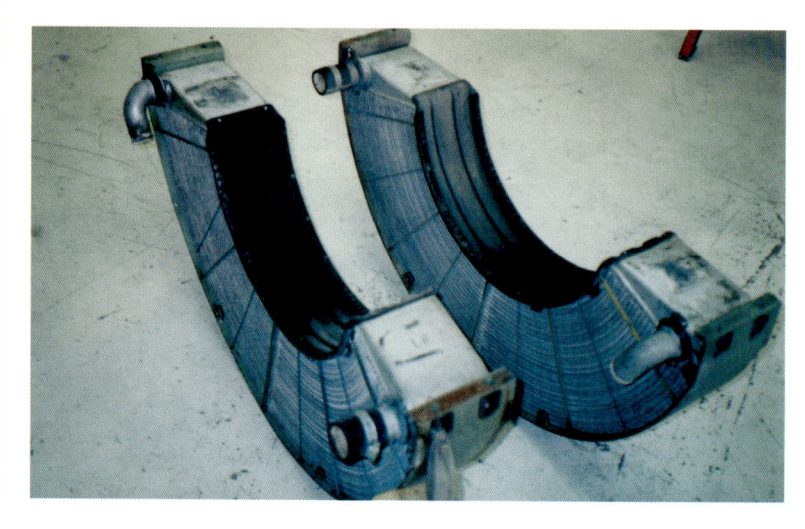

**ABOVE** The restored engine back in the airframe with the cowl gills fitted and the radiator mounting ring, before installation of the radiator.

**LEFT** The radiator fitted to its ring frame. The silver-coloured plate is the propeller backplate, surrounded by the spinner mounting disc.

133
THE ENGINEER'S VIEW

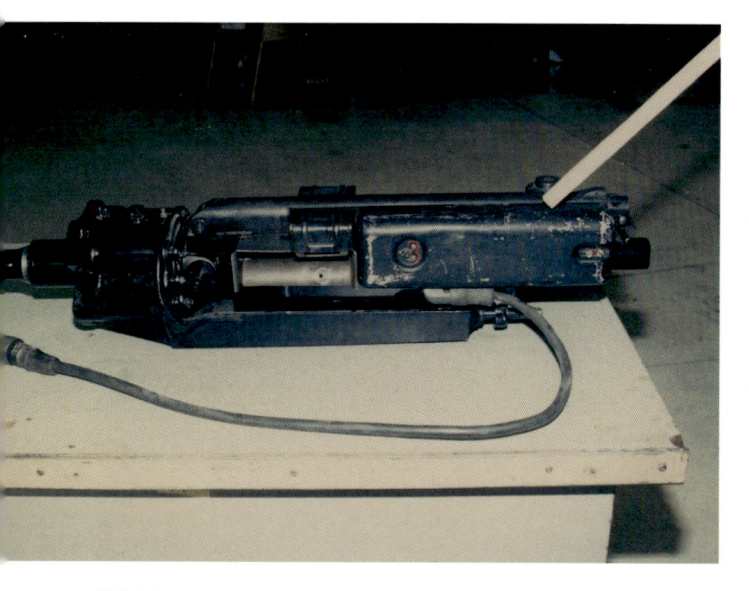

**LEFT** Deactivated weapons are fitted to the aircraft. Here an MG151/20 cannon complete with mount and electric cocking unit is shown prior to installation.

**BELOW LEFT** Wing root starboard cannon fitted in weapons bay complete with electrical wiring.

**BELOW** The restored ammunition boxes showing the loading diagram for the belted rounds. Each box could hold 250 rounds of 20mm ammunition.

**BOTTOM** Original radio racks were sourced and fitted for the restoration.

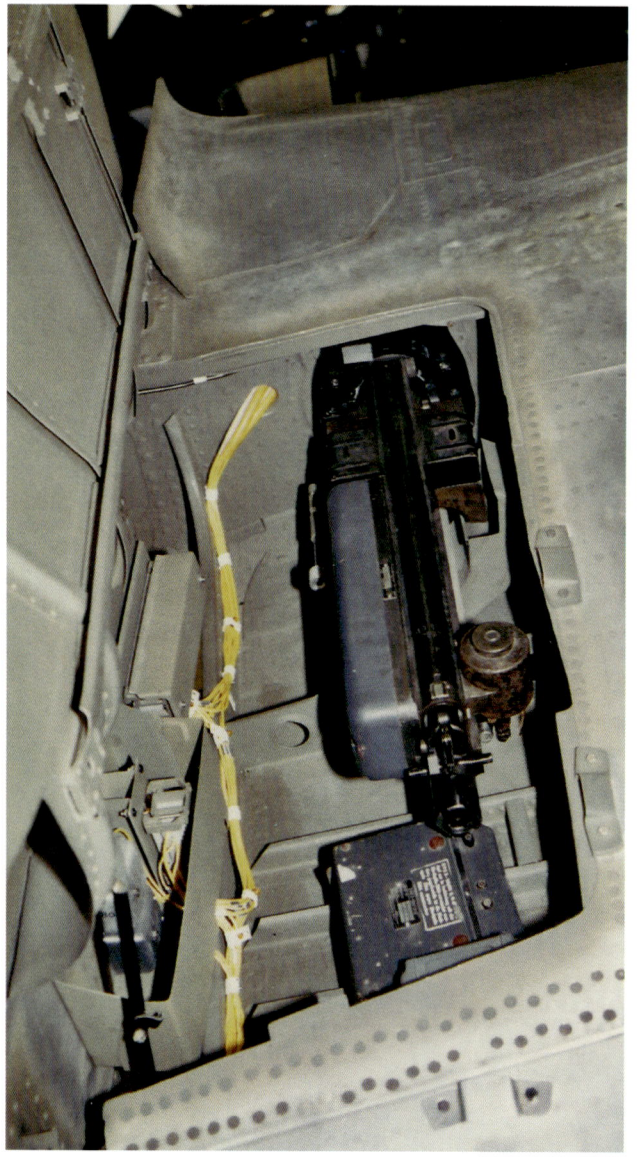

**ABOVE** Racks in place in the fuselage bay ready for wiring to be completed.

**ABOVE RIGHT** The hatch containing the FuG16ZY radio on the starboard fuselage side of the Fw190 D-13. The hatch cover is made of wood.

**RIGHT** The aircraft is jacked up to allow removal of the undercarriage for restoration.

**RIGHT** The cockpit part-way through restoration. The central panel is in primer at this stage.

**BELOW** Two views of the completed cockpit finished to authentic original standard. The tan-coloured strip is an authentic finishing touch.

**LEFT AND CENTRE** Attention to detail is obvious in these photos of the immaculately refurbished Junkers Jumo 213 engine fitted to the D-13 model restored by GossHawk Unlimited in 2004. *(All photos GossHawk Unlimited Inc.)*

**BOTTOM LEFT** The flaps on this aircraft are built of wood in order to save on dwindling stocks of aluminium during the final stages of the war. The gauge can be seen through a small aperture in the upper wing, to indicate to the pilot the flap setting.

**BELOW** In the rear of the fuselage, an authentic acetate cover is installed, something that will rarely be seen but nevertheless should be in place. Its purpose is to prevent seepage into the cockpit of exhaust gases. The black grommets allow cables and tubing to pass through.

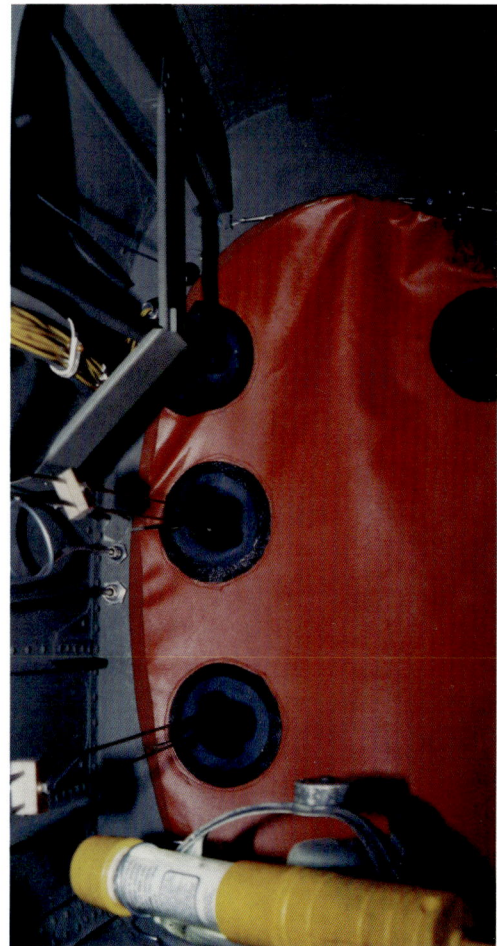

The company's next involvement with the famous German fighter was the completion of the restoration of the Fw190 A-5 that is now owned by the FHC. It was discovered as a derelict but largely intact airframe in Russia in the late 1980s and airlifted by helicopter from the forest near Leningrad where it had lain since it crashed in 1943. Restoration was begun by JME Aviation in the UK and completed by GossHawk in 2010. To date, it is the only original airframe flying with the authentic (and extremely rare) BMW801 engine. Again, the emphasis was to restore the aircraft as faithfully as possible to its operational state, using as many parts as practicable from the original aircraft.

With all this experience gained on the real thing, it was hardly surprising that when local businessman and warbird enthusiast Dan Kirkland decided to purchase one of the Flug Werk kits, he should come to Dave Goss to complete it for him. The kits are despatched in a fairly basic form and don't come with a set of build instructions. GossHawk needed to fabricate a number of parts in order to make them fit properly, and the wing leading edges, mainwheel doors and wing/fuselage fillet panels all needed to be made from scratch. The result is a stunning reproduction of the Luftwaffe fighter, painted in the authentic personal markings of Josef 'Pips' Priller who, together with his wingman, flew a strafing attack over the D-Day invasion beaches on 6 June 1944.

The latest project to grace the GossHawk workshops is the rebuild of an original Fw190 F-8 that will be restored to flight with a BMW engine installed. The aircraft crashed in Norway in 1945 and is now owned by the Collings Foundation. This is a 'ground up' project and, as ever, Dave intends it to be his best yet. Attention to detail is evident in everything in the restoration, down to the reproduction of the manufacturer's original ink stamps used to mark the aluminium with the individual factory code. A fair percentage of parts from the aircraft will be restored and put back into the restoration, and it will therefore be a faithful restoration of the original aircraft. In a few years' time the skies will once again welcome the sight and sound of another genuine Fw190, thanks to the skills and determination of Dave Goss and his team.

Since its inception in 1995, GossHawk has grown considerably, and the company now employs around 12 full-time staff, including Dave's wife, Connie, and his daughter, Lindsey. Connie runs the administration, which included, in the early days, transcribing all Dave's handwritten paper notes to electronic format. Dave is unashamedly 'old school' and very much hands on, and leaves the keyboard side to Connie and Lindsey. While handling PR for the company, Lindsey has also been helping her father in the workshop since she was six years old. Nowadays she is an accomplished mechanic, as well as a fly away engineer when larger aircraft, such as the PB4Y-2 Privateer maintained by GossHawk, take longer trips around the country. Lindsey is equally at home changing a cylinder as she is updating the company website or Facebook page.

**BELOW** Stages of construction of an Fw190 fuselage by GossHawk Unlimited. A 3D drawing of the fuselage is drafted on computer in order to see the structure in perspective. *(All photos GossHawk Unlimited Inc.)*

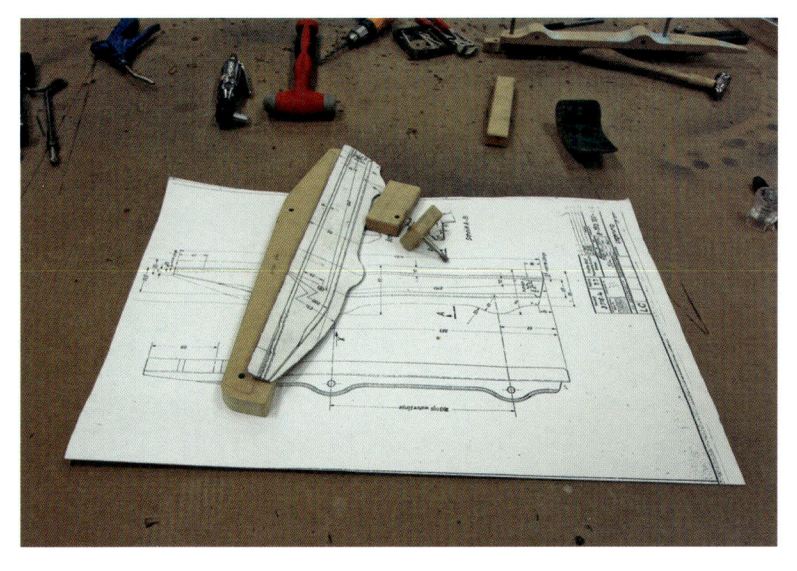

**ABOVE** By using an original Focke-Wulf drawing, a wooden form block is constructed to be used to shape a new part. In this case it is an upper step support angle.

**RIGHT** The aluminium is formed around the wooden block.

**BELOW** Original parts such as this doubler frame for the fuselage equipment hatch can be used as templates for copying rivet hole patterns.

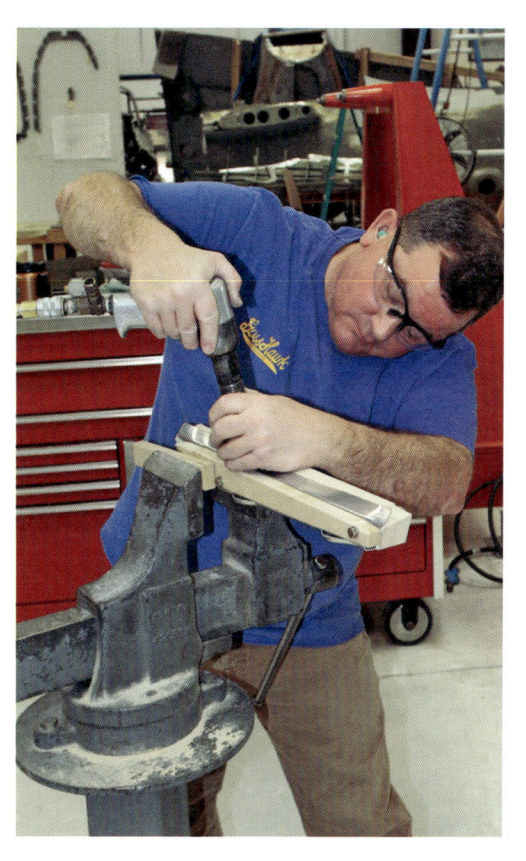

**RIGHT** The new doubler has been worked between form blocks to the exact size and shape of the original.

**RIGHT** Old and new canopy support rails.

**RIGHT** Some small parts need to be remade, such as this fuel primer port on the left.

**LEFT** Some original parts can be recovered and have been restored, such as the pilot's step and hand-hold.

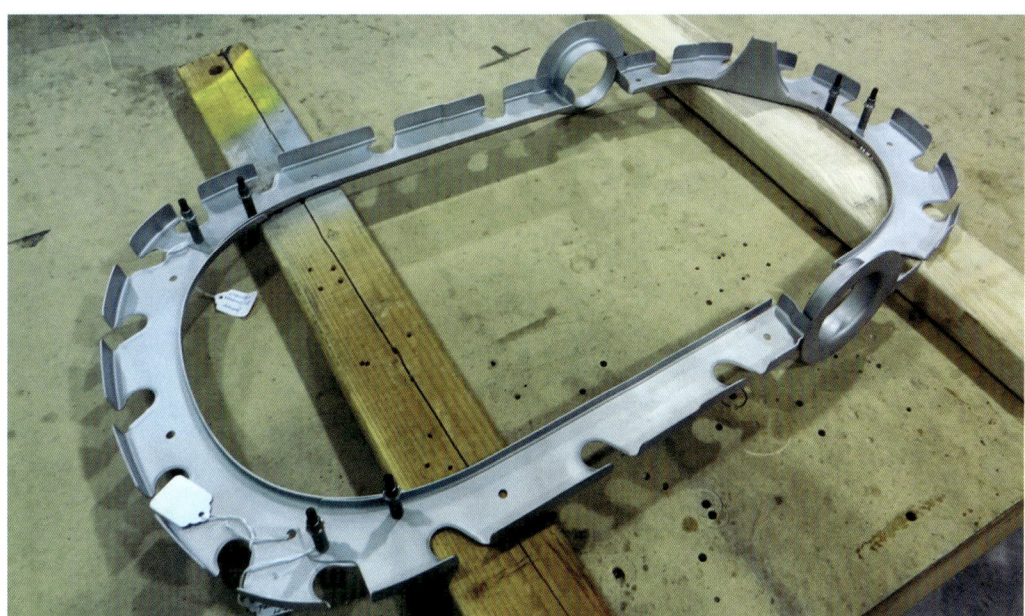

**LEFT** Frame 13 after fabrication. Parts that have been hand-formed need to undergo a heat treatment process to restore the temper of the aluminium.

**LEFT** These frame parts have returned from heat treatment and are placed back in form blocks to retain their shapes until they can be placed in the fuselage fixture.

**ABOVE** A selection of frames and other components awaiting mounting in the fixture.

**RIGHT** Rear fuselage frames 9a to 14 can be seen mounted in the fuselage fixture (jig) in order to correctly align everything during the build.

**LEFT** Stringers are being added to the left side of the rear fuselage. Note the doubler around the equipment hatch and how the stringers terminate at frame 12.

**BELOW** Fuselage doubler strips being installed at frame 12 where the stringers meet.

**ABOVE** Skinning of the rear fuselage has begun, and construction of the forward section is under way. Note the four longerons extending from frame 8 in the centre to the structural steel frame 1 (part of the firewall). The cockpit floor is not yet in place but will sit above the fuel tank bays, of which the bulkheads for the forward bay have been installed.

**RIGHT** Fabrication of the rear fuel tank bay. The cockpit floor will locate above and the side frames will attach to the outer skin.

143
THE ENGINEER'S VIEW

**RIGHT** With the cockpit floor fabricated and in place, there is the opportunity to trial-fit some components. Here the left-hand cockpit side console is shown together with the engine power lever and friction adjustment knob. Once all skins and panels have been drilled for rivet patterns, they will be removed and sent for anodising as protection against corrosion. Focke-Wulf did not paint interior surfaces.

**RIGHT** On the left-hand side, several components are being trial-fitted. The windscreen support frame casting, the cockpit canopy frame and pilot's seat are all temporarily in place. The rear fuel tank bay structure is now complete.

**RIGHT** Rear fuselage skins, having been anodised, are riveted into place. The diamond shaped rivet pattern is reinforcement around the lifting tube at frame 13. *(All photos Graeme Douglas, courtesy GossHawk Unlimited Inc.)*

144
FOCKE-WULF FW190 MANUAL

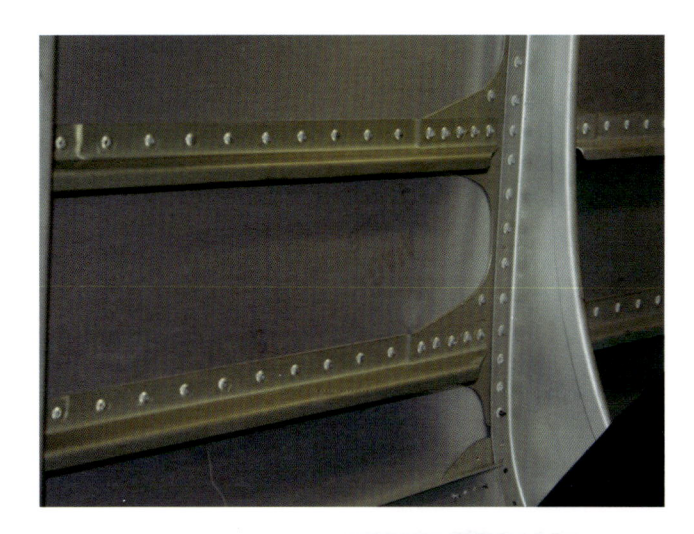

**ABOVE** Stringers are Z-section construction. Here at frame 12 they are joggled where they meet the doubler. It is just possible to make out the reproduction ink stamp on the skin, as applied by each sub-assembly manufacturer.

**ABOVE RIGHT** Forward fuselage skin is held in place by skin pins for rivet pattern drilling. When completed, this skin will be anodised before being riveted finally into place.

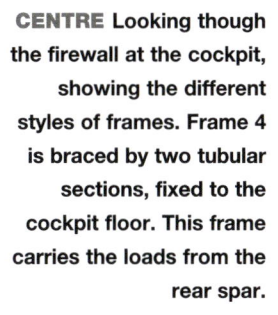

**CENTRE** Looking though the firewall at the cockpit, showing the different styles of frames. Frame 4 is braced by two tubular sections, fixed to the cockpit floor. This frame carries the loads from the rear spar.

**RIGHT** The top decking on the rear fuselage is a compound curve and difficult to reproduce. Flush riveting is evident in this view.

**RIGHT** One of several fuel tank panels held by GossHawk. A new panel will need to be made, as corrosion is clearly evident.

**BELOW** There are plenty of original parts to go back into the aircraft. For example, a restored master compass will be fitted into the rear fuselage.

**BOTTOM** An auxiliary tank (for fuel or MW50) will be installed behind the pilot's cockpit.

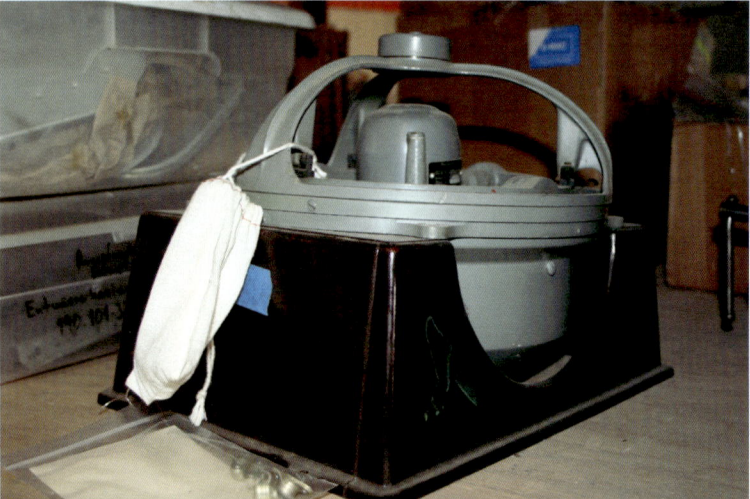

**BELOW** In the cockpit, an original control stick will of course be fitted.

# Periodic maintenance schedule – Fw190 A-series aircraft

## Daily inspection
- Test oleo leg pressure before flight.
- Check condition of tyres, looking for signs of creeping.
- Check brake lines for signs of leaking.
- Inspect fuselage for signs of skin damage. Check all inspection doors for security.
- Check flying controls for free movement at stick and rudder bar.
- Check control surfaces, bearings of flaps, tailplane etc. Check electrical connections.

## Every 6 hours
- Check fit and security of pipe unions in the pressure lines of the engine. Tighten all clips.

## Every 12½ hours
- Check security of cowlings, tank covers, inspection doors, etc.
- Clean fuel filter of selector valve assembly.
- Clean oil filter.
- Check filling pressure of pressure chamber and top up as required with compressed air.
- Check full range of operation of electric propeller switch.

## Every 25 hours
- Carry out work detailed for 12½-hour inspection.
- Perform compression checks on engine.
- Check condition of spark plugs.
- Check all cables and connections.
- Clean engine oil filter.
- Remove sediment from the Kommandogerät hydraulic system.
- Check security and tightness of pressure ventilation system.
- Clean fuel filter of engine injection pump. This is to be repeated at the next 25-hour inspection and thereafter every 50 hours.

## Every 50 hours
- Carry out work detailed for 25-hour inspection.
- Check wear of generator carbon brushes.

## Every 100 hours
- Carry out work detailed for 50-hour inspection.
- Drain oil from engine, oil cooler and oil tank and pump. Change oil.
- Check fuel injection nozzles for spray pressure and angle.
- Perform top overhaul of engine in accordance with RLM maintenance instructions.
- Grease propeller worm gear.

## Every 250 hours
- Complete overhaul of the airframe.
- Complete overhaul of engine in accordance with RLM maintenance instructions.

## After every 14 days
- Check oleo leg pressure.
- Check undercarriage operation, indicators and warning systems for correct operation.
- Check navigation lights for operation and free from damage.

## Every month
- Check condition and security of all radio and aerial leads.
- Inspect entire radio system.
- Recharge battery.
- Check carbon brushes on all electric motors.
- Check ignition system.
- Inspect all electrical leads for damage.

## Every two months
- Test altimeter.
- Check all instrument dial containers for air-tightness.

## Every three months
- Perform a compass swing.

## After every 25 take-offs
- Jack up aircraft, clean and perform retraction and lowering tests.
- Carry out brake test.

# Sources

## Books and periodicals

Arthy, Andrew and Jessen, Morten, *Focke-Wulf Fw190 in North Africa* (Hersham, Surrey: Classic Publications, 2004).

Boiten, Theo and Bowman, Martin, *Battles with the Luftwaffe* (London: Harper Collins, 2001).

Brown, Eric 'Winkle', *Wings On My Sleeve* (London: Weidenfeld & Nicolson, 2006).

Brown, Eric, *Wings of the Luftwaffe* (Manchester: Crécy Publishing, 2013).

Franks, Richard A., *The Focke-Wulf Fw190 D and Ta152 Airframe and Miniatures No 3, a complete guide to the Luftwaffe's Last Piston-Engined Fighters* (Bedford: Valiant Wings Publishing Ltd, 2012).

Hermann, Dietmar, 'Der Panzervogel der Luftwaffe', *Flugzeug Classic*, 8/2014 (Munich: GeraMond Verlag GmbH, 2014).

Hirschel, Ernst Heinrich and Prem, Horst, *Gero Madelung Aeronautical Research in Germany; From Lilienthal until Today, Volume 147* (Berlin, Heidelberg, New York: Springer Science & Business Media, 2003).

Jakobs, Fred, Kröschel, Robert and Pierer, Christian, *BMW Dimensions, BMW Aero Engines: Milestones in Aviation from the Beginnings to the Present* (Munich: BMW Group Classic, 2009).

Johnson, Air Vice-Marshal 'Johnnie', *Wing Leader* (Manchester: Crécy Publishing, 2004).

Kosin, Rüdiger, *The German Fighter since 1915* (London: Putnam, 1988).

Lowe, Malcolm V., *Production Line to Front Line, Focke-Wulf Fw190* (Oxford: Osprey, 2003).

Nowarra, Heinz J., *The Focke-Wulf 190, A Famous German Fighter* (Letchworth: Harleyford Publications, 1965).

Nowarra, Heinz J., *Aircraft and Legend, Focke-Wulf Fw190 & Ta152* (Sparkford: Haynes Publishing, 1988).

O'Leary, Michael, 'Mission over Normandy', *Warbirds International,* Volume 34/No. 7 (California: 2015).

Price, Alfred, *Focke-Wulf Fw190 in Combat* (Stroud: The History Press, 2009).

Ryle, E. Brown and Laing, Malcolm, *Walk Around Number 10 Fw190 D* (Texas: Squadron/Signal Publications, 1997).

Smith, J. Richard and Creek, Eddie J., *Focke-Wulf Fw190, Volume Three 1944–1945* (Manchester: Crécy Publishing, 2014).

Weal, John, *Focke-Wulf Fw190, Aces of the Western Front* (Oxford: Osprey Publishing, 1996).

Weal, John, *Focke-Wulf Fw190, Aces of the Eastern Front* (Oxford: Osprey Publishing, 2008).

West, Kenneth S., *The Captive Luftwaffe* (London: Putnam, 1978).

## Technical material

D. (Luft) T.2190 A-5/A-6 Aircraft Handbook, Technisches Amt (Berlin: 1943).

D. (Luft) T.2190 A-5/A-6 Engine Servicing and Maintenance, Technisches Amt (Berlin: 1943).

D. (Luft) T.2190 A-8 Aircraft Handbook, Technisches Amt (Berlin: 1944).

Description and Operating Instructions, Kommandogerät für BMW801 A, C, D, G Flugmotorenbaugesellschaft (Munich: 1943).

Flugmotoren und Strahltriebwerke by Kyrill von Gersdorff and Kurt Grasmann, Bernard & Graefe Verlag (Munich: 1981).

Handbook for BMW801 C and 801 D, BMW Flugmotorenbaugesellschaft (Munich: 1942).

Handbook for Fw190 Airplane F-TR-1102-ID (publisher and date not specified).

Handbook for Jumo 213 A-1 and C-0, Junkers Flugzeug und Motorenwerk (Dessau: 1943).

L.Dv. T. 2152 H-0/F1 Operating Instructions and Pilots' Notes for Ta152 H-0, Oberkommando der Luftwaffe (Berlin: 1945).

Pilot's Handbook of Flight Operating Instructions for Focke-Wulf 190 compiled by Technical Data Laboratory, Wright Field (Dayton, Ohio: 1943).

Service Manual for Jumo 213 A-1, Junkers Flugzeug und Motorenwerk (Dessau: 1943).

Werkschrift 2190 D-9 Aircraft Handbuch, part 8A Weapons Systems, Oberkommando der Luftwaffe (Rechlin: 1944).

Werkschrift 2190 D-9 Aircraft Handbuch, part 8C Special Weapons Systems, Oberkommando der Luftwaffe (Berlin: 1945).

# Appendix 1

## Rüstsatz field conversion kits fitted to the A-8 series*

R1 MG151/20 4 × 20mm cannon in 2 underwing gondolas replace 2 × 20mm outer wing weapons**
R2 MK108 30mm outer wing cannon replace 20mm weapons inside the wing
R3 MK103 30mm outer wing cannon replace 20mm weapons beneath each wing**
R4 MK103 30mm outer wing cannon replace 20mm weapons inside each wing **
R5 Fitment of 115l fuselage fuel tank, initial designation, abandoned when tank fitted as standard**
R6 W. Gr21 unguided mortar launchers under each wing
R7 Sturm role, extra armour around cockpit, windscreen and cowling with standard weapons
R8 Sturm role, armament as R2 and with extra armour added as with R7
R11 Bad weather variant with course steering autopilot, radio range approach equipment and heated windscreen
R12 Equipped as the R11 but with MK108 cannon as with the R2.

*Most Umrüst-Bausatz (factory modification kits) were later redesignated as Rüstsatz (field conversion kits).
**Planned, but either did not enter production or only limited use.

**BELOW** An Fw190 A-5 fitted with a MK103 cannon beneath the wing, which became the little-used R3 kit. *(via Aviation-images.com)*

# Appendix 2

## Surviving, substantially complete FW190 airframes and airworthy Flug Werk replicas

**BELOW** This example of the D series is the world's only D-13 version. Note the air intake for the supercharger is on the starboard side for the Jumo engine; with experimental DB-engined aircraft, the intake was on the port side. The aircraft is shown here at the Museum of Flight. It is now owned by the Flying Heritage Collection, Seattle, USA. *(Bob Harrington)*

Around 30 original airframes are still in existence. Listing them has not been easy, however. Most are based in the United States, owned by private museums and individuals who often like to keep their projects 'under the radar'. What is apparent, though, is that a number of projects are in progress which should come to fruition in a few years. They will hopefully see a return to the skies of a number of Fw190 A, F and D models flying with original BMW or Junkers engines. To give the reader an indication of what to expect, where aircraft have been issued with a North American civil registration (N) these are shown, and while this does not guarantee that these aircraft will eventually be restored to airworthiness status, it at least indicates their owner's intention to do so. Deciding what constitutes a replica, a new-build or an original airframe is not always straightforward. There are no hard and fast definitions, but the author offers the following guidance based on nothing more than his opinion. The Flug Werk replicas were constructed as new-builds; that is, they are based as far as possible on original Focke-Wulf drawings and specifications, but where possible using modern materials and equipment to save weight and improve safety. All systems are custom built by each owner using modern parts. They are clearly not original. In order for an airframe to be deemed original, even after restoration, it should contain substantial parts and a data plate that can be traced to a specific Werk-Nummer. A reproduction can be defined as a machine constructed predominantly from new material, which structurally has significant changes to the original design and has no data plate link with an original aircraft. There will be those who will question my definitions, but clearly a Flug Werk replica fitted with an original tailwheel (for example) from 1944 does not constitute an original aircraft from 1944, as, sadly, some like to pretend.

The following list refers only to original Focke-Wulf airframes; airworthy Flug Werk replicas are shown separately.

| W Nr | Series | Status | Remarks |
|---|---|---|---|
| 125425* | Fw190 A-2 | DW | Flew as Yellow 16 with JG5, after ditching in December 1943 recovered from Norwegian Sea in 2006, displayed at Herdla Museum, Norway. |
| 125476 | Fw190 A-2 | UAR | Originally flew with JG5 as Yellow 9, currently registered to Texas owner, USA, as N6152P. |
| 132219 | Fw190 A-3 | USR | Crashed in Norway October 1943, JG5 as Black 3. Sent to USA for restoration, but returned to Bodo, Norway, 2009. |
| 151227 | Fw190 A-5 | A/W | Discovered in forest near St Petersburg, 1989, restored to airworthiness by JME and GossHawk and now the only 190 flying with BMW engine. Based at Flying Heritage Collection, Seattle, Washington, USA. Reg. as N19027. |
| 550214 | Fw190 A-6 | SD | Night-fighter variant, captured at the end of the war. Displayed at South African National Museum of Military History, Johannesburg. |
| 550470 | Fw190 A-6 | ND | Operated by JG26, restored with Ash engine and parts from other wrecks. Privately owned, registered in Florida, USA, as N126JG. |
| 170393 | Fw190 A-8 | SD | Largely reconstructed from original parts and Flug Werk additions and displayed at Luftfahrtmuseum, Hanover, Laatzen, Germany, as Yellow 11, flew with JG1. |
| 173889 | Fw190 A-8 | ND | Operated by JG1 as Yellow 4, owned by Mark Timken, USA, location unknown. |
| 350177 | Fw190 A-8 | ND | Recovered from Norway, operated by JG5, Military Aviation Museum, Virginia Beach, USA. Reg. as N4247L. |
| 730924 | NC 900 | SD | French-built version of Fw190 A-7/A-8, Musée de L'Air, Paris, France. |
| 732070 | Fw190 A-8 | ND | Formerly of JG5, crashed 1945, restored and displayed, previously at Texas Air Museum but current location unknown. |
| 732183 | Fw190 A-8 | SD | Flown by JG5, shot down over Norway, recovered and displayed as Blue 4, Virginia Beach Museum, USA, N90FW. |
| ??5467 | Fw190 A-8 | ND | Formerly reg. as N43906, now lapsed, current location unknown (poss. at Virginia Beach). |
| 733682 | Fw190 A-8 | SD | Originally operated as part of Mistel composite, captured after the war. Displayed at RAF Museum, Cosford, UK. |
| 210096 | Fw190 D-9 | UAR | Owned by Collings Foundation, Mass, USA. Reg. as N190CF. |
| 210968 | Fw190 D-9 | USR | Flew with JG26 under restoration at Luftwaffe Museum, Berlin, Germany. |
| 211028 | Fw190 D-9 | UAR | Flew with JG26. Remains believed to be under restoration to fly at Virginia Beach Museum, USA. |
| 400616 | Fw190 D-9 | SD | From JG54, restored, displayed at Usedom, Germany. Sold 2015. |
| 601088 | Fw190 D-9 | SD | Operated by JG3, captured and taken to the US for testing postwar, on display at NMUSAF, Dayton, Ohio, USA, where it is on loan from the National Air and Space Museum. |
| 836017 | Fw190 D-13 | SD | From JG26, acquired by US forces for testing, fully restored by GossHawk. Now on display at Flying Heritage Collection, Seattle, USA. |
| 670071 | Fw190 F-3 | DW | Centre section with wing displayed as wreck, operated by SG1. Flugplatz Museum, Cottbus, Germany. |
| Unknown | Fw190 F-8 | ND | Wing section from SG5, marked as White 5. In USA, but current location unknown. |
| 583573 | Fw190 F-8 | ND | Once registered as N190ML, now deregistered, possibly in Fort Wayne, Indiana, USA. |

SD = Static display, A/W = Airworthy, USR = Under static restoration, DW = Displayed as wreck, WR = Wreckage not on display, ND = Not on public display, UAR = Under airworthy restoration

RIGHT The only surviving example of the Ta152, this is an H-0 model captured in Denmark by the British, the aircraft having served with JG301 as 'Green 4'. Handed over to American forces, it was given FE (Foreign Equipment) number 112 and shipped to the USA for evaluation. Now owned by the National Air and Space Museum, it has remained in storage for many years with, sadly, no apparent plans to restore and display it.
*(Jonathan Falconer collection)*

| W Nr | Series | Status | Remarks |
|---|---|---|---|
| ??5415 | Fw190 F-8 | ND | At one point under restoration in New Zealand, current location unknown. |
| 930838 | Fw190 F-8 | ND | Formerly operated by SG2, remains stored in Aeronautical Museum, Belgrade, Serbia. |
| 931862 | Fw190 F-8 | UAR | From JG5, crashed in Norway during combat in 1945, now owned by Collings Foundation, under restoration to fly with BMW engine. |
| 931884 | Fw190 F-8 | SD | Captured at the end of the war from SG2, test flown after the war in the US. Now restored and displayed in Smithsonian National Air and Space Museum facility at Chantilly, Virginia, USA. |
| 584219 | Fw190 F-8 | SD | Factory converted into a two-seat version from original configuration in 1944. Captured in Denmark at end of the war and flown to Britain. Now in RAF Museum, Hendon, London, UK, the only two-seater in existence. |
| 150020 | Ta152 H-0 | ND | Operated by JG301 and captured in Denmark, evaluated in the US post-war. Stored at the NASM storage facility, Maryland, USA, awaiting restoration. |

\* Werk-Nummer often prefixed with a 0, omitted here

| AIRWORTHY FLUG WERK REPLICAS (Designated FW190 A-8/N) | |
|---|---|
| 990001 | ZK-RFR based at Omaka, New Zealand, owned by Chariots of Fire (formerly D-FWWC). Damaged in landing accident April 2015. |
| 990002 | N447FW based at Beverton, Oregon, USA, owned by Wulf LLC (previously owned by Jerry Yagen). |
| 990003 | D-FWMV based in Germany, damaged in belly landing July 2014, undergoing repairs. |
| 990004 | Formerly N4190 previously owned by Don Hanson. Although containing some parts from original A-8 173056, it is almost all Flug Werk. Flown for first time in November 2015 in Australia as VH-WLF. |
| 990005 | N190BR with Tu-2 engine installation. Based at Virginia Beach, USA, owned by Jerry Yagen/Military Aviation Museum. |
| 990010 | N190RF based at Chino, California, and Urbana, Illinois, USA, on loan to Planes of Fame. Powered by P+W 2800 engine. |
| 990016 | N190DK based at Casa Grande, Arizona, USA, owned by Dan Kirkland, flown again after rebuild in 2015. |
| 990017 | Private owner, Germany, registered as D-FWJS. |

# Appendix 3

## German terms and abbreviations

**Atü** Atmosphären Überdruck, pressure measurement.
**Bediengerät** See Kommandogerät.
**BMW** Bayerische Motoren Werke AG.
**Erhöhte Notleistung** (Increased emergency performance). System that boosted engine power for short periods by increasing supercharger boost pressure.
**Erprobungsstelle** (Testing ground) abb E-Stelle Military testing and evaluation centre.
**FuG** Funk Gerät. (lit. radio device). General term for radio equipment of any type.
**FW** Flug Werk GmbH.
**Fw** Focke-Wulf Flugzeugbau GmbH.
**GM 1** Göring Mischung (Göring's mixture). Code for nitrous oxide injection system used to boost engine power by increasing the amount of oxygen in the fuel mixture.
**Gruppe** Sub-unit of a Geschwader, each Gruppe (group) comprising between three and five Staffel.
**Höhenjäger** High-altitude fighter.
**Jagdgeschwader** (JG) Daylight-fighting unit of the Luftwaffe, equivalent to a wing. Each JG comprised three or four Gruppen.
**Jagdbomber** Fighter-bomber, commonly known as Jabo, term applied to the F-series Fw190.
**Jagdbomber mit vergrösserter Reichweite** Fighter bomber with increased range, commonly contracted to Jabo-Rei. A term used for the Fw190 G series.
**Jumo** Contraction of Junkers Motoren, aircraft engine manufacturer.
**Kommandogerät** Control device used on BMW801 engine for adjusting engine settings via mechanical-hydraulic linkages. A similar unit for the Junkers Jumo engine was known as the Motorbediengerät or MBG (engine operating device).
**Motorkanone** Cannon designed to fire through the propeller shaft of an engine.
**MW50** Methanol-Wasser (methanol-water) injection for increasing the power of aero engines. Developed for the BMW801 but not put into production, because of problems; it was successfully used on the Jumo 213 along with GM 1.
**Nachtjagdgeschwader (NJG)** Luftwaffe night-fighting wing.
**Revi** (Reflex gunsight). Generic term for Reflexvisier.
**RLM** Reichsluftfahrtministerium, Ministry of Aviation of the Third Reich.

**ABOVE** A preserved Fw190 A-6 near Johannesburg, South Africa. This aircraft is believed to have served with a night-fighter unit before being captured. Note the underwing gondola housing a 30mm cannon. *(Andreas Zeitler)*

**Rotte** A pair of aircraft, leader and his wingman.
**Rüstsatz** Field modification kits usually to provide various armament options (R).
**Schlachtgeschwader (SchlG or SG)** Ground-attack wing.
**Schnellkampfgeschwader (SKG)** Fast fighter-bomber wing.
**Schwarm** Four-aircraft flight, comprising of two Rotten.
**Stab** Staff flight, senior flying officers commanding a Geschwader or Gruppe.
**Staffel** Equivalent to a squadron, each Staffel comprising 12 to 16 aircraft.
**Stammkennzeichen** Four-letter radio code letters applied to an aircraft at the factory, usually overpainted with unit markings when the aircraft arrived in theatre.
**Technisches Amt** TA, the technical design bureau of the RLM.
**Umrüst-Bausatz** Factory-installed conversion kits to provide various capabilities or Armaments (U).
**VDM** Vereinigte Deutsche Metallwerke AG, propeller manufacturer.
**Versuch** Experiment (literally), term applied to research aircraft, not necessarily a prototype (V).
**Viermot** Fighter pilot slang for four-engined bomber.
**W Nr** Werk-Nummer, German aircraft serial number.

Luftwaffe unit abbreviations: When identifying Gruppen or Staffeln within a Geschwader the convention is to write II./JG26, to indicate the second Gruppe of JG26, for example, and 4./JG26 to indicate the fourth Staffel of JG26.

# Appendix 4

## Conversion factors

As the Fw190 was designed and built using metric (SI) units, these have been used throughout the book. Readers of a certain age (the author included) and those from North America may need some assistance converting unfamiliar units into imperial (English) measurements.

| Length | 10mm = 1cm = 0.394in |
| --- | --- |
| | 1m = 3.28ft |
| | 1km = 1,000m = 3,280ft = 0.621 mile = 0.539 nautical mile |
| Area | 1cm² = 0.155in² |
| | 1m² = 10.76ft² |
| Volume | 1cm³ = 0.061in³ |
| | 1,000cm³ = 1l = 61.02in³ |
| | 1l = 0.22 Imperial gallon = 0.26 US gallon |
| Weight | 1kg = 2.2lb |
| | 1 metric ton (tonne) = 1,000kg = 0.984 long ton (British) = 1.1 short ton (US) |
| Speed | 1kph = 0.621mph = 0.539 knot (nautical mile per hour) |
| Pressure | 1kg/cm² = 1ata = 0.98bar = 0.98Atü = 14.22psi |
| | 100mbar = 1.45psi = 2.95inHg |
| | Atmospheric pressure at sea level is given as 1,013mbar = 29.92inHg |
| Power | 1 metric horsepower (PS) = 0.986 international horsepower (HP) = 735.5 watts |
| Temperature | To convert temperature in °C to °F multiply the figure by 1.8 and add 32; to convert from °F to °C, subtract 32 from the figure and multiply by 0.55. |

# Appendix 5

## Useful addresses

**Aircraft Engine Historical Society (AEHS)**
http://www.enginehistory.org/index.php
*Website of society dedicated to all types of historic engines.*

**GossHawk Unlimited Inc.**
3184 N Rockwell Ave. Casa Grande, Arizona 85122, USA
Tel: +001 520-423-2622
Email: Info@gosshawkunlimited.com
http://www.gosshawkunlimited.com/
*Restoration and maintenance of vintage and warbird aircraft including the Fw190 and FW190 replicas.*

**Vintage V12s, Inc. and Vintage Radials**
1582 Goodrick Drive, #1
Tehachapi, California 93561, USA
Tel: +001 661-822-1503
http://vintagev12s.com/home.htm
http://vintageradials.com/index.htm
*Rebuild and repair of in-line and radial engines, including the BMW801.*

# Index

Accidents and losses 8, 25, 39-42, 44, 47, 55, 120, 138
AEG 16
Aerials 23, 40
Aerostar SA, Romania 106
AGO 22, 24-25
Airfields and air bases
  Beaumont-le-Roger, France 42
  Casa Grande 125
  Debin-Irema, Poland 45
  Kairouan, Tunisia 51
  Lille-Vendeville, France 41
  Manching, Germany 9, 120, 122-123
  Montecorvino, Italy 50
  Neubiberg, Germany 43
  Payne Field, Washington, USA 10
  RAF Pembrey, Wales 51-52
  RAF West Malling, Kent 39
  Rechlin, Luftwaffe testing airfield 18, 20, 26, 97
  St Trond, Belgium 25, 54
  Schipol, Holland 42
Airworthy examples 10-11, 105, 116, 130, 138, 150-152
Albatross Aircraft Co 16
American pilot's report on Fw190 D-9 29
Arado 22, 24, 30
Armament 18, 20, 23, 25-26, 28, 31, 35, 59, 66, 77-81
  ammunition 78-79, 134
  bombs 30, 39, 45, 50, 81
  cannon 22-25, 28, 30-31, 35, 41, 47, 59, 77-79, 131, 134, 153
  fusing panel 80
  machine guns 18, 21-24, 41, 47, 77
  mortars 25, 41, 59, 66
  rockets 81
  Rüstsätze (field modification kits) 23, 77, 149
  special weapons 80-81
  synchronising mechanisms 79
  Umrüst-Bausatz 'U' sets (factory modification kits) 20, 23, 30, 77
  upward firing cannons (Schräge Musik project) 80
Armée de l'Air 55
Armour protection 30, 41-42, 45, 106

Battle of Bizerte 50
Battle of Britain 40
Battle of Stalingrad 45, 47
Battle of the Bulge 55
Battle of Tunis 50
Beethoven-Gerät aircraft combination (Mistel/Mistletoe) 48-49
Begleitgruppen (escort groups) 41
Blaser, Rudolf 18
Boeing
  B-17 Flying Fortress 41-42, 130
  737 106
Books 148
  *Battles with the Luftwaffe*, Theo Boiten and Martin Bowman 43
  *Fw190 in North Africa*, Andrew Arthy and Morten Jessen 51
  *Wings of the Luftwaffe*, Eric Brown 6, 35, 54
  *Wings on my Sleeve*, Eric Brown 29
Brendel Joachim 47

Brown, Captain Eric 'Winkle' 29, 51, 54
Burath, Lt Eberhard 42-43
Butcher Bird nickname 8

Cameras 80, 84
Canterbury attack 40
Captured aircraft 13, 25, 35, 39-40, 43, 49, 51-54, 57, 95, 126, 129, 152
Chaff (aluminium foil) 40
Champlin Fighter Museum, USA 130
Cockpit 18, 20, 29-30, 41, 47, 52, 59, 62-63, 107, 110, 121-122, 124, 136, 143-146
  autopilot 30, 83
  canopy 17-18, 25-27, 30-31, 35, 41, 63-66, 124, 140
  canopy opening, closing and locking 66, 122, 126
  consoles 64, 66, 76, 80, 84, 110, 131, 144
  controls 47, 64, 66, 83
  floor 63, 131, 143-144
  gunsight 63
  heating 26
  instrument panels 20, 34, 49, 63-64, 123, 136
  instruments 63-64, 111, 117
  noise level 29, 113, 121
  pilot's step 141
  preparation 122
  pressurised 25-27, 35
  seat 29, 63, 144
  windscreen 63, 84, 144
Colling, Claus 117, 120
Collings Foundation 138
Cologne bombing 40
Comparison with allied fighters 52-53
Consolidated
  B-24 Liberator 41-42, 44
  PB4Y-2 Privateer 138
Construction 17-18, 20, 57, 131
  dispersed factories 22, 59
  Flug Werk replica kits 106-117
  in France 55
  outside contractors 22-25, 30, 59
  production lines 22
Control surfaces 17-18
Cost of ownership 117
Cowlings 17, 24-25, 27, 50, 83, 98, 108, 132-133
  air intakes 8, 89, 108, 150
  tropical air filters 30, 50
Curtiss
  Hawk 12, 38
  P-40 Warhawk 50-51

D-Day 44, 138
  Sword Beach 44
Deutsches Museum, Munich 96, 99
Dornier Do217 39, 88
Douglas Boston 39
Drawings 139, 150
Duckstein, Martin 88

El Alamein, Egypt 49
Electrical system and motors 17, 29, 35, 47, 66-67, 69-71, 76-77, 79, 110, 117, 124, 134
  magnetos 91, 103
Emergency equipment 84

Emergency power systems 81-83
Emergency procedures 127
Empennage (tail unit) 30, 66-67
  control surfaces 66
  elevators 67, 72, 125
  fin 20, 67
  rudder 67, 72-73, 114, 123-124
  tailplane 17, 20, 67
  vertical stabiliser 67
Engine boost system 25, 81-83
Engine components 87-103
  accessory drive 91
  camshafts 99-100
  connecting rods 99
  crankcase 88-89, 98, 122
  crankshaft 88-90, 98
  cylinder heads 89-90, 99-100, 103, 121
  cylinders 87, 89-90
  Kommandogerät (control device) 23, 91-95
  pistons 89-90, 99
  reduction gear 90, 99-101
  turbo-supercharger 15, 26, 89, 91, 95, 101, 103
  valve gear 90
Engine cooling system 17, 23, 25, 98, 101-102, 110, 117, 132-133
Engine overheating 18, 20, 23, 82, 89
Engine installation 26, 83
Engine lubrication system 90, 93, 102-103
Engine starting 127
Engines 25
  Allison 26, 53
  BMW radial 10, 24, 30, 83, 87, 108, 138, 150
  BMW 132 88
  BMW 139 17, 20, 88
  BMW 801 20, 26-27, 82, 87-96, 138; C-0 20, 88; C-1 20-22; C-2 23; D-2 23, 25, 83, 88, 93; M 88; S 88; T 88; TS 25; TU 25, 83
  Bramo 88
  Bramo 329 88
  DB601 17
  DB603 26, 31, 97; L 31
  DB605 122
  Dongan HS-7 106
  Jumo 27-28, 65, 87, 106, 132, 150
  Jumo 210 96
  Jumo 211 27, 98
  Jumo 213 27, 29, 31, 96-103, 137; A 97; A-1 27-28, 100, 103; C 100; E 28, 31, 35, 97-98; F 97; F-1 28
  Junkers V-12 96
  Pratt & Whitney Hornet 88
  Rolls-Royce 26
  Rolls-Royce Merlin 60-series 53
  Shvetsov ASh-82 106, 108, 117; ASh-82T 12
  Wright Cyclone 106
Exhaust systems 26-27, 53, 83, 89, 92, 100

Faber, Oblt Arnim 51-52, 57
Fieseler 23-25, 27
First flights 11, 18, 20, 34, 113, 116, 120-126
Flight controls 52, 63, 72-73, 107, 123, 131

Flug Werk replica kits 6, 8-9, 11-12, 70-72, 105-117, 119-128, 130, 138, 150, 152
FW190 A-8/N 106, 120, 152
FW190 D-9 106
Flying Heritage Collection (FHC) 10, 24, 131, 138, 150
Focke, Heinrich 16
Focke-Wulf Flugzeugbau AG 16
Focke-Wulf Flugzeugbau GmbH 12, 16
  Aslau factory 25
  Bremen airport factory 15-18, 22-23, 37
  Cottbus factory 25, 27-28, 35
  Marienburg dispersed plant 22
Focke-Wulf Fw58 Weihe (Harrier) 16
Focke-Wulf Fw189 Uhu (Eagle Owl) 16-17
Focke-Wulf Fw190
  A-series 9, 20-25, 29-30, 47, 55, 64, 81, 88, 126-127, 147, 150
  A-0 pre-production 15, 20-21, 26, 30; A-0/U4 30
  A-1 21-23, 26, 38
  A-2 22-23, 37
  A3 23, 51-52
  A-4 23, 30, 39, 50, 52; A-4/U 23, 30
  A-5 10, 13, 23-24, 30-31, 50, 55, 138; A-5/U 30; A-5/U3 45
  A-6 24, 30, 55, 153
  A-7 24-25, 29
  A-8 22, 25, 28, 30-31, 42, 44, 58-60, 63, 77, 79, 81-82, 85, 106, 149; A-8/R1 58; A-8/R2 54; A-8/R8 41-42
  A-9 25, 27, 30, 40
  A-10 25
  Aa-3 55
  B-series (experimental) 25-26
  B-0 26
  B-1 26
  C-series (experimental) 25-27
  C-0 26-27
  C-1 26-27
  D-series 9, 25, 31, 34-35, 55, 67, 96-97, 150
  D-0 (pre-production) 27
  D1 and D-2 27
  D-3 to D8 (unused designations) 27
  D-9 27-29, 85, 131
  D-10 (not built) 28
  D-11 28
  D-12 28
  D-13 28, 64, 68, 77-78, 129-137, 150
  F-series 9, 23, 31, 47, 50, 55, 81, 84, 88, 150
  F-1 30
  F-2 30, 45
  F-3 30
  F-4 to F-7 (unbuilt projects) 30
  F-8 30-31, 43, 48, 54, 81, 138
  F-9 30
  G-series (Jabo-Rei) 9, 23, 30-31, 47, 50, 55, 81, 84, 88
  G-1 (A-4/U8) 30
  G-2 (A-5/U8) 30
  G-3 13, 30-31, 50, 81
  G-4 to G-7 (unbuilt projects) 31
  G-8 31

S-series (trainers) 31
 S-5 and S-8 (two-seat) 31
 V1 (Versuch) 16-18
 V2 20
 V3 and V4 20
 V5 and V6 20
 V13 26
Focke-Wulf 200 Kondor 16
Focke-Wulf Ta152 9, 16, 27, 29-31, 34-35, 64, 152
 A-series 31
 B-series 31
 C-series 31, 34
 E-series 34
 H-series 9, 12, 31, 34-35, 96-97
 H-0 35, 152
 H-1 31, 35, 85
Franco, General 11
Fuel system and tanks 18, 20, 25, 30-31, 35, 49, 63, 74-75, 82-83, 90-93, 121-122, 132, 140, 143-144, 146
 drop tanks 6, 23, 30, 39, 44, 59, 74, 80-81
 injection system 30, 34, 90-92
 pumps 66, 92
Fuselages 17, 20-21, 27-28, 31, 34-35, 59, 62-63, 107-108, 117, 132, 137-146
 extension 12, 24, 27-28, 67
 interior fittings 62
 rivets 144-145
 skinning 143-145

Gautreaux, Rusty 116
German Army 51
 Afrika Korps 49
 Ninth Army 47
 Second Panzer Army 47
Göring, Reichsmarschall Hermann 19, 54
Goss, Connie and Lindsey 138
Goss, Dave 117, 130-131
GossHawk Unlimited 117, 119, 130-131, 137-138, 146, 154
Gotha 16
Götz, Major Franz 129

Hamburg bombing 40-41
Handling characteristics and stability 18, 20, 29, 47, 52, 54, 120
Hanson, Don 116
Hawker
 Hurricane 39, 130
 Typhoon 53, 55
Heinkel 16
 He219 97
Hermann, Oberst Hans-Joachim 40-41
Hispano Buchón 130
Hitler, Adolf 9, 11, 16, 44
Hydraulic system 17-18, 29, 31, 35, 95

Ilyushin Il-2 47

JME Aviation 138
Johnson, AVM James 'Johnnie' 38
Junkers group 19
Junkers aircraft manufacturing company 96
 Ju52 19
 Ju87 Stuka 47
 Ju88 40, 48-49, 55, 88
 Ju188 97
Junkers Motorenwerk (Jumo) 96, 98
Junkers, Hugo 19

Käther, Willy 16
Kirkland, Dan 138
Kittel, Otto 47

Kriegsmarine 39
 *Gneisenau* 39
 *Prinz Eugen* 39
 *Scharnhorst* 39

Landing and approach 29, 47, 53, 116, 120, 124-125
 Approach Check List 125, 127
 wheels up 54, 120
Lichte, Dr Ing. August 97
Lockheed
 P-38 Lightning 50-51, 53; P-38F 53; P-38J 29
 P-80 Shooting Star 29
*Longest Day, The* film 44
Luftwaffe 12, 16-17, 19, 26, 34, 38, 40-42, 44, 47-48, 50, 55, 83, 120
 Luftflotte 4 48
 1./JG1 42
 JG2 40
 II./JG2 51
 9./JG2 42
 JG3 44
 JG4 54
 5./JG4 25
 JG10 81
 JG 26 22, 40-41, 44, 129
 II./JG26 38, 42
 JG51 47
 JG54 47
 JG300 Wilde Sau 40
 JG301 35, 41, 152
 JG302 41
 KG30 48
 KG200 48-49
 1./NJG10 40
 II./SchlG1 47
 6 Stafel 45
 SchlG4 51
 II./SG2 48
 6.SG10 43
 SKG10 40
 II./SKG10 39

Maintenance schedule 147
Manoeuvrability 29, 53
 radius of turn 29, 53
 rate of roll 29, 53
Markings and code letters 13, 18, 25, 40, 42, 44, 48-49, 52, 57, 113, 129, 138, 152
Materials 26, 131, 137, 150
Messerschmitt 16
 Bf109 16-17, 38, 40, 47-48, 55, 120, 122, 129-130; Bf109 G 41
 Me262 45
Messerschmitt, Willy 19
Milch, Erhard 19
Mimetail 27
Mittelhuber, Ludwig 16
Museum of Flight 150

National Air and Space Museum 152
National Museum of the United States Air Force 131
National Test Pilot School, USA 120
Norddeutsche Dornier 24-25, 30
North American P-51 Mustang 8, 26, 28, 34, 39, 41, 55, 120, 122; P-51A Mk IA 53; P-51D 29
Nose 27-28, 31
 engine panels 126
Nowotny, Major Walter 45, 47

Oil system and cooling 8, 18, 20-21, 41, 75-76, 83, 89, 92-93, 102, 117, 121-122, 125-126
Operating limitations and settings 127
Operation Barbarossa (invasion of Soviet Union) 44

Operation Bodenplatte (base plate) 25, 54-55
Operation Eisenhammer (iron hammer) 48-49
Operation Jubilee (Dieppe raid) 39
Operation Torch 49
Operation Zerberus (Channel Dash) 39
Operation Zitadelle (Citadel) 47
Oxygen system 18, 35, 63, 66-67, 83-84, 121

Painting 108, 112
Performance 12, 29, 34
 acceleration 53
 altitude 26, 28, 34
 climb 53
 diving 53
 range 47
 speed 20, 35, 53
Petlyakov Pe-2 47
Pilots operating instructions 126-127
Plasa, Klaus 11, 113, 116, 119-122, 124, 126
Polikarpov I-16 Rata 17
Pre-flight checks 121, 126-127
Priller, Major Josef 'Pips' 44, 138
Production figures 9, 22-25, 28, 30-31, 35
 engines 98
 export 55
 replica kits 106, 117
Propeller and shaft 17, 22-23, 25-26, 66, 76, 90, 99-100, 110, 123

Radar 40-41
Radio equipment 23, 63, 66; 83-84, 111, 113, 121, 124, 126, 134-135
RAF Museum 81
Red Army 55
Republic P-47 Thunderbolt 41
RLM (German Ministry of Aviation) 16-17, 19-20, 25, 34, 83, 88
 building 19
 prototype system 19, 26
Roles 12, 20
 armed photo-reconnaissance 23
 battlefield support 30, 48, 51
 bomber attack fighter 24, 41-42
 fighter bomber (Jabo) 23, 30-31, 39, 47
 fighter-reconnaissance 34
 ground attack 12, 23, 25, 29-31, 41, 43, 45, 50, 55, 84
 high-altitude interception 12, 26, 29, 34-35
 hit-and-run attacks 39-40
 long-range fighter-bomber (Jabo-Rei) 12, 23
 medium-level fighter 31
 night-fighter 30, 40-41, 53, 55, 153
 radar-equipped night fighter 24
 Sturmbock (battering ram) 44
 torpedo-armed 26
 Wilde Sau 40-41
Romanian Air Force 55
Royal Air Force (RAF) 26, 37, 39, 52, 57
 Air Fighting Development Unit (AFDU)
 Bomber Command 40
 Fighter Command 52
Royal Hungarian National Air Force (MKHL) 55
Rudorffer, Ob Erich 51

Sander, Hans 18
Schnoor, Hauptmann 42
Seyffardt, Lt Fritz 47

SNCAC aircraft company 55
 NC900 55
Soviet Air Force (VVS) 55
Soviet 16th Air Army 47
Spanish Civil War 11, 17
Specifications 85
 BMW801 D-2 engine 93
 Fw190 A-8 85
 Fw190 D-9 85
 Jumo 213 A-1 engine 103
 length 24, 27
 Ta152 H-1 85
 weight 17, 20, 41, 106
 wingspan 26
Speer, Albert 19
Spinners 17-18, 20, 28, 117
Stores racks
 underbelly (fuselage) 6, 13, 23, 25, 30, 66, 69, 79-81
 under wing 13, 30, 81
 ventral 30
Sturmgruppen (storm groups) 41-42, 44
Supermarine
 Seafire 52
 Spitfire 8, 44, 50, 55, 130; Mk V 12, 38-39, 52; Mk Vb 53; Mk IX 6, 12, 39, 53-54; Mk XII 53
Surviving (preserved) Fw190 airframes 130, 150-153

Tail unit – see Empennage
Take-offs 53, 115, 120, 123
 Before-Take-Off-Checks 123, 127
Tank, Prof Kurt 8-9, 16-17, 25, 29, 34, 38, 54, 96
Taxiing 29, 53, 114, 122, 125, 127
Test flying 9, 18, 23, 113, 119, 123-124, 126
Theatres of operation
 Ardennes 54-55
 Eastern (Russian) Front 24, 43-45, 47-49, 55, 81
 Kursk 47-49
 Mediterranean campaign 49-51
 Normandy campaign 42, 44, 54
 North African campaign 49-51
 Western Front – Europe 38-39, 42
Transall C-160 120
Treaty of Versailles 88
Turkish Air Force 55

Udet, Ernst 17
Undercarriage 18, 25, 29, 31, 35, 66, 69-72, 107, 109, 111, 127, 135
 brakes 125-126
 retraction sequence 69-71
 tailwheel 66-67, 71-72, 106, 122-123, 126
 wheels 106
USAAF 49, 55
 95th Bomb Group 42
 492nd Bomb Group 44
 404th Fighter Group 25, 54
US Air Material Command 29

Versailles Treaty 9
Vought Corsair 120

Weserflug 25
Wings 12, 20, 24, 26-27, 30-31, 35, 41, 68-69, 106-109, 117
 ailerons 17, 72-73, 124
 flaps 29, 47, 69, 111, 115, 123-125, 131, 137
 leading edge 69, 138
 main spar 68, 107, 109
Wodarczyk, Heinz 44
Wulf, Georg 16
Wurmheller, Ob Josef 42